The Time of My Life

Peter Bird Martin

Edition: 5/17/2020.

Generated: August 13, 2020 at 3:46pm.

ii

Contents

List of Figures

Foreword

My World ... and Welcome to It

You're about to read a series of anecdotes – *true* anecdotes – about my life. They're mainly about my professional life, with a lot of family life and personal linkage thrown in.

Many of the stories are about lucky breaks I took advantage of, but there are a few I *didn't* take advantage of, and looking back, *should* have. One of these involved a pleasant, intelligent television actor named William Windom.

When I arrived as Senior Editor of TIME's Television Section in 1968, Windom had already made his mark as a solid, believable, often-funny character actor on TV's Hallmark Hall of Fame, "Robert Montgomery Presents", and "The Twilight Zone." In 1969, to my eye and taste, he hit his solid stride in an intelligent, upper-Middle series of tasteful, humorous tales based on yarns written by that *New Yorker* legend, James Thurber. They were called "My World, and Welcome to It." In them, Windom played a milquetoasty, Thurber-like character whose imagined heroic actions wreaked havoc in his personal and family life.

The show was a delight, and at just the right intellectual level to make Windom a good candidate for an in-depth profile article in TIME. I said as much at a Friday story-planning meeting of Television-Section writers and researchers. Quicker-than-quick, a group lunch with Mr. Windom was set up for the following Wednesday.

We Martins were living in Yorktown Heights in Westchester County in those days, and I was commuting to Manhattan on a New York Central train that ran along the Hudson River from Croton-on-Hudson, to Ossining, to Tarrytown, to Yonkers, and finally to Grand Central Station.

On Wednesday morning, who should get on the train at Tarrytown but William Windom? He must have been visiting a friend in Pocantico Hills (or maybe Nyack at the end of the Tappan Zee Bridge, just across the river) and was taking the train into town for *that TIME magazine lunch.* Those commuter trains had seats for three on one side of the aisle and seats for two on the other. The seats for two were less crowded than the three-seaters, but they were gone by the time we got to Tarrytown and Windom had to take one of the three-seat numbers just two rows ahead of me. He was carrying a copy of the *New York Times* and he was only the second person on the seat. There was still room for a third.

A Mittyish idea popped. I would get up, move forward two rows, and plop my hefty rump and broad shoulders into the third seat on the aisle, next to Windom. When he twisted and turned in the middle seat to read the *Times* (in those days it was a full-sized, broadsheet paper eight columns wide), he'd be a widespread, messy menace to those on either side of him.

Words would be spat. "Can't you fold a paper like a *civilized* person? Can't you keep your elbows to yourself? *This* is the way you do it!"

I'd grab his paper and fold it, lengthwise, into thirds. (I'd been taught the commuter triple-fold by my high-school journalism teacher, Margaret Hay.) I'd smack the paper back into his hands.

"People like you should be *banned* on these trains! I don't know what the hell's become of manners in Tarrytown!"

We'd then sit in furious silence to Dobbs Ferry, or maybe 125th Street. We'd glare at each other as we stalked off the train at Grand Central.

That noon, at lunch on the 34th Floor of the TIME-LIFE Building in Manhattan, he'd walk into a small private dining room to meet the writers and researchers of TIME's Television Section. *And* the Senior Editor.

Eyes would widen. "You! You! You S.O.B.!" Laughs would be belly-laughed, and a legend would be born.

Never happened. My Mitty moment had chickened out in Tarrytown.

Chapter 1

Copy Boy

The year was 1950. Harry Truman was President of the United States. John Sloan Dickey was President of Dartmouth College. Wisconsin Senator Joseph McCarthy was riding high, chasing people he identified as Communists or Communist sympathizers out of the Government. I was 21 years old, in my junior year at Dartmouth in Hanover NH, preparing a term paper for my Journalism course, English 401, with Professor Eric P. Kelly.

English 401 was a "gut course," Dartmouth slang for a course offering an easy ride rather than a serious slog of research, lectures and study. The textbook was not a book. It was a daily copy of the *New York Times*, bought at the Dartmouth Bookstore, plus a mailed subscription to another American daily newspaper. My other paper was the *St. Louis Post-Dispatch*. I had been introduced to it by an English teacher at Lower Merion Senior High School in Ardmore, Pennsylvania, a remarkable and admirable woman named Margaret Fleck Hay. In those days the *P-D*, as I later learned to call it, was a regular on anyone's list of "Ten Best American Newspapers." [1]

---

[1]

Among other admirers of Mrs. Hay in the Class of 1946 was my friend, James ("Jim") Billington, who went on to become the near-permanent U.S. Librarian of Congress.

Another Lower Merion classmate who achieved national fame was Ed Hiestand, who worked professionally for advertising agencies like Batton, Barton, Durstine and Osborne. He was a member of a weekend group of us "boys" who rarely had dates with girls, and wandered around Lower Merion Township in family cars on Friday and Saturday nights going to sock hops, other people's parties, and drive-in restaurants. We sang what we thought

In English 401 we didn't study journalism, we *imbibed* it. Every Tuesday, Thursday, and Saturday morning at 10 o'clock I walked into Professor Kelly's classroom on the second floor of Reed Hall in Hanover with a carry-out container of coffee, a muffin, a notebook, and copies of the *Times* and the *P-D*. I sat down, drank my coffee, ate my muffin, read my papers, compared their coverage of the same continuing story, made some notes, and chatted about the day's news with my classmates. It was perfect preparation for adult daily life, especially the daily life of a a commuter who took a train to a major city to go to work as a journalist.

In my case, the continuing story was Wisconsin Senator Joseph McCarthy's relentless campaign against the infiltration of "godless Communism" into American society and government. The *P-D* was no friend of McCarthy and McCarthyism. Nor was I. The paper followed his Red-baiting trail across America, and assigned reporters to go to towns and cities where McCarthy was speaking, to keep track of his campaign against American "subversives." The more I read, the more I admired the *P-D*. The more I admired, the more unscrupulous I became. Unashamedly, I assembled my term paper, week by week, from *Post-Dispatch* coverage.

There were no "hour exams," no quizzes, no final examination in English 401. Just a long, original paper. Professor Kelly gave me a B+ for the paper, perhaps because he knew how easy it was for me. I gave the *Post-Dispatch* an A+, and decided I wanted to work there as a reporter after I graduated.

My father was a journalist. From the time I could understand anything adult at all, I understood how much fun he had and how much he loved the work. From my teens on I knew that I, too, wanted to be a reporter and writer.

---

were "bawdy" songs. Borrowing a group name from World War II, we called ourselves "The Raiders" and when Ed died a group of us at his funeral in suburban Philadelphia gathered at graveside and sang one of his most famous ditties:

> Mister Clean gets rid of dirt and grease and grime
> just in a minute,
> Mister Clean will clean your whole house
> and everything that's in it.
> Mister Clean, Mister Clean, Mister Clean.

In high school I took a journalism course from the remarkable Mrs. Hay and wrote for the school paper. When I got to Hanover I "heeled" (which is to say, "tried out") for the daily college newspaper, The "*Dartmouth*." I made the grade, wrote for the paper, and took Professor Kelly's course.

[Eventually I also became an Editor of the "*Dartmouth*" And in my senior year, got fired. But that's another bit of memoir. See page 35.]

The more I read about McCarthy and McCarthyism in the *Post-Dispatch*, the more I wanted to start my newspaper work there. But how? As you can see from the way I went about my McCarthy research, my favorite way was the easy way. I went to my father and told him I wanted a job at the paper. Did he know anyone who might help?

He did. One of his good friends at the *Saturday Evening Post* was Jack Alexander, a talented magazine writer who got his start — where else? — at the *St. Louis Post-Dispatch*. Mr. Alexander phoned a friend at the *P-D*, and I was on as a copy boy, the lowest-ranking editorial job on any publication, anywhere, anytime, anyhow. The friend suggested that I get a room at the downtown St. Louis YMCA ($49.50 a month) at 1528 Locust Street, four blocks from the newspaper office at 12th and Olive.

In those days, before everywhere air conditioning, St. Louis summers were as famously and inhumanely humid as the Mississippi River, which ran along the ancient levee just 12 blocks east of the office. They were also inhumanely *hot*. I've italicized *hot*. It deserves it. Summer daytime temperatures ran regularly over 100 degrees Fahrenheit, and a lot of nighttimes, too. One of my occasional east-coast affectations was to wear brown-leather loafers with thick, crepe-rubber soles. After I'd walked the egg-frying sidewalks from Union Station to the Y, and from the Y to the *Post-Dispatch* building, those soles melted out sideways like snowshoes. They didn't spring back. I had to throw them away.

My work was more manual than mental, more repetitive than creative, more strain than brain. The *P-D* published four editions a day: a "City" edition at 9 a.m. for newsstand sales in the morning; a "Home" edition for early afternoon street-by-street delivery to subscribing customers; a "One-Star Final" to be picked up at newsstands by readers who got off work by 3 or 4 p.m.; and a "Two-Star Final", the last edition of the day.

The presses occupied two floors of the *P-D* building, the ground floor and a floor below. You could see the presses through sidewalk windows, and you could feel their thunder inside and outside.

Each weekday and Saturday, when a press run ended, the papers were strapped into 50-pound bundles. A copy boy then had to heft a bundle onto his shoulder and climb a narrow interior metal stairway four flights to the City Room, where reporters and editors grabbed copies and checked their work for vanity reads, typos and possible problems. Saturday evenings, the same thing happened with the Sunday papers.

A copy boy also had to keep track of the work of stringers. "Stringers" were independent journalists or reporters on other papers who covered cities, towns and even states outside of St. Louis on a part-time basis for the *P-D*. Some places were relatively close, like East St. Louis and Belleville, across the river in Illinois; others were farther afield, like Granite City and Cape Girardeau, Missouri.

In the old, old days, stringers were paid for the number of column-inches their stories filled in the papers they "strung" for. Balls of actual string, labeled with the stringer's name, were kept in a drawer by the head copy boy. Each time one of the stringer's stories was published in the *P-D*, the copy boy measured the column inches with a piece of string, and tied the string to the labeled ball in the drawer. At the end of the month, the ball was unwound and measured, and the stringer was paid, inch by inch.

Then there were individual tasks. "Coffee," the City Editor, Ray Crowley, would say to Gene, the head copy boy who sat on a bench behind the City Desk.

"Go get coffee for Mr. Crowley," Gene would say to one of the boys on the bench.

The first time it happened to me, I hopped up and went down the back stairs to the alley behind the building. Just down the alley was Beffa's Buffet, the place where all the copy boys bought lunch sandwiches. Beffa's had pre-

Beffa Brothers Buffet, St. Louis, circa 1952.

cooked hamburgers, which they dipped in a sauce of meat juice, topped the burger with a slice of American cheese, and encased it all in a slightly sweet roll. Experienced boys would say "dip the lid," and Beffa's counterman would dip the top slice of roll lightly in the hot hamburger juice and put it on top of the cheese. The combination of meat juice and slightly melted cheese was delicious. I can remember the taste even now, 70-plus years later.

For Mr. Crowley I ordered a coffee to go from Beffa's, got a couple of packets of sugar and two little containers of milk. I paid, and headed back to the office.

I put the coffee, sugar and milk on the corner of his desk. He was busy, but he must have heard the coffee arrive. Without looking, he put his hand out and touched the container. He frowned, glanced at the container, pulled off the lid, and looked inside. Then he poured the coffee into a spittoon under his desk.

"Gene," he said. "Tell the new boy where to get my coffee."

From then on I went to Speck's, a squeaky-clean, upscale cafeteria on Washington Boulevard at 12th Street.

"Coffee for Ray Crowley," I would say. And each morning I put a beautiful, shiny, *glass* container of coffee, already sugared, with "just a speck" of cream, on Mr. Crowley's desk.

A year later, in the spring of 1951 just before I graduated, I sang baritone on the spring concert tour of the Dartmouth Glee Club. In Dayton, Ohio, I ducked out of the post-concert party and boarded an overnight Pullman to St. Louis. Next morning, by appointment, I was in the *P-D* city room being interviewed for a reporter's job by Ray Crowley, newly promoted to City Editor.

By chance, a *Holiday* magazine photographer was there, taking pictures for an upcoming feature-article on the city of St. Louis. He snapped me in my bow-tie and gabardine suit, and Mr. Crowley interviewing me. Back in Philadelphia (*Holiday* and the *Saturday Evening Post* were both published there by the Curtis Publishing Company), he took the photo of me and Mr. Crowley to my father.

"How come you took the picture?" my father said. "Did you see an iconic moment there, the fresh kid reporter being interviewed by the crusty old editor?"

"No," said the photographer. "It was the spittoon."

Would-be reporter Peter Martin being interviewed for his first job in the "City Room" of the *St. Louis Post Dispatch* by Raymond Crowley, City Editor. Note the spittoon.

Chapter 2

Ordinary Seaman

Before World War II, my Uncle Larry (my Father's older brother, Lawrence Janney Martin) was an executive of the Ediphone Corporation, which made and sold office voice-transcribing machines. He lived in Alexandria, Va., just across the Potomac River from Washington, D.C. During the War he agreed to serve as a "dollar-a-year" official of America's Lend-Lease Program, which provided war materiel to U.S. allies. In the spring of 1946, as the war ended, he had access to the hundreds of American cargo ships and tankers that had been loaned or leased to Britain, Russia, France and other allies during the war, and were being returned and tied up, stem to stern and stern to stem, in the Hudson River north of New York City.

That year I was turning 16, due to graduate from high school in June. Without consulting me, my father and Uncle Larry decided I should fulfill that standard boyhood dream and "Go to Sea." The only reason the dream was a possible one for me was the end of Lend-Lease. Seaworthy ships could be rented from the U.S. Government, cheap, by steamship companies, and as a result my uncle had a lot of friends at those companies. A pal of his at Moore-McCormack Lines enabled me to get U.S. Merchant Seaman's papers, as well as "permits" to ship out as a new member of the Sailors' Union of the Pacific (S.U.P.) and the National Maritime Union (N.M.U.). As part of the process, the friend also wrote a letter guaranteeing me a job as an "Ordinary Seaman" aboard a Moore-McCormack ship.

SS/*Marine Jumper* underway, probably during builders' trials in early 1945.

In June a bottle of Scotch whiskey (provided by my father) persuaded
Max Kornblatt, the dispatcher at the S.U.P. hiring hall on Manhattan's lower
Wall Street, to call out my name for an Ordinary Seaman's berth aboard the
SS/*Marine Jumper*, newly docked at Pier 42, "North River" (the Hudson).
It was a modern, oil-fired, "C-4" cargo vessel that had been converted to a
troopship during the war and fitted with tiers of bunks from top to bottom.
In 1946 she was carrying hundreds of university-exchange students across the
Atlantic from New York to England, France and Norway — and back.

I got details of the ship's location from Mr. Kornblatt (who never thanked
me for the Scotch), gathered my gear from the locker that went with my fifty-
cent-a-night cot at the Seamen's Church Institute on The Bowery, and reported to the *Marine Jumper's* chief mate. He checked my papers, signed me

Harry Lundeberg, president of the International Seamen's Union (1938-1957) and Secretary/Treasurer of the Sailors' Union of the Pacific, wearing his "Stetson".

on, and told me I was on the "twelve-to-four watch." He had someone show me to the forecastle ("foc'sl"), where I and my three watch-mates had bunks, lockers and a shared sink.

I was 16, going to sea for the first time! Even though the idea was my Father's and Uncle Larry's, I bought wholeheartedly into the dream. As luck would have it, the rules of the "Sailors' Union of the Pacific" required its officers to go to sea once a year to keep them in touch with a) their trade, b) their fellow seamen, c) the seafaring world and d) the sea itself. Result: With me aboard the *Marine Jumper* on my maiden voyage was the Secretary-Treasurer and leading spirit of the S.U.P., Norway-born Harry Lundeberg, sailing as the ship's Boatswain ("Bo'sun").

A tough, charismatic labor organizer and seaman in the bad old union-busting days of the 1930s, Norway-born Harry Lundeberg had been through his own particular hells, both aboard ship and dockside, during picketing and head-bashing strikes. He led his militant fellow seamen through picket-line battles with hired company thugs and deputy sheriffs. Their badge of identity was, of all things, a white cotton golf hat, known throughout the seafaring labor world as a "Lundeberg Stetson."

As Boatswain on the *Marine Jumper*, Lundeberg was the foreman in charge of all daily work done at sea by sailors when they weren't "on watch." Sailing with Lundeberg (as bodyguards, I figured out later) were three massive, Norwegian, Able-Bodied Seamen. All three of them were members of my twelve-to-four watch. Two of them, Ola and Trygve, were in the foc'sl when I arrived on board. They showed me my bunk and locker, and as I hung my clothes I told them I'd never been to sea before, and needed their help. To their ever-lasting credit (and maybe to Harry Lundeberg's), they didn't laugh or tease me like the raw landlubber I was.

Ola did crack a few been-here-done-that smiles, though, as they began to walk and talk me through what the twelve-to-four watch — and my life at sea — was all about. At sea and under way, days and nights were divided into four-hour "watches," four men to a watch. During their watch, those four — under the command of one of the ship's "mates" — were responsible for sailing the ship.

One of the four of us steered the ship from Noon or Midnight to 1 p.m. or 1 a.m. A second stood lookout on the "wing" of the bridge, just outside the wheel-house, from 1:00 to 2:00. A third became lookout on the ship's bow from 2:00 to 3:00. The fourth was on "standby below" from 3:00 to 4:00, making fresh coffee for the next watch or a quick sandwich for himself. On succeeding days, the four-hour schedule rotated, man by man, hour by hour, day and night, watch by watch.

As we walked, my watchmates showed me how to find the galley (kitchen), the "head" (toilets and showers), the bridge, the wheel house, and the bow. Along the way, we were joined by the third Norwegian on our watch. His name? "I'm Ola too," he said.

Ola too? Another Ola? I could see confusion ahead. "If you don't mind," I said, "I'm going to call you 'Toola,' for 'Ola Two.' That way, we won't get confused." They all laughed, so I guessed it was going to be okay.

They took me to the "slop chest" (the ship's shop for the crew), where they practically ordered me to buy leather-palmed gloves for rope handling when we tied up or cast off. In the wheel house they showed me the illuminated compasses and course indicators and the small steel and large wooden wheels for steering. Inside the point of the bow, they told me how to work the two-way squawk box that communicated with the bridge.

With the same seriousness they used to explain the difference between the small steel wheel (it controlled electric motors that moved the immense rudder effortlessly and remotely) and the large wooden one (it moved the rudder directly, by hydraulics, and took more time and effort), they told me why it was necessary to crack open an egg and drop it, shell and all, into the grounds when I was making coffee in the giant urn (the shell absorbed bitterness, they said).

We were scheduled to cast off that afternoon and evening during the four-to-eight and eight-to-twelve watches, and I would be below for the first hour of our twelve-to-four watch. After that, I was told to show up on the bridge at 1 a.m. for my hour of wheel-watch. I would be steering the ship after we left New York Harbor and were on the open Atlantic.

It sounded like a good plan — except for the weather. It had begun to rain and blow in the afternoon as some 400 college kids tromped their bedrolls and backpacks up the gangway and stumbled, fumbled and tumbled their way down the steel ladder-staircases to the stacks and racks of bunks in the hold. And back *up* the ladders. And *down* the ladders. Despite the weather, they wanted to poke into everything on the ship and, it seemed, the higher the better.

They were endlessly being shooed off the bridge and the wings of the bridge, and they loved hanging out in and around the "gun tubs," the circular steel enclosures that had provided shoulder-high protection for the Coast Guard artillerymen who'd manned the anti-submarine defense guns during the war. The guns and Coast-Guard swabbies were gone, but not the tubs.

Torrential rain was blowing sideways by the time Boatswain Lundeberg called us on deck to cast off. Tug boats were ready, fore and aft, to pull us away from the dock. We were "doubled up" (two hawsers to the dock from the bow, two from the stern). As we "singled up" I was overjoyed to have the gloves, but I cursed myself for leaving my slicker in the locker as rain sluiced down my T-shirt and jeans.

Deck Crew SS/*Marine Jumper* summer, 1946. Boatswain Harry Lundeberg (2nd from left, rear row) was president of my first union, the Sailors' Union of the Pacific. (Me, seated, front row, far left) White golf caps were called "Lundeberg Stetsons."

Without heavy gloves, you'd have no hands left after you handled the hawsers, which are long lengths of hemp rope two or three inches thick. They're rough and tough. Wet, they must weigh about ten pounds a foot.

My first time at casting off I was not much help, but I could see and hear what it was all about. Deck hands on the ship slacked off the hawsers until the dock stevedores could lift their looped ends off the bollards and drop them into the mucky river water between the ship and the pier. The hawsers were then run around massive, electric-powered winches, which pulled them in so we seamen could snake them back and forth and back and forth, by hand, on the deck. It's not intricate, but the patterns had to be even and you had to know what you were doing. And do it fast. I didn't.

After we cast off, there were still several hours before my twelve-to-four watch was scheduled to go on duty. Ola showed me the way to the "finley," the warm interior air space high on catwalks above the ship's engines. I wrung out my sopping clothes, hung them over steel railings to dry, and hit the sack.

"Let go your cocks, and grab your socks!" At our foc'sle doorway the overhead light snapped on and the wake-up shout from the eight-to-twelve stand-by rang loud.

"Rise and shine for the Moore-Mac Line! The weather still sucks!"

We groped for clothes — including my slicker, this time — and splashed water on our faces. As the Twelve-to-Four stand-by, I headed for the galley. Ola went to the bow, Trygve went up to the wing of the bridge and Toola headed for the wheelhouse. Outside, wind and rain were in our faces and wet darkness was everywhere. So were vessels. Deep-throated horns meant big ones, medium-deep meant middle-size (tugboats? ferries?), poop-poops meant fishing boats or power boats. They sounded from left and right, from astern, sometimes almost dead-ahead.

In the galley I scouted up the makings of a half-pound cheeseburger, dug out a pan, and began cooking. I put a bun in the toaster, cut a slice of onion, found some mayo and ketchup, and poured myself a large glass of milk. A feast! I ate fast, then loaded the coffee urn with water, a full can of ground coffee, and a broken raw egg. When the brew stopped bubbling, I poured myself a cup. A cup? No! A mug! Two!

Full, I climbed the ladder to the wing of the bridge, and ducked inside, Except for the light of the course indicators, it was dark, but I could make out the bulk of Toola standing at the small electric wheel. As I went in, an unknown hand gripped my elbow.

"Who are you?" said the hand's voice, close to my ear.

"Martin, sir," I said. "I'm the Ordinary Seaman on the Twelve-to-Four watch."

The voice stayed low. "I'm the Junior Third Mate, Martin. This is my watch, and we've got a problem. The captain's drunk, and he thinks he's getting us out of the harbor. We're under way, and we don't even have the pilot aboard yet. The captain'll be running in from the wing, shouting course corrections. You've got to answer him, but *don't* switch to the course he gives you. Answer, but stick to the course you're on until *I* give you a correction. But after the time it would take for you to switch to the course *he* gave, call out that you're steering the course. Got that?"

I was green and stung with surprise, but I was fairly quick. "Yes, sir," I said.

"Now relieve the man at the wheel." I went over to Toola, and he backed away.

Toola whispered: "It takes fifteen or twenty seconds to come to a new course."

I put my hands on the wheel, and almost immediately a man came running in from the wing of the bridge through the doorway on my right. It must have been the captain. "Steer one-eighteen!" he yelled. He ran through the wheelhouse and out the doorway to the bridge wing on the left.

"Steer one-eighteen!" I yelled after him, and began counting to myself. One one thousand, two one thousand, three one thousand, four one thousand, five ... At fifteen one thousand I called out, "Steering one-eighteen!"

The mate came over and said, quietly, "Steer one-ten."

We were steering one-twenty-two at the time, and I turned the wheel to point the ship 12 degrees to the left. Nothing happened. What seemed like an awfully long time went by. Then, slowly, slowly, the indicator began to move. One-twenty-one. One-twenty. One-nineteen. One-eighteen. One-seventeen. One-sixteen. One-fifteen. One-fourteen. One-thirteen. One-twelve. One-eleven. One-ten.

But steering thousands of tons of steel ship in water is not like steering a car. One-oh-nine. One-oh-eight. I thought about it, and turned the wheel a bit to the right. One-oh-seven. One-oh-six. One-oh-five. I brought the wheel to dead-center. One-oh-four. One-oh-three. At One-oh-two (to my immense and overwhelming relief) the numbers stopped changing. I turned the wheel slightly left.

The indicator stayed at One-oh-two. Then it moved to One-oh-three. One-oh-four. One-oh-five. One-oh-six.

I may not be a fast learner, but I'm a learner. I brought the wheel back to dead center. One-oh-seven. One-oh-eight. One-oh-nine. The mate came over and looked over my shoulder at the indicator.

"I said one-*ten*!" he said, with a bit of quiet emphasis. As he spoke, the indicator moved to One-ten, and stopped. "Oh," he said. "Hold to that for now."

The captain appeared at the right entry to the bridge wing. "What are we steering?" he shouted.

"One-eighteen!" I called back.

"Steer One-twelve!" he ordered.

"Steer One-twelve!" I called back. He ran back to the right wing of the bridge and I began to count to myself... .

And so it went.

My first lesson in steering a ship continued for my hour of wheel duty (Steering One-twelve! ... Steer One-sixteen! Steer One-sixteen. ... Steering One-sixteen! ...Steer One-twenty! Steer One-twenty ... Steering One-twenty! ...)

When it came time for my hour of bow-watch, and we passed the Overhauls Lightship on the way out of the Harbor, I was exhausted, mentally, emotionally and intestinally. I turned off the squawk box. I leaned out over the leeward side of the bow. And I threw up my cheeseburger.

* * * *

Three days later, at sea in calmer weather, the lessons — and my learning curve — eased off. At breakfast, Boatswain Lundeberg came over and introduced himself.

"I'm Harry Lundeberg," he said.

"I know," I said. "I'm Peter Martin"

"I know," he said. "That was a good show, leaving New York."

"Thank you."

"Let's have a cup of coffee in the mess at ten bells."

[At sea, time is measured in half-hour chunks between the beginnings and ends of eight-hour watches. "Ten Bells" in the morning is 9 a.m.]

"Yes, Sir."

"And don't call me Sir. Call me Harry."

"Yes, Harry."

At ten bells I found the Boatswain sitting at the crew table in the mess hall.

"Grab a cup of coffee and sit down," he said. "How old are you?"

"Sixteen, Sir."

"Call me Harry," he corrected. "I figured you were about sixteen. Do you go to school?"

"I just graduated from high school," I said.

"And what next?"

"I'm planning on going to college."

"A college punk," he said.

"What's a college punk?" I said.

"It's a college or high-school kid, shipping out for the fun of it. For *adventure*, to see the world, or whatever. And taking a berth and a job away from a working sailor who needs it, and needs the pay. As a college boy, would you keep going to sea?"

"Maybe summers." I said. "I don't know."

"If you do, I can promise summers of hell. Regular sailors give punks a hard time. Teasing, chewing out, the lousiest jobs, roughing up once in a while. Sometimes worse."

"Worse?"

"It can get worse. Some voyages and turnarounds get long. Four, five months without a home port. Life's not normal for a seaman. A seaman's mind is not always normal. It can get in a twist. For no good reason or no reason at all, he can start to hate the man on the next watch. Or in the next bunk. In a storm at sea it could be man-overboard, and who would know?"

"Does this really happen?"

"It *can* happen. It *has* happened. But times are changing, and shipping out is changing. And sailors' lives are changing. This whole business is changing. We've worked all these years to make sailors' lives better, and we may have made them *too* good. We get good pay for shorter voyages, overtime for work when we're not on watch, first-class food at meals, respect for unions and union men. We've left the rest of the shipping business behind — so far behind that before too long, shipping companies won't be able to compete with the Liberians, the Greeks, the Indonesians, even the Chinese. If you've got goods to ship, you'll ship it in a Liberian ship, or an Indonesian ship — anything but a U.S. ship."

"What can you do about it?"

"Except for another war, when we would *have* to use American bottoms, not a fucking thing that I can see right now. And by then, there may not *be* any American bottoms. When that day comes, though, or *before* that day comes, we're going to need people like you, out of college. What do you figure on doing when you're through with college?"

"Journalism, I think. My father's a journalist, and he's had a good life."

"Well for now, keep going to sea. Don't worry about this college punk thing. Pay no attention if they get on your case. We're going to need people like you, with college and good thinking. You won't be bothered on *this* trip. You've got good watch mates. They saw how you handled the captain and the ship that night. They'll look after you."

They did. We sailed first to Southhampton on the south coast of England, and I could see by the thin eyes and mottled skins of the Brits what all those war years of poor food and living in bomb shelters had done. Then Le Havre, on the coast of France across the English Channel. There *wasn't* any Le Havre after all those years of bombing and war — just acre after acre of concrete rubble, some flattened into streets and storage areas, some just rubble.

The crew had some shore leave coming, and many of them went ashore to the bars and night life that had re-risen along those ruined streets. I was on gangway watch at three bells one night when I heard faint voices calling from between the warehouses.

"Pete! Oh, Pete!" I looked, but I couldn't see anyone.

"Pete! Pete!" came the call again.

"Where are you?"

"Over here!" I could see a smudge of white between a couple of the dockside buildings.

"We need blankets! Three of them!" The voice was that of Jack Daly, Ordinary Seaman on the Four-to-Eight watch.

"Bring them over! Please!"

I went down to the Four-to-Eight forecastle, picked three blankets from the beds, walked down the gangway, and over to the path between the warehouses. Jack and two of his watchmates stood there, bent over. *Stark naked.* Stripped and robbed of everything — *every thing* — on their way back to the ship. It wasn't cold, but I could swear they were shivering. They wrapped themselves in the blankets.

"We should have asked for shoes," Jack said. Even without walking, they were limping. Their feet were in terrible condition from the rubble. They hobbled back to the gangway, climbed it, and went to find antiseptic and bandages.

Trygve, Ola, Toola and I went ashore the next night. We found some Belgian beer for me, some *aquavit* for them (and one for me; tasted slightly licoricey), and practiced a little French on some women in a bar who seemed to want to talk with us. Then, without incident, we walked back to the ship — with our clothes and shoes on.

The *Marine Jumper* kept on, across the North Sea to the entrance of the Oslofjord. A Norwegian pilot came aboard to guide and command us up the narrow, miles-long fjord, between lovely, steep, green hills. The pilot asked Toola which of us would be at the wheel. Toola smiled, and pointed at me.

I took the wooden, hydraulic wheel and the pilot took the engine telegraph to signal "slow ahead" to the engine room. He gave me course corrections as we moved, carefully, deliberately, slowly, slowly, up the narrow waterway. The captain, sober, stood by as we arrived alongside the tugboats waiting to nudge us into the dock. Toola took the wheel, and the pilot left the bridge. Before he went, the pilot shook my hand.

"Good," he said.

I was proud.

Chapter 3

Venezuela - And Sexual Adventures!

"Maybe summers," I'd said to Harry Lundeberg when he asked whether I'd keep going to sea after my travels to Europe in 1946 — and the first summer that came along was the summer of '47.

In 1946 my Uncle Larry not only arranged for me to become a "permit member" of the Sailors Union of the Pacific, a "white-shoe" and largely white-skinned affiliate of the American Federation of Labor. He also arranged permit status for me in the National Maritime Union — the N.M.U., affiliated with the CIO and home to a great number of Spanish-speaking sailors, many from Puerto Rico.

As the 1947 spring dwindled and summer drew nigh I wondered to myself: Why not give the N.M.U. a try? Its hiring hall in Manhattan was an eye-catcher — the side of the building was an architectural blend of stylized port-holes and ocean waves. And its membership was much larger and more ethnically mixed than that of the S.U.P. The N.M.U. President, Joseph ("Joe") Curran, was having a well-publicized flirtation with the American far Left, and a peek inside it could be interesting.

I took a train from Philadelphia to New York, signed up for a cot at the Seamens' Church Institute, showed my permit and seaman's papers at the hiring hall, and went on the waiting list for the next opening on an American ship for a member of the deck, engine, or steward's crew. For old time's sake, I checked in at the S.U.P. hiring hall and found that all members, permit or otherwise, were being asked to walk a picket line at the New York Stock Exchange. The A.F.L. was trying to organize the Exchange's clerks, and was applying pressure. Just for the experience, I borrowed a Lundeberg Stetson, went over to the Exchange at Broad and Wall Streets, took a sign and walked the picketing circle on the sidewalk outside.

But not for long. I didn't want to miss a possible N.M.U. call-up, and went back to the hiring hall to wait. It took another three days, but my name was called out for a job in the steward's department of a United States Lines' passenger ship, the SS/*Washington*. The vessel's wartime role as the wartime troopship *Mount Vernon* over, it was being refitted and put back into scheduled transatlantic passenger service. I reported to the ship and the Chief Steward. He took a look at me and my papers and told me that I would be a "Dishwashing Machine Technician."

When I got to the ship's kitchen, I found the reason. All other members of the *Washington's* stewards' department were Puerto Rican, and I was the only one who could read "technical" English. In the refitting, all dishwashing machines for the passenger dining rooms had been replaced by new ones, and the instructions were in English. My job, I was told, was to turn the machines on as dishes came out at the end of a meal, and turn them off again when the dishes were washed. No handling of plates, no food scraping, no garbage dumping, no stacking was required. Just turn the machines on. And off.

As it turned out, I had plenty of time to myself. My bunk was in the bow of the ship, with no distracting exterior portholes. The lights were always on, but not bright enough to read by. There was a deck for the crew, but it was under the rear passenger deck, out of sight of sky and sun, and there were no chairs or benches — only flat-topped steel bollards. I had no conversational Spanish, and *¿Como está usted?* didn't go very far.

I ate well. The ship had "stabilizers" underwater on its sides and didn't roll or pitch much, but even slight motion caused many passengers to eschew eating, or even chewing. Dinner and dessert plates would come out untouched.

Plenty of pasta and stew were served to the crew, but on steak or chop nights we on dishwasher detail could feast on grilled red meat, followed by cake, berry pie, or chocolate mousse.

This was all very well, but when we arrived at Cobh ("Cork"), Ireland, Southhampton and Calais, we in the stewards department were not allowed to go ashore. From the edges of the crew's deck we could admire the green hills of Ireland or scan the docks of England or France. But that was all.

When we got back to New York I could have signed on for another voyage. Instead, I signed off and went home to suburban Philadelphia.

There, I discovered, an entrepreneurial friend of my father's was taking advantage of the end of Lend-Lease by renting World War II tankers to companies shipping crude oil from Venezuela's Lake Maracaibo to refineries in Texas and Pennsylvania. From there, they were moving refined petroleum products to coastal cities on both American seaboards.

The tankers were "T-2"s, of which 481 were built during the war to carry small cargos and refuel larger ships at sea. One of them — the SS*Julesburg* (named for an 1865 battle between U.S. soldiers and Native Americans in Colorado) — was built in Mobile, Alabama. It accidentally sank hip-deep during sea trials off the coast of Louisiana, and as the story went, salvage companies were too busy to raise and refit it until after the war.

When my father ran into the entrepreneur that spring, the ship had been raised and towed into a drydock in Algiers, a port town across the Mississippi River from New Orleans. The *Julesburg* was being refitted and soon would be ready for its first working voyage. A crew was needed. I was experienced, as my father knew, but no experience was required of the rest of the crew. Did I have friends who would like to go along?

I did, and I quickly recruited a couple of Lower Merion High School classmates, Bob Allen and Lon (Real Name: Alonzo) Horsey, to come along. I was a deckhand and Ordinary Seaman because of my 1946 experience, but Bob and Lon would have to be in the Steward's Department, serving meals and doing housekeeping for the ship's officers. Bob was a literary type who'd worked with me on the weekly school newspaper, the *Merionite*. Lon, our like-

Lilly Christine, a New Orleans Bourbon Street attraction.

able class president, was a brainy gymnast who was solid high-bar muscle from the waist up but stood and walked on pipestem legs because of childhood poliomyelitis. He went on after college to study and practice Law.

The shipping company paid our way south by train, and told us to report to the *Julesburg* in Algiers. But when we got there, the ship was far from ready to re-launch and sail. A room was booked (and *paid for*) in the downtown Roosevelt Hotel ("home of the Sazerac Lounge"!). We were ordered to report to the ship each morning for a *"per-diem"* food and living allowance *in cash*. Otherwise, we were on our own.

The ship's purser (an undergraduate at Swarthmore College) guessed that it would take another week or ten days to finish work on the ship. What more could you give a trio of 17-year-olds on their first outing in wicked New Orleans? Wow!

We did young-tourist things, like wandering through the overground cemeteries (the city's water-level in some places was too high for dry-as-a-bone burials) and exploring Tulane University. We rode the streetcar named "Desire." Besides to-and-from Algiers every day, we sailed on ferries on the Mississippi. We listened to Dixieland jazz bands. We walked the ways and by-ways of the city and Algiers by day, and peeked in at sexy Bourbon-Street night-club acts from outside sidewalks by night. We splurged on a beer or three and watched Lilly Christine (the "Cat Girl") do back-bends to drink "champagne" from straight-up martini glasses balanced separately (and *unglued*) on the tops of her right and left breasts without using her hands (and without spilling a drop!).

One night, as we turned away from a night-club entrance after a particularly non-sexy "sexy" performance, a cab driver came up.

"Would you like to see a *real* sex show?" he said.

"Yes," one or two of us said. I think I was one of them.

"Come with me," he said. We walked around a corner and got into his cab.

"It'll cost you ten dollars apiece," he said.

"Ten dollars!" Lon said. "*Apiece?*"

"Let's call it five dollars apiece," the driver said. "Fifteen, total."

We paid the money, and the cab took off. I can't tell you where it went, exactly, but we were in wide, empty streets when it stopped. The driver pointed down a block of what looked like four-or-five-storey apartment buildings and handed us (me) a doorknob with a rectangular spine attached.

"Halfway down that block you'll find a street door without a knob," he said. "This will fit it. Put it in, turn it. The sex show's upstairs."

We got out and went down the deserted sidewalk. Sure enough, on the right we came to a street-level door with no knob. I inserted the doorknob spine, turned it, and the door opened onto a staircase. There was a hallway at the top, leading to a lighted room at the rear. We walked along until we got to the room. It was an apartment living room, a bit on the shabby side. An old couch and a couple of overstuffed chairs stood inside. On them were two youngish women, in what I guess you'd call negligées.

One of them said, "Hello. How can we help you?"

"A cab driver brought us here," I said. "He said we could see a sex show."

One of the women got up. "Have a seat," she said. "I'll get another show-girl." She walked out of the room.

We sat, saying nothing. I was wondering whether we were going to have to pay for the show. My folding money was stored safely in my shoe, and getting it out would be kind of awkward. The woman who had gone out came back with another woman, also in a negligée.

"What kind of sex show were you looking for?" said the first woman. She and the "showgirl" sat down.

"I don't know," I said. "The driver just said there would be a sex show here."

I didn't say anything. Lon and Bob didn't say anything. Neither did the women. At last the two women who'd sat down, got up. They took off their negligées. They lay down on the spotted carpet and began to pretend to lick each other. They didn't actually touch. The third woman didn't say anything. She just sat there.

At last the first girl said, "We can't do a good sex show here. I think we need to move to the other rooms to do a sex show." She stood up and put her negligée back on.

Lon, Bob and I sat for a minute or two. Finally, I got up.

"I'm leaving," I said. I headed for the door and went down the stairs. The door to the street was open. Without the knob, I couldn't close it. I tried to pull it shut, but the latch wouldn't catch. I went out, leaving it open.

As I tried to figure out which way was back downtown, I heard voices. "Pete! Pete! Wait up, Pete! Wait up!"

Lon, Bob and I walked until we got to a street where there was more traf-fic. We hailed a cab and rode home to the Roosevelt.

The next morning, as we ate breakfast in our favorite diner, who should we see at the back of the room but two of the women from the night before? We hesitated, then waved virtuously at them.

They waved back.

Chapter 4

Tales of the Daily D

My football career ended with a torn *meniscus* at Lower Merion Senior High School in Ardmore, PA in 1945 — but I didn't know it, thank goodness. The end came in a searing flash as I was running full-tilt down the practice field. My "team" had punted, and I was supposed to tackle the receiver. I glanced up to find the flight of the ball, not noticing that Bob Davis, another player, had knelt in my path. I hit Bob, hard. My lower left leg stayed locked against him. My upper body, all 175 pounds of it, kept going. The knee between my lower leg and upper body was stretched to the separation point. The connective cartilage — the *meniscus* — was torn, and I had what was known in those days as a "trick knee."

I limped for days. When I felt better I played football, but at unpredictable times, when the knee underwent unexpected stress, it "went out." I limped around, and kept playing football, but the knee kept "going out."

Surgery happened. Today, a trick knee can be repaired and can heal. In those days it was believed that a *meniscus*, being cartilage, *couldn't* heal. The only thing you could do was cut it out and throw it away. Mine was thrown away.

I tried to play football when I left high school and went to Dartmouth, but at unexpected times the knee kept "going out." During spring practice my senior year, the line coach, John Del Isola ("Johnny Del"), took me aside and gave me some of the best football advice I ever had.

"You're not having fun," he said. "Stop trying to play football."

I did.

I had a pretty decent singing voice and became a baritone in the Dartmouth Glee Club. I could write pretty well, and I "heeled" (tried out) as a reporter and writer for the campus daily newspaper, *The Dartmouth*.

Part of the heeling process were stints as "Night Editor" for the paper. In those days the paper was printed on a large flat-bed press in the back of a building on Allen Street in Hanover. Using a molten-lead "Linotype" machine, a fast and able print-shop typist named "Ed" molded written articles and headlines into lines of solid-lead type, and locked the type into "forms" for printing.

Photographs were more complicated. They had to be engraved on copper plates in another town by another process a day or two in advance, nailed onto wooden blocks, shipped back to Hanover, and tucked into the printing "forms" with the lines of molded lead type as tight as possible around them. An expandable metal device called a "quoin" (pronounced "coin") went in next, to twist the lines of type and wooden blocks into an immoveable mass with a special wrench called a "quoin key."

When all was ready, Ed inked the type and photo plates, rolled paper over them, and produced printed "proofs." The Night Editor read the proofs. If he found "typos" (typographical errors), he asked Ed to mold new, replacement lines of type. When they were in place and new proofs were read, the Night Editor told Ed to start the press and begin printing the morning paper.

The year of my night-editing was 1948, and Harry Truman, the Democratic Vice President who'd succeeded Franklin Roosevelt, was being challenged for the presidency by the racket-busting former District Attorney and Republican Governor from New York State, Thomas E. Dewey. Truman may have been President, but politically he was a nobody — a Democratic hack from the Nowhere State of Missouri. Anybody and Everybody who knew anything about American politics knew that Dewey was sure to win.

This included the top editors of the daily *Dartmouth*. To illustrate the front page of the election-morning issue, they had ordered up an oversized, freshly engraved photo-portrait of Thomas E. Dewey. The idea was that when the final results came in after midnight on election day, the Night Editor could compose a front-page headline, get the first couple of paragraphs of the Associated Press news-wire election story Linotyped by Ed, check the proofs, and go to bed — where the top editors would already comfortably be.

But at midnight the results were not final. Far from it. Ed and I watched the vote count creep upward for Truman — and, at about 3:00 a.m., he was clearly ahead. It was time to put the paper — and ourselves — to bed. I wrote a banner headline to run on the front page over the top story: "TRUMAN LEADING IN UPSET"

But what about that front-page photo? In our collection of old, cast-lead, one-column Truman photos we had nothing anywhere near the size of the four-column Dewey extravaganza. No article could fill the space. Ed and I stood looking at the form, with Dewey looking triumphantly up from his upside-down copper engraving.

"Loosen the form, Ed," I said.

He took the quoin key from his apron pocket, and loosened the quoin and the wooden block under Dewey.

"Take it out," I said.

He lifted the Dewey engraving out of the form.

"Turn it around."

"Turn it around?"

"Turn it around, so it prints upside-down. And lock it in."

Next morning, on the floor outside my dorm-room at 410 Russell Sage Hall, the face of Thomas E. Dewey, his moustache where his forehead should have been, looked up at me and my roommates. "TRUMAN LEADING IN UPSET" said the headline. The same happened at every other door on the Hanover campus, and most other doors in Hanover. (In those days, there was no other daily paper in town.)

When they heard why, my roommates cheered and pounded my back.

But what would the reaction be at the Managing Editor's daily noontime criticism session at The *Dartmouth* office in Robinson Hall? Night Editors were supposed to close the paper, not re-design it.

The office door was shut as I walked into Robinson Hall. I opened it.

Silence. The room was full of *Dartmouth* staffers, all staring.

Then, Applause.

Chapter 5

When Worlds Collide

I'm not going to *over*check the *facts* underlying this memoir chunk. My son Bill (William Thornton Martin III, named for his paternal grandfather and great-grandfather), who lives and breathes computer languages and cyber-security, may do so. He has been converting my writing into the book are now holding. He's a great researcher, fact-finder, and fact-checker. I owe most of the photographs, footnotes, illustrations, and solid factual exposition you've been reading to his searches and research.

The happenings in this chapter began toward the end of my third undergraduate year as a writer and budding editor of the daily *Dartmouth* in Hanover, New Hampshire. I was at the end of my Junior year, and the newspaper's out-bound Senior-class directorate met to elect its successors.

So it came to pass in May, 1950, at the age of 20, I was elected "Features Editor" of the "D" (as it was known). Theodore ("Ted") Laskin was elected Editor-in-Chief.

Politically, the times were interesting. The Korean war began that June, and Joseph McCarthy, a Republican U.S. Senator from Wisconsin, kept discovering "dangerous" Communists in the State Department, in the Armed Forces, in the White House, in Congress, and in just about every arm and organ of government. We "moderates" and "liberals" described what he was doing as a "witch hunt."

Ted Laskin was solidly, firmly Left. He wrote columns and editorials supporting left-wing causes and issues, and was particularly vocal about the plight of a Dartmouth graduate named William Remington, who had been arrested and jailed for associations and activities in support of far-left organizations banned under provisions of something called the "Smith Act."

I was ignorant about the particulars of the Smith Act and too immature to have decided what I *was*, politically. But if you're a left-handed hammer like Ted Laskin, every nail must seem bent to the right. Since my father worked for the conservative *Saturday Evening Post*, I must have looked like a right-wing spike to Ted.

That summer I went to sea, to Venezuela and Texas, as an Ordinary Seaman aboard the tanker SS/*Julesburg*. When I returned to Hanover to begin my Senior Year I got to work to find, assign and write "feature" assignments for the daily "D". As a member of the newspaper's "directorate," I also had a responsibility to write an editorial once a month. The editorials were long, and expressed opinions about events and issues both on and off the Dartmouth campus.

For my first editorial, I focused on railway strikes. There were a lot of them going around. It seemed to me there wasn't a day or a week when U.S. economic activity wasn't being brought to a screeching halt by railway strikes. A particularly damaging one that fall was called by the union of railway "firemen," striking for higher pay and permanent space and status in the locomotives of American freight and passenger trains.

In the recesses of my mind, railway firemen were recalled by a line in one of my Uncle Larry's favorite folk songs, "The Wreck of the Old Ninety-Seven". At the end of the song, the engineer was "found in the wreck with his hand on the throttle; he was scalded to death by steam." Before that happened, "he turned and said to his old black fireman, 'shovel on a little more coal, 'cause when we hit that wide old mountain, you're going to see old Ninety-Seven roll!'"

Railway firemen, obviously, were originally aboard locomotives to keep coal fires burning and steam pressure high enough to keep the pistons moving and the wheels driving. But in a diesel-powered age? With no fires to stoke, they were little more than backup humans. In an emergency, if something like a heart attack or sprained thumb befell the engineer, a fireman could stop the train. Otherwise, his function was quaint, but limited.

I did a bit of research in the *Encyclopedia Americana* and back copies of the *New York Times,* and wrote a semi-humorous editorial urging the replacement of "firemen" with backup engineers or under-employed brakemen. I checked the grammar, made sure it was the right length to fill the *Daily D* editorial column, left it on Ted Laskin's desk, and went back to my dorm ... or, maybe, to Hanover's Nugget Theater to "flick out" (take in a movie).

In ways mysterious to me, the editorial got to the linotypist on Allen Street, was set in molten lead, and appeared on Page Two of the newspaper the next morning.

Even before I got to the editorial meeting that day, warning flags were flying. Friends outside the newspaper office in Robinson Hall said that Ted Laskin was furious. Looking like a gathering tornado, he walked into the reporters' meeting room and told me to come to his office.

"That editorial!" he shouted when I got there. "What did you mean by it? Why didn't you tell me you were writing it?"

"I didn't know I was supposed to," I said. "All I knew was that we had to take our turn writing editorials, and my turn came around yesterday. I left it on your desk."

"I didn't have time to read it!" Ted said. "You made the paper look sophomoric, and me like an idiot!"

"How come?" I asked.

"You don't understand the Labor Movement! That strike was not just about firemen and locomotives! It was about the history of the *Labor Movement,* and the worldwide struggle of workers for equity!"

Ted didn't *capitalize* and *italicize* Labor, and Movement, but the upper case and italics were in his voice. I don't like shouting arguments, and I could see we were headed for one.

Trying to be Mr. Calm, I said. "I think you're reading too much into this."

"Reading too much!" he said. "Reading too much? You're not reading enough! The rise of Labor is the underlying force behind what's happening in the world, and *you* want to get workers out of *locomotives*! Look at what's happening in eastern Europe! The workers are finally taking charge! It's a workers' revolution!"

"I think who's taking charge in eastern Europe is the Communist Party, not the workers," I said. "I had a Czech girl friend, Milena Pichova, who came to the United States as a war refugee when the Germans invaded her country in 1939. We were both eleven or twelve at the time. We were friends all the way through grammar school and high school in suburban Philadelphia, but when the war ended she decided to go back to Czechoslovakia and help rebuild her country. She went to Law School at Charles University in Prague.

"To help her and her family through post-war food shortages I arranged to send CARE packages, and we wrote long letters back and forth — at least for much of her first year in Law School. She mentioned that she and her family were under some kind of suspicion because she'd lived in the West, and she asked me to stop sending the CARE packages. Then her letters began reminding me how 'Socialist' she had been when we were together at Plymouth Meeting Friends School and Lower Merion Senior High School in Pennsylvania. She 'reminded' me of how 'misunderstood' she had become because of her 'Socialist' principles. Those reminders were total nonsense.

"It became obvious to me that all this talk about her high-school "socialism" was for other people who were reading her mail, not me. Then came a letter in which she begged me to stop writing to her. Then, silence.

"Ted," I said to the Editor-in-Chief, "she was silenced by her fear of the Communist dictatorship."

Ted wasn't yelling any more. His voice was cold and final. "That does it," he said. "You understand nothing. As long as I'm editor, not another word of yours will ever appear in this newspaper!"

I was fired.

And no word I'd written ever appeared in the paper again.

Years later, when I was a writer at TIME magazine, I worked with an immigrant Czech researcher named Desa Pavlu. Casually, I asked her one day if she had ever known Milena Pichova.

"Milena!" she said. "We were at Charles University together! At the end of the first year I could see what the Communists were up to, and decided to come back to the States. I tried to persuade Milena to come with me, but she was determined to stay, and improve the situation. They sent her to some kind of rehabilitation camp. She was beaten to death."

Years after I met Desa, I got approval from my TIME bosses to organize the Iron-Curtain color-photography project described in the "David and Elzbieta" chapter of this book. See page 185. To make latter-day Czech Communists squirm a bit, when I got to Prague I told my official guides I had an old friend who had lived in Prague and attended Charles University after the Germans left. She had disappeared. I wanted to find her and interview her friends and family. I gave them Milena's old address, and insisted that they take me there so I could ask neighbors what had happened to her, and where she had gone. We went, and they knocked on doors and asked the questions I wanted asked. Within myself, I was pleased that the neighbors realized that *someone* remembered — and the official guides understood the same.

I was not the only Dartmouth person bothered by Ted Laskin's editorial tilt. Many alumni subscribed to the paper by mail to keep in touch with what was going on at the College, and they let President John Dickey know how they felt about the left-wing editorials. Dickey believed in freedom of the Press and freedom of speech, and he often spoke up on Laskin's behalf.

Each week, as part of his presidential routine, Dickey met with Laskin in his office in Parkhurst Hall. It was said that Ted gauged his effectiveness by the temperature of Dickey's presidential pique.

Such was the situation one day in the winter of 1951, when Ted stepped in to Parkhurst for his weekly meeting. But Dickey was quite composed, and the conversation seemed abnormally normal. Finally, Ted could no longer stand the calm.

"Did you read my editorial today?" he asked the President.

"Ted," said Dickey, "I can read you, or I can defend you. But I can't do both."

Chapter 6

The Cub Reporter Meets Walter S. Rogers

Being a cub reporter at the *St. Louis Post-Dispatch* in 1950 was fun. Well ... a *lot of it* was fun. Learning the newspaper's "style" rules took a while.

It may look Midwestern on the map, but St. Louis was a Southern city. You could almost capitalize and italicize *Southern*. If a man or (rare) woman in a news story was black, or what later became *Afro-American,* he or she was "negro." Not "a Negro." No capitalization, no indefinite article, no exceptions, no explication, no matter — negro. Nice Equivalent: black. Un-nice equivalent: nigger.

For a 22-year-old from the northeastern U.S., it was hard (but after a couple of lectures at the copy desk not *totally* hard) to identify a holdup man or a hit-and-run driver as "negro." But in usual, non-racial language, the kind of language you'd use in an article about a school-board election or an obituary, the word would stick in the throat of your Royal Typewriter.

Just try writing "Funeral services for Walter P. Jones, 82, former Executive Vice President of the First National Bank of East St. Louis, will be at the Bopp undertaking establishment at 2:30 p.m, Friday, May 6. Mr. Jones, negro, was also past President of the Rotary Club of East St. Louis ..."

It's not easy. You also had to learn that, no matter what it called itself, an organization that took care of the dead was never a "Funeral Home" or the "Gates of Heaven" or a "Cremation Service." It was an "undertaking establishment." No bells, whistles, trumpets or capital letters. An "undertaking establishment." Period.

Young reporters also "broke in" on the "beats." This is "beat" as in "a police beat in Canarsie" (where nothing ever happened, and cops being punished in New York were compelled to serve). On the *P-D*, the "beats" were the Civil Courts beat, the Federal Court beat, the Police Beat and the St. Louis County beat.

If you were new at the paper, the Police Beat was usually where you found yourself on a Saturday night from 6 p.m. to 2 a.m., when other 20-year-olds were out playing and partying, and newspaper presses had stopped printing Sunday-morning editions. Both the *P-D* and its competitor (the *St. Louis Globe-Democrat*) were closed to any "late-breaking" stories. If the Anheuser-Busch brewery in South St. Louis caught on fire, the Police-Beat man was there to report it. Otherwise, the Police-Beat man sat in the press room at Police Headquarters at 12th Street and Olive Boulevard, listened to the Police Radio, and played Gin Rummy with the *St. Louis Globe-Democrat* Police-Beat man and an occasional off-duty detective. I got pretty darned good at Police-Beat gin rummy, and eventually won enough to buy three new tires for my 1947 Studebaker Commander.

Only once was I prodded out of my press-room chair — when a report came over the Police Radio of an "assault" at 14th and Olive. This was only two blocks away from where I was sitting, and the *Globe* man was out of the room. I got up, walked the two blocks west to 14th, looked down the street and saw a cluster of people looking up at the back of one of the decrepit, four-story, apartment buildings. Wooden staircases went up the back to the apartments' upper floors, and I asked a bystander what was going on.

"Fellow came home drunk" — it was Saturday night, after all — "and got into a fight with his wife. She took a kitchen knife, and killed him. That's her, over there."

A homicide! I went over to the woman, told her I was from the *Post-Dispatch*, and asked what had happened. The bystander had it right. Her husband had come home drunk while she was making his supper. They got into a fight, and he swung a chair at her. She grabbed the knife and hit out at him. The knife caught him in the neck, and he fell down at the top landing of the outside stairs. She got a neighbor to call the police, and went downstairs to wait for them. They hadn't arrived yet. I got her name, her husband's name, their address, his employer's name, and their *ages*. (Cub reporters learned their trade as a result of snarls from the City Editor. One snarl, often snarled: "What was her *age*, Martin? Her *age*?) I climbed the flight ot stairs to check — and earned a red badge of courage and initiative — a drip of the victim's blood on my gabardine suit.

I got all the essential information, went back to Police Headquarters, and called the Assistant City Editor. At home. From my notes, I read the details to him.

"What was that address, Martin?"

"Thirteen-thirty-eight Olive."

"What?" (A tone of disbelief.)

"Thirteen-thirty-eight Olive."

Disbelief was replaced by Anger. The Assistant City Editor knew his St. Louis neighborhoods, and he recognized a negro address when he heard it.

"That's a *cutting*, Martin! We don't cover *cuttings* in the *Post-Dispatch*!" The phone got slammed down.

When the *Globe* man got back, I learned they didn't cover *cuttings* — or other Saturday-night assaults in negro neighborhoods — in the *Globe*, either.

Live and learn.

Deadliest of all was the Civil Courts Beat. Day by day, the Beat-Man had to check with the clerks of each of the eight or ten courts in the Civil Courts Building to find out whether any "interesting" cases had been filed. None ever were.

The Beat-Man also had to check whether any interesting divorces were on the Civil-Courts docket. None ever were.

The Beat-Man also had to check whether any interesting wills had been filed for probate. None ever were.

Trouble was, all the interesting St. Louis people — and most of the interesting St. Louis money — had moved west, away from the city's decaying Mississippi-River docks and levees, and away from the city's sweltering old downtown enclaves, to St. Louis County — to the country clubs and Lords&Taylors of air-conditioned Ladue, and Clayton, and University City, and Creve Coeur. The Germans — the Busches and the Anheusers and the Griesediecks — still made beer and money in south St. Louis, but they invested it remotely or spent it at Nieman-Marcus in Dallas.

A dusty phone sat on the Beat-Man's desk in the downtown Civil-Courts Building, but it almost never rang.

Imagine my surprise then, when late one spring morning in March or April, it rang. I picked it up. An unfamiliar voice said, "This is Walter Rogers. I'm with the Institute of Current World Affairs in New York. It's been suggested that you might benefit from spending two years writing from subSaharan Africa. Are you interested?"

It took a few seconds to drink it in, but I had to be honest. "I'm interested," I said. "But I know very little about Africa."

"That's the idea," said the voice. "Why don't you come to New York? We can talk about it."

It took a while to explain my proposed and mysterious New York disappearance to my editors (I was going to *miss* a Saturday night at Police Headquarters!), but three weeks later — with a ticket paid for by Mr. Rogers — I boarded an Eastern Airlines four-engined Constellation aircraft at Lambert-St. Louis Field and flew to La Guardia Airport outside New York City. Following instructions, I took a taxi to the Iroquois Hotel on West 44th Street in Manhattan. It eventually became a revived, restored, multi-starred, boutique showplace, but then it was pretty much a no-place. A dump.

I spent the night, walked the next morning to the corner of 43rd Street and Fifth Avenue, and rode an elevator up to the eleventh floor of the Guaranty Trust Company building. Waiting for me in the outermost of a modest suite of offices was a neat, organized woman named Helen Pluntze. And, beyond her, a rangey, late-middle-aged Walter S. Rogers.

Founding Executive Director Walter Rogers

Mr. Rogers (I never called him anything else) was ... *ordinary.* He had a short crop of grey hair receding from a forehead that had already reached the top of his head. He wore thick eyeglasses, a white shirt, grey trousers (a jacket that matched hung on the back of his office door), and an unremarkable necktie. He sat behind an ordinary desk beneath (as I recall) a painting of what looked like a Spanish grandee. He smoked thin brown cigars in a holder, and flicked the ashes into a waste basket at the end of the desk. When he wanted to make a conversational point, he flicked with an emphasis that frequently dislodged the cigar past the waste basket onto the carpet. From the burn marks in the carpet, you could see that he was often emphatic.

As a young Chicagoan (I found out later), Walter Rogers had studied night-school law and gone to work, first as a journalist and second as secretary to a man named Charles Richard Crane. Crane was one of two brothers who'd inherited a New Jersey family company that made brass fittings for the plumbing industry. When the flush toilet was invented early in the 20th Cen-

Charles R. Crane in 1909, the year he was appointed Minister to China by President William Howard Taft.

tury (and was successfully marketed in Britain by Thomas Crapper — later *Sir* Thomas Crapper) America woke up to the possibilities and potential of indoor plumbing.

The Crane Brothers' father realized that the "crapper" (so called by Brits and U.S. doughboys returning from Europe and World War I) would bring *indoors*, watery functions previously done *outdoors*, in an outhouse or at the kitchen sink. He more-or-less *invented* the American bathroom, and the Crane Company began making and selling matching fixtures and faucets, shower curtains and wallpaper, stylish tubs and basins.

The Cranes became very rich and Charles Crane, not fancying a career in plumbing supplies, sold his half of the company to his brother John for a reputed $14 million. That doesn't sound like much in these billionized days, but back in the 1920s a "millionaire" was, well, a MILLIONAIRE. Charles

Crane became a world traveler, a desert fruit-grower (California dates and figs), and a peripatetic philanthropist, funding Middle Eastern universities (Roberts College in Lebanon and American Universities in Yemen and Cairo) and underwriting irrigating visionaries in desertified Yemen and Saudi Arabia.

He hired Walter Rogers as his secretary, and Rogers sailed and traveled the world with him, acting as his agent, discovering and delivering significant amounts of money to ambitious Sheiks, impoverished monarchs, Bolshevik revolutionaries and enlightened American dreamers and politicians. Crane became a principal backer of the presidential campaign of former New Jersey Governor Woodrow Wilson. He was Chairman of Wilson's Finance Committee, and traveled with Wilson to the Versailles Peace Conference after the First World War.

Along the way, Rogers became an expert in the young science of international telecommunications. After Crane died, Rogers became the administrator and dispenser of income from his fortune. He and Crane's son John founded the Institute of Current World Affairs (ICWA) in 1923 to provide fellowships that would enable young Americans to gain the same sort of international understanding that British and French diplomats and scholars took with them to Versailles.

World War II brought ICWA's fellowship program pretty much to a halt, but Rogers kept sending ICWA's "Fellows" out to study and write about all reachable regions of the world — to Latin America, Canada, the Middle East and, as it became possible, Africa, Europe and Asia. At war's end Rogers' and Crane's tight little band of academic and journalistic scholars and writers were among the few sources of anything like in-depth international understanding for American students and the public at large.

Realizing this, the Ford and Rockefeller Foundations supplemented ICWA's international study resources, and Walter Rogers began looking farther and wider for potential scholars and writers. He created a corps of academics, called the American Universities Field Staff (AUFS), to teach international subjects and topics at participating U.S. colleges and universities. He broadened his search for ICWA Fellows to man both organizations. I, and dozens of other Ford- and Rockefeller-funded ICWA Fellows and AUFS "Associates" (as the latter were known), were the result.

In the late 1940s and early '50s when I encountered him, Rogers lived his life seeking, finding, funding, guiding and managing young ICWA Fellows and AUFS Associates. He traveled (by train and ship, never by plane) on scouting trips to American, Canadian and British friends with international experience and contacts. One of these (as I also later learned) was John Sloan Dickey, who as a young man had broken off a State Department Career at the end of World War II to become President of Dartmouth College.

Visited many years later by an oral historian with a tape recorder, Dickey remembered, "He was very twentieth-century-rural in appearance. He used to show up at my office without any warning or appointment, looking like he'd just put the hoe down. He was always interesting company, and we'd walk over to the Hanover Inn and gossip in the rocking chairs on the porch. We'd catch up, and then he'd want to know whether I'd come across any young writers who were learning about interesting areas of the world ... "

World War II closed the world to Rogers' Fellows — and to all American academic researchers, for that matter. At the end of the war, U.S. universities and newspapers had precious few professors and serious international writers informing students and the reading public about international issues.

Now, back to June of 1953, and my first meeting with Mr. Rogers in his New York office. It's a bit dim in my mind, but I'm sure he asked whether I'd done any international traveling. I told him that my new wife, a lovely, lively, public-spirited woman named Julie (Julia Lawnin Gordon), and I had spent our honeymoon aboard a refrigerated ship of United Fruit's "Great White Fleet," sailing up and down the Caribbean coast of Central America visiting banana plantations and loading cargoes of the still-green fruit for delivery to New Orleans and thousands of American grocery stores beyond. Julie and I spent a lot of time riding narrow-gauge railways into the plantations, learning about banana cultivating and harvesting, learning about banana transportation, storage and marketing — and, along the way, eating banana cake, banana pie, banana fritters, banana salads, banana daiquiris, bananas raw, and bananas flambé.

And, naturally, I told him about my two teenage summers in the U.S. Merchant Marine, working as a crew-member on passenger ships and oil tankers to and from Europe and Latin America.

Mr. Rogers told me about the writing fellowships of the Institute of Current World Affairs. The ideal Fellow, he said, would be an intelligent young man just arrived in some part of the World from Mars. He would look about him, learn the local language, observe the human activity around him, apply his values and understanding, and then write to a friend or relative back on Mars what was happening in this new land or society, and what it meant.

How often would Mr. Rogers expect a Fellow to write one of these reports?

"When he knew enough to write about it, he would write about it."

Mr. Rogers already had a Fellow in subSaharan Africa, a geographer named Edwin S. ("Ned") Munger. He had earned a Ph.D. from the University of Chicago and was already doing some adjunct teaching at the California Institute of Technology in Pasadena.

Teaching *Geography* at CalTech?

"Someone out there decided that scientists in high-tech fields needed to understand the world. They signed on for teaching visits from Institute Fellows who'd joined the American Universities Field Staff, and they liked what Munger brought them. Now he stops in there and teaches African geography once a year. I think they're going to offer him a full professorship."

The conversation went on like this for quite a while. Then Mr. Rogers suggested that I cross Fifth Avenue and meet a friend of his, Henry Allen Moe, for lunch. Moe and Rogers were close friends, and Moe was just launching a series of fellowships for the newly founded Guggenheim Foundation. Since they were both spending foundation money on new international ventures, Moe and Rogers were in and out of each other's offices several times a week. After lunch, Mr. Rogers wanted me to come back to 522 Fifth and meet a man named Phillips Talbot, who had recently returned from an ICWA fellowship in India and was managing the American Universities Field Staff from an office a few flights below.

Martin building apartment (upper left) at 5592 Waterman Boulevard.

Somewhat dizzy from all this international talk, I returned to the ICWA office, said goodbye to Mr. Rogers and Miss Pluntze, went back to the Iriquois Hotel, and St. Louis, and the "beats."

A couple of weeks later came another Walter Rogers phone call. He wanted to come to St. Louis and meet Julie. Could he stay with us a few days, or could we get him a hotel room?

We had an old-fashioned floor-through apartment on the top floor of a two-sided, three-up and three-down apartment building in western St. Louis at 5592 Waterman Boulevard. Julie's mother and father came from old Illinois and Missouri families, and we had fully furnished the place with wedding gifts. We had a library, a dining room, and a guest bedroom. Any empty chinks we filled with chairs and side tables from her family home. Of course he would stay with us.

I was at work the morning he arrived, and Julie met him at St. Louis' Union Station. There was some confusion because Daylight Savings Time, which skipped across the country in unpredictable and uneven patterns in those days, was in effect where he'd come from but not in St. Louis. Or vice-versa. At any rate, Julie spent some time searching the vastness of that immense station for him, and he for her. Neither looked like the other expected, and by the time I got home that afternoon they were deep in discussion about whether standardized rules were good or bad for a society.

We talked that way over drinks and dinner, and so to bed — early, because Mr. Rogers had had a hard day of train travel and he wanted to go to work with me the next morning. Which was also early.

After breakfast Mr. Rogers and I took the bus downtown to the *Post-Dispatch* building. I explained to Sam Armstrong, then the City Editor, who Rogers was and why he was there. Sam, a good man, understood that Mr. Rogers just wanted to see what a day's work for me was all about, and how I went about it. I established Mr. Rogers in a visitor's chair near my place in the back row of desks in the City Room and explained procedures. For cub reporters, the City Editor had a folder full of stories from that morning's rival *Globe-Democrat* — stories that the *Post-Dispatch* hadn't covered. The *P-D* reporter was supposed to re-report each one of them, making phone calls, getting earlier stories out of the "morgue" (our library files), checking addresses and names. He (there were no female reporters) had to re-check the Globe's facts, adding things that the *Globe* had missed, or under-reported. Tedious and boring work.

If a newsworthy event suddenly happened, the City Editor could shout a reporter's name and call him up to the desk and tell him to go out and report the story. This didn't happen many days, but it was great when it did. You could turn over all your re-reporting to another new guy and get out of the building.

When Mr. Rogers was there (perhaps *because* he *was* there) one of those moments came for me. Some workman had fallen down the shaft of a freight elevator of a warehouse near the riverfront and emergency vehicles and crews were on the way.

"Martin!" came the call, and I went up to Sam Armstrong's desk. Sam gave me the details he had from the *P-D* reporter at police headquarters and said (bless his heart; this didn't always happen), "Take a cab."

I gathered my notebook and Mr. Rogers, turned my re-reporting stuff over to fellow cub reporter Jim Deakin, and headed out of the office. When we got to the warehouse I found the cop on the case, found out where the accident had happened, and headed for it. The workman had tried to leap on to the open-fronted, slow-moving elevator as it passed the fifth floor, but didn't quite make it. He hit the top opening of the fifth-floor level and his legs got caught. He didn't quite get cut in half (no story ever quite lives up to its potential), but he got pushed off the elevator and fell down the shaft. When I got to the basement they were fishing his body out of the oil and waste next to the giant spring that was supposed to keep an out-of-control elevator from hitting bottom. I dashed off to the warehouse office to get the man's name, address, identity, *age*, and family circumstances, and look for a phone I could use to call the story in to the office. When all was done, I looked around for Mr. Rogers, but he was nowhere to be seen, or found. Finally, one of the office people told me that he'd identified himself to the office staff, said he was with the *Post-Dispatch* reporter, but had a train to catch, and left.

That evening, he phoned. He *did* have a train to catch, he said. He'd gone back to the apartment, got the superintendent to let him in, packed his stuff, and headed off to Union Station. He thanked me for the dinner and the overnight, thanked me for letting him follow me on assignment, and cleared up whatever misunderstanding I had about Daylight Saving Time. He told me to thank Julie, said I'd be hearing from him. Then, silence.

It was almost as if the visit had never happened. The beats went on. April ended. May came, and was almost gone when the phone at the Civil Courts Building rang again.

"Well, your fellowship's been approved. Where would you like to begin?"

"Where would you like me to start?"

"There's an important election going on in Southern Rhodesia," said Mr. Rogers. "Journalists like elections, because a lot gets said about a country's problems, and politicians don't mind talking about them. In fact, they *want* to talk about them. I'd suggest you start in Salisbury, Southern Rhodesia. How soon can you start? Oh, and can you get a couple of letters of reference? The Ford Foundation needs them."

"I've got to tell the people here that this has happened," I said, "and find out how soon they can replace me."

"Get back to me when you know," he said.

"I will," I said. And we hung up.

Julie, of course, had questions. Did you thank him? Where will we live? Where is Salisbury, Southern Rhodesia? How do we get there? What's the weather like there? How much will we have to live on? How long is a fellowship?

Miss Pluntze had most of the answers. Fellowships last until Mr. Rogers and the Fellow agree that they've run their course and the Fellow is ready to move on. Travel out and back would be first class, and I should make the bookings. You couldn't take a ship to Southern Rhodesia; she had checked and found that British Overseas Airways was the only way to get there. When we were ready to go, Julie and I should fly to New York and spend a day or so with her and Mr. Rogers going over details.

Being the organized person she was, Julie got busy. Southern Rhodesia? Salisbury? Hmmm. She spread the word on her network, and the word came back. Of *course* she had a connection in Southern Rhodesia! Betsy Mayfield, a well-to-do daughter of a St. Louis family, had married a British guy named Barnaby Howard. He was the second son of a British Lord, or something like that, and he and Betsy had gone off to a Southern Rhodesian town named Umtali to establish a tobacco farm. We should look him up when we got there.

Another St. Louisan had a British friend named Courtauld, a British chemical-industry magnate who'd moved himself, his family, and a fabulous art collection to an estate in rural Southern Rhodesia. Julie began to assemble a Rhodesian "Who's Who" and "Who's Where."

I looked for Southern Rhodesia travel books. They were scarce. I looked for Southern Rhodesia news in newspapers and magazines. It was just as scarce. I found that the Prime Minister of Southern Rhodesia was a man named Godfrey Huggins. *Sir* Godfrey Huggins, in fact. The government was parliamentary, traffic drove Britannically left, their subequatorial summer was our winter, and currency was measured in pounds, shillings and pence. The colony was a mere 65 years old, spawned by a group of British freebooters organized by an empire-builder named Cecil Rhodes to expand the colony across the Limpopo River into the kingdom of a Matabele tribal king named Lobengula, who had been "persuaded" to turn over the region's mineral rights to the British South Africa Company.

The colony's main worry was South Africa, just south of its border, where a newly dominant government of Dutch-descended "*Afrikaners*" was introducing a legal form of racial separation called "*apartheid*" to replace the more relaxed British discrimination that had prevailed since the British won the Boer War in the 19th Century.

Such was my history and political science lesson.

Chapter 7

Off to Rhodesia

Back in 1953, before Southern Rhodesia became Zimbabwe, it was colored British pink on the map, in the middle of the hoped-for British "Cape-to-Cairo" Africa. It was just south of the Equator and north of the gold and diamond mines of the Union of South Africa. Its southern border was Rudyard Kipling's "grey-green, greasy Limpopo River." To the east lay Mozambique — "Portuguese East Africa" — on the Indian Ocean, balanced by Angola, or "Portuguese West", across the continent on the south Atlantic.

To the north was Northern Rhodesia (now Zambia) and, beyond that, the Belgian Congo (Zaire, or the Democratic Republic of Congo). Northern Rhodesia's copper resources (the "Copper belt") were found and exploited long after Cecil Rhodes organized the annexation of Southern Rhodesia to South Africa in 1899. Besides copper, the principal exports of Southern and Northern Rhodesia in the 1950s were high-grade "Virginia" cigarette tobacco, and asbestos. Because of a lack of east-west roads and rails, these had to be exported through South Africa or (in a minor trickle) through the ports of Portuguese East Africa.

The vast majority of the Rhodesian population, both North and South, were tribal black Africans — Shona and Matabele. The economies of both colonies — *and* the easy life of the white colonials — depended on the cheap labor they represented, as did the gold-and-diamond-based economy of the Union of South Africa.

White settlers, mostly British liberals, white racists and in-betweens, dominated Northern and Southern Rhodesian politics. In South Africa, political power had migrated from the English-speaking winners of the 19th-Century Boer War to *Afrikaans-speaking* descendants of the Dutch and French Calvinist explorers and pioneers who arrived to establish victualing stations and farms to serve 15th, 16th and 17th-century shipping routes between Europe and Asia. What were Belgian, French, German, Spanish, Indian, Chinese and Middle-eastern settlers like farther north? Exploiters and Colonists

Walter S. Rogers, founder of the foundation known as the Institute of Current World Affairs (ICWA), and Ned Munger, who preceded me as an ICWA Fellow in Central Africa, knew. Or knew a lot. Although I write knowledgably now, I knew next-to-nothing then. My bride Julie and I were both products of an insular, isolated, college-educated, white, American middle class. Liberal and well-intentioned, to be sure, but ignorant.

Full of excitement and adventure, we flew from St. Louis to New York first, then on to Salisbury, the capital of Southern Rhodesia.

"We'll start you off at $5,000 a year," Mr. Rogers said when we arrived at his New York office at 522 Fifth Avenue. "We'll open an account for you downstairs here at the Guaranty Trust Company. In Salisbury, open an account in a bank with international connections so we can transfer funds to you by wire. When you find out whether the stipend is too much or too little, we can adjust it. There'll also be a $10,000 life-insurance policy."

I had been earning $69.50 a week as a reporter at the *St. Louis Post-Dispatch*. Until I could sit down somewhere quiet and multiply it out, I didn't know how much that was a year. It turned out to be $3,614. Five thousand dollars was quite a raise for the Martins.

"Keep track of your expenses and send me an accounting each month," said Helen Pluntze.

"I want you to write without worry," said Mr. Rogers. "Your newsletters will be mimeographed and sent to friends of mine and the Institute who might benefit from seeing them. You can have a personal list of up to 100 people to receive them by mail. But under *no circumstances* will your newsletters go back to Africa. I don't want the people you're writing about to see what you're saying, and put pressure on you to change your views."

"How often do you want me to write?" I'd asked this at our first meeting, but I wanted to be sure about deadlines.

Again the answer: "When you know enough about something to write about it, write about it."

I had already come up with my own personal answer: In St. Louis, I could research and write a long-form "feature story" in two weeks. For Africa, I would set myself a deadline of a newsletter every two weeks. Two a month. Twenty-four a year. Forty-eight in two years.

What about transportation in Africa? We'd sold our 1947 Studebaker Commander before we left St. Louis. Could we buy a car?

"Look at the situation when you get there," said Mr. Rogers. "If you need a car, make a case for it."

Miss Pluntze made our reservations on British Overseas Airlines — a good thing, since I would never have had the first-class nerve to make the first-class bookings she made. We flew in the early evening from Idlewild Airport on Long Island (now JFK) on a piston-powered Boeing four-engine "Stratocruiser." Airborne, we ate dinner seated across from each other at a table set with linen and solid silverware in the plane's upstairs dining room. We landed briefly at Gander, Newfoundland, while the crew made up our beds — pull-down *bunks*, with side-curtains, mattresses, blankets and pillows, like those in a U.S. Pullman rail car.

We then flew overnight and over the Atlantic to Heathrow Airport, outside London, and were served breakfast in the Stratocruiser dining room before changing to a DeHaviland "Comet II" (the first commercial jet airliner).

As we waited at Heathrow, we got a special sendoff. The royal aircraft was rolled alongside us, a Bentley limousine pulled up, the queen's flag was unfurled from a small pole at the top of the plane, and their royal highnesses Elizabeth II and the Duke of Edinborough strolled across the tarmac and up the gangway. They gave little waves, the flag was taken in, the door was closed, and they took off for a royal tour of Ireland.

Boeing 377 Stratocruiser

Our Comet took off for Rome, Cairo, Khartoum, and Livingston, Northern
Rhodesia, where we were to get off. (The Comet went on, eventually, to Johannesburg, South Africa.) The jetliner was a notable "first" for Britain, but
it was hard on the ears — or at least *half* the passengers' ears. The jet engines were built into the aircraft's wings, and their high-pitched exhausts pro-
truded from the back of the wings, just in front of the rear half of the cabin
seats. Their whine made conversation and sleep difficult on long flights —
and flights from England, to Italy, Egypt, Sudan and Northern Rhodesia were
long.

In *Northern* Rhodesia, we transferred to a small DeHaviland "Twin Ot-
ter" propjet for the short flight to Salisbury, *Southern* Rhodesia. And in Salisbury, at the end of our two-day journey, Miss Pluntze's planning hit its first
snag. The flight from Northern to Southern Rhodesia was part of our overall ticket — but we had no Southern Rhodesia pounds (only American travelers' checks) to pay for a cab ride into town. Up stepped our introduction
to Rhodesian hospitality and friendship, Ken and Irene Cunningham. The
Cunninghams were Brits who — like many others — had left memories of a
chilly, hungry, shortage-wracked England-at-war to seek a warmer post-war

world where *they* — not austerity — were in charge. Ken was sales manager of Puzey & Diss, the Morris automobile agency in Salisbury. See page 371.

Out came the Cunningham wallet, out came a Rhodesian ten-pound note (then worth US$28.30) and with it, Ken's instructions to a black African cab driver to take us to Meikle's Hotel. Meikle's was a British colonist's dream of a safe retreat from the white man's burden. It occupied an entire Salisbury city block, stood a colonnaded, restrained, two stories high next to a palm-edged park, and had bathtubs so long that a full-grown Brit (or American) could not simultaneously rest his head against the top of the tub and touch his feet to the bottom. That's a run-on sentence, but (except for "Bubble and Squeak" and other pre-dessert "savouries" at the evening meal, and the constant presence of silent waiters in red fezzes ready to fetch whiskeys and "pink gins" when the command "Boy!" was sounded) it says one of the atmospheric things that need saying about a British hotel in central Africa in the colonial 1950s.

Julie and I drank it all in. We rested, ate, imbibed, and wandered the neighborhood. We walked to Barclay's Bank (D.C.O. — "Dominion, Colonial and Overseas") to cash a traveler's check and open a pound-sterling checking account. We found a copy of the daily *Rhodesia Herald* to begin checking housing rentals. (To my eye and reading, the paper seemed straightforward, honest and well-edited.) We took a cab to Puzey & Diss to repay Ken Cunningham's ten-pound loan — and looked over the supply of available Morris automobiles in case we ever needed to buy one. (The Morris Minor was too small, the MG-TD two-seater too sporty and convertible, but the Morris Oxford seemed sturdy and the right size for adults — even sleeping adults.)

The "rainy season" starts in the sub-Equatorial "winter" (a moderately warm June to November with occasional downpours) in Salisbury — but canny Rhodesian merchants and city-planners protected their customers and citizens by covering the sidewalks with shelters of corrugated steel or asbestos. Most eateries and drinkeries were straightforwardly British — but there were enough occasional Indian restaurants on tree-lined back streets to seem interesting. It didn't happen to us, but we noticed when some black Africans

Meikles Hotel, Salisbury, Southern Rhodesia, in the 1950s.

Our Morris Oxford, sturdy and sleepable. Julie in the passenger seat.

(known generally as "Natives") saw a white Rhodesian approaching on the sidewalk (often wearing a hat), they stepped out of the way onto the street.

On one side of Meikle's was flowery Cecil Square, and across Cecil Square was the *Rhodesia Herald* newspaper office. I was going to need a research resource, and aside from a proper public library, the closest thing to it I could think of was a newspaper's "morgue," where all previous stories about a particular topic are clipped, filed and stored. Also, reporters and editors keep reference books on their office shelves and know everything that's going on in a city or a country. I went in, identified myself to a passing person as a newspaperman from the United States, and asked to see the managing editor. David ("Taffy") Williams quickly appeared with a broad smile and a warm welcome.

Taffy was, as you can tell, a Welshman ("Taffy was a Welshman, Taffy was a thief, Taffy came to my house and stole a side of beef..."). Taffy was not only a Welshman, Taffy was a treasure. He was an instant friend of every newsman who ever came to town. Within minutes we were sharing tea, he was hearing my fellowship story, and he was inviting me — and Julie — to join the Herald's weekly, Friday-night poker "school" (actually a regular poker game), held around bottles of Lion and Castle lager beer (not chilled, but "off the shelf") at the newspaper office. We signed on for the "school", and Taffy not only gave me the run of the *Herald* morgue, he loaned me a reporter's unoccupied desk and told me to come in, use the "loo", make telephone calls, and "have a cuppa" (tea) whenever the need or urge arose.

After a week of getting the "feel" of Salisbury, I also got the Meikles bill. It was more than 100 pounds (US$280), and it jolted Julie and me into immediate action. We got busy with "estate agents," and it took only three or four days to find Rosemary de Souza, an English-speaking, Portuguese-descended artist who was going back to Europe for a long holiday. She would rent us her stuccoed-brick, modern, two-bedroom house in suburban "Eastlea" *furnished* — not only with furniture, linens, pots and pans, but with two live-in African servants — for 25 pounds a month (US$70). Rosemary paid "Cook-boy" Nomeas and "Garden-boy" Aaron $9.80 and $4.25, respectively — a month. She wanted them there when she got back from her holiday.

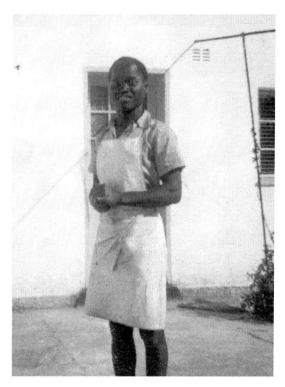

Aaron, our garden boy in Eastlea, Salisbury.

Nomeas and Aaron didn't live in Miss de Souza's house; they lived in the separate, tiny, back-yard "*piccanin' kaia*" ("little house," in the bastardized-Zulu "kitchen kaffir" language that white "masters" and "madams" used to give orders to household workers). Nomeas and Aaron were actually locked out of the main house itself at the end of each working day, and had to spend the night in the *kaia*. They couldn't leave the premises without a special written "pass" from "madam" or me. In the morning, "madam" or "master" unlocked the kitchen door, left shoes to be shined in the kitchen, and went back to bed — to be re-awakened by the clatter of tea (and toast, if desired) being placed outside the bedroom door at a pre-assigned time.

"They're good boys," Rosemary said. "Nyasaland boys." For some reason, Nyasaland "boys" (grown African men, actually) from Nyasaland, the neighboring British colony to the northeast, were considered to be the best, the most polite, the most manageable black servants in all of Southern Rhodesia.

Our daily reading of the *Rhodesia Herald* left no doubt that Walter Rogers was right: a major election was under way in the Rhodesias and Nyasaland. The new *Afrikaner* government of South Africa was busily writing rigid *apartheid* into rigid law south of the Limpopo. Fearful of its echo effect to the north, the Prime Ministers of Southern Rhodesia, Northern Rhodesia and Nyasaland (and their legislatures) had scheduled a referendum to create a single, self-governing "Federation of The Rhodesias and Nyasaland" in which traditional British Law would remain constant — and serve as a barrier to the hard, racist *apartheid* law the three Premiers (and their legislators) feared would breed eventual rebellion and bloodshed in their colonies.

It was time for me to get the journalistic part of my fellowship started. I asked Taffy how he was covering the election. He was sending reporters to political rallies and meetings. There were plenty of white Rhodesians and Nyasalanders just as fearful of the vast majority of blacks around them as white *Afrikaners* and English-speaking South Africans were of "natives" and other non-whites who outnumbered them by something like twenty to one. Recalling the American Civil War, "Europeans" (whites) most fearful of the "liberalism" of Southern Rhodesia's Godfrey Huggins, Northern Rhodesia's Roy

Wilensky and Nyasaland's Malcolm Barrow, were organizing themselves into a "Confederate" Party (I kid you not) under the leadership of a transplanted South African greengrocer named Percy Newton.

Taffy offered to let me tag along with his reporters covering the election, and I didn't say No. But I was starting from too far behind for anything like comprehension and in-depth understanding to result from "tagging along." The *Herald* kept calling the election "historic," and indeed, there was too much history behind it to even begin to *think* about it, let alone *write* about it. I needed to learn that history from people who understood it and, if possible, people who were making it.

There was no public road or rail transportation in either of the two Rhodesias or Nyasaland. No buses, no passenger trains, no rental cars. In fact there were no *paved* roads at all between the three tiny capitals (Salisbury, Lusaka, Blantyre). The "highway" between Salisbury and the important Southern Rhodesian tobacco-farming town of Umtali, for example, was a "strip road" consisting, literally, of two strips of asphalt an axle-length apart. On either side of the road, and in the center, was tall grass. You drove with your wheels on the asphalt strips. When a car or truck came in the opposite direction, you pulled Britannically off to the left, with your right-hand wheels on one of the strips and your left wheels off the road completely, in the grass. You passed each other with supreme caution and swung back onto the strips when you had passed each other. With luck and nerve, you could travel 30 miles in a day.

You had to be prepared for trouble. In rainy season, streams could rise with amazing swiftness, and low-lying stretches of road might disappear under water completely. There were hard-surface fords that could be crossed carefully, but if the water had risen above the foot-high posts at the edge of the fords you should stop until the water went down — there might be no strip road there at all. You could then turn back, but the water might have risen behind you, and the previous ford could be gone as well. What was then necessary was a high-pressure Primus stove, cooking and drinking water, a teapot, cooking pot, tea leaves, and pasta. And maybe oatmeal and canned ("tinned") soup as well. You could be stranded there for hours, or days.

The terrain was ruggedly gorgeous, but there were thousands of square miles to cover. I wrote to Walter Rogers and explained that a personal car was the only solution. He agreed, and I bought a Morris Oxford four-door sedan for 680 pounds (a little under US$2,000) from — of course — Ken Cunningham, of Puzey & Diss.

Eager to get down to work, I wrote a letter to Southern Rhodesia Prime Minister Huggins, explaining who I was and what I was doing in his colony. I asked for a chance to meet and talk with him. I took it around to his office in Salisbury and left it with one of the "Peter B. Martin" calling cards Mr. Rogers had provided, with the upper right-hand corner folded down. According to some "language of cards" I'd heard about when I got the cards, the fold meant that I was "requesting an interview." Looking back, I guess it took a lot of nerve, but I had turned 24 the month I arrived, and the election was scheduled for December. There was no time to waste — and no phone in the Eastlea house, so I asked Sir Godfrey to call Meikle's hotel and leave a message.

Ten — maybe eleven — days later, a Meikle's car pulled up in front of our rented house at 42 Fereday Drive in suburban Eastlea, and the driver handed Nomeas an envelope. It was from the Office of the Prime Minister. "I would be delighted to meet you," said the note. "Please telephone my office for an appointment."

I drove to the red-painted public phone booth down the street, dropped in my two-penny coins, dialed the number, and pressed button "A" when a female voice was heard. Then I pressed button "B". "Prime Minister's office," a voice said. I told her who I was, and that I was responding to a request to call.

"Oh, Mister Martin, the Prime Minister would like you to lunch with him at the Salisbury Club on Tuesday next, at twelve-thirty, if it's convenient." I said it was convenient, indeed. I would be there. Where was the Salisbury Club? She gave me the address. She also warned me that the P.M. was "a bit hard of hearing," so I should speak "distinctly."

The Salisbury Club was a sizable, proper Salisbury house across a broad sidewalk and a line of Jacaranda trees near the middle of town. I gave my name to a guard, and was shown past the bar and across a large dining room to a table directly under a bronze statue.

"Welcome to Southern Rhodesia," said the Prime Minister. "*I* welcome you, and so does Cecil Rhodes. The statue is of him."

"Quite impressive," I probably said, distinctly. The lunch happened more than 60 years before this writing, and I'm recalling from memory. But I've been in the club — Salisbury's been renamed Harare ("hah-rah-RAY"), and the club became the Harare Club — since then, and the statue's still there. It's still bronze. It's still Cecil Rhodes, funder of the Rhodes Scholarships and namesake of Rhodesia. And it's still impressive.

I told Sir Godfrey it was good of him to call me, and added something about the continued efficacy of the language of cards.

"It wasn't just your note," he said. "I knew you were coming thanks to Barnaby Howard. He's a good friend. When you get the chance, you should drive up to Umtali and visit him and Betsy. It's a splendid drive and will give you a good sense of the landscape of Rhodesia. His tobacco crop is first-rate, and his farm is just under the mountains on the border of Mozambique."

I gave Sir Godfrey a quick history of the Institute of Current World Affairs — how it was born out of Charles Crane's financial support of the work and thinking of Woodrow Wilson, and how Crane had accompanied Wilson to the Versailles peace conference. Wilson brought no American territorial claims to the conference, but as Crane observed and listened to each day's dismemberment of the Ottoman and German empires, he found himself wishing the American participants had had the same depth and familiarity with international issues as the French and British delegates. Through international immersion, he and Walter Rogers hoped to give Fellows of the Institute the same sort of familiarity.

"Admirable!" said Huggins. "What a fine idea, to give young people like you a chance to travel and learn about us. What do you have to do in return?"

"Grow, I suppose. Grow through experience. And, maybe, someday, grow and do likewise."

"Is that all?"

"Oh ... And *write*. We have to write reports on what we're learning. Those reports get circulated to friends of Mr. Rogers and Mr. Crane and friends of the Institute of Current World Affairs."

"What will you be doing here in Southern Rhodesia?"

"Traveling, and watching your progress toward creating a Federation of the Rhodesian colonies as, it seems, a counterbalance to what's happening in South Africa. And writing about it. I'm a journalist, you know."

"The colonies *and the protectorate*. The Rhodesias are self-governing colonies, but Nyasaland is still a protectorate, you know. Do you have introductions to Sir Roy Wilensky and Malcolm Barrow?" (Wilensky, Prime Minister of Northern Rhodesia, was a onetime boxer, railway engineer and labor-union organizer. Malcolm Barrow in Nyasaland was a true colonialist, owner/manager of a tea plantation.)

"No," I said.

"Well, you shall have them. On one condition. That is, you satisfy my envy, my curiosity, and my need. You will be traveling about, taking the pulse of the electorate, as you journalists like to say, and you will have some idea of how the election is *going*. I will have no such ear to the ground. I will only hear what my aides and assistants tell me, and they will tell me what they think I want to hear. I envy what you'll learn, what you'll *know*, what you'll understand. So, in return for introductions to Wilensky and Barrow, I want to have lunch with you, here, every five or six weeks, and I want you to tell me, in all frankness, how it's going."

"You want me to spy on your country?"

"You've got the wrong 'ah' before the last syllable. It's *reportage* I need, not *espionage*. And there's one more thing *you'll* need, and don't yet know you need: a good reference library. There's no such thing as a solid, accessible library in either one of the Rhodesias, and until we get a decent university, there won't be. But we do have a parliament, and a good parliamentary library. I will introduce you to the parliamentary librarian, and put her on your team, as well. Does this sound like a good arrangement?"

"Excellent."

"Done!"

We shook hands. And ate some more first-class lunch, and a savoury, and cheese. And drank some fine coffee. And shook hands again.

Julie and I began buying fresh vegetables at "Vitagreeens," Percy Newton's Salisbury store. Percy was not only a greengrocer, he was a truck gardener proud of what he grew and sold. He was often in the Salisbury store, and Julie and I met him and struck up a friendly acquaintanceship. He and his wife played Contract Bridge, and so did Julie and I. As regular as poker at the *Herald* poker school, we began to eat suppers and play Bridge with Percy and his wife. Julie taught them handy Bridge rules ("If on the left the dummy lies, lead through strength if you are wise") and he told us why he and his party were so conservative.

"These *munts* are just down out of the trees," he'd say. "They have no idea how to run a farm, let alone a country." As all the books about Rhodesia and South Africa told us, black Africans as a people were collectively known as "Bantu." That was the polite, anthropological, Zulu-language, group plural. The Shona singular for an individual person was "*muntu.*" Racists like Newton shortened this down to "*munt*" and pluralized it back up to "*munts.*" It was their equivalent of "niggers."

Southern Rhodesia was getting ready for its first-ever parliamentary election, and Percy was extremely busy, organizing his Confederate Party. From scratch. From the bottom up. He considered me a "visiting foreign journalist," and as such invited me to the Party's organizational, principles-writing, first meeting on Friday, July 24, 1953.

It was held in the shabby, yellow-stuccoed "Athenaeum Hall" on Jameson Avenue, and I was given a folding chair at the press table. The old wooden floor was so unevenly worn that only three of the chair's four legs could touch the floor at the same time. The meeting was called to order promptly at 10 a.m., and it was an eye-opener. The Chairman, Col. G. R. Musgrave, a white farmer and old British soldier from the Mrewa District south of Salisbury, gave the keynote speech.

"By far the most important item in the Confederate Party manifesto is the Native Policy," he said, "and if Europeans [whites] and Natives are going to live and prosper in this Federation we cannot delay any longer in taking a firm and united stand in this connection... The Confederate Party wishes to make it quite clear that it supports the Federation but at the same time wishes to leave no one in doubt that the final aim of the Party is dual development — that is, development of Europeans and Natives along their own lines. That is the only way. One has only to look back in history to see the failures which can be attributed to the experiment of multi-racial societies when the races have consisted of Europeans and African Natives or Europeans and Asiatics."

At a tea break, I had a short chat with Colonel Musgrave. "This is the most important clause in the Confederate Party's statement of principles," he said. "Natives will certainly be allowed to find employment in European areas. They are not to be fenced in. We only mean to keep them out of our politics and out of our beds."

This deep-South sentiment was shared by quite a few Southern Rhodesians who'd moved north from South Africa or south from Great Britain. Even Taffy Williams, who edited the *Rhodesia Herald* with an admirable open-mindedness, called black Africans "munts." When Julie and I began to have trouble with Nomeas's promptness in showing up to prepare dinner for guests, we mentioned it at one of Taffy's Friday poker sessions.

"Oh, those *munts*!" Taffy said. "You can't rely on them. You've got to teach them a lesson. I've got a pair of handcuffs I double over my fist to beat them when they get cheeky. Just say the word, and I'll bring them over and have a little talk with Nomeas."

We never did. I had my own little talk with Nomeas, and said that I knew I couldn't fire him because Miss de Souza wanted him there when she returned, but I wanted my "Madam" to be able to rely on him. He began showing up on time.

And so it went. In the Morris Oxford, Julie and I drove through tsetse-fly decontamination tents into Northern Rhodesia and Nyasaland. We were amazed at the copper-financed elegance (freshly sautéed *trout, boned at the table* by a transplanted Parisian waiter) of the brand-new Ridgeway Hotel in Lusaka, capital of Northern Rhodesia. And stunned by the sheer colonial-ness of Blantyre, the capital of Nyasaland ("A *tip* for polishing the shoes you leave outside your hotel-room door? A penny or two, *at most*. Better, nothing. That's the trouble with you Americans. You spoil our Natives.")

I spent several nights drinking whisky with Roy Wilensky in Lusaka, listening to him curse the British Colonial Office for over-administering Northern Rhodesia. And Julie and I watched preparations for an amazing colonists' evening with Rupert Buquet, a friend of Sir Malcolm Barrows' who grew tung nuts near Lake Nyasa. Buquet didn't exactly *grow* tung nuts, the oils of which were used in quick-drying paints and enamels in the days before synthetics. The tung nuts *grew* all by themselves, on trees. Twice a year, when they were ready for harvest, Rupert had his "boys" lay tarpaulins under the trees and shake them. The accumulated nuts were put in bags and placed on racks along the road. The Tung Nut Marketing Board picked them up, and Buquet received a cheque.

Then came the celebration. Buquet consulted *Larousse Gastronomique* and a few other gourmet cookbooks. He planned a proper banquet on the wide, roofed verandah of his plantation home. He wrote orders for ingredients, and spices, and condiments, and sent them off to Harrod's and Fortnum & Mason in London. Slowly, slowly, the packets came in, and were stored in the larder, or the fridge, or in Rupert's lockup cupboard. Invitations were printed. Gilded chairs and rental tables for eight were ordered. Table cloths, napkins, finger bowls and champagne glasses were counted. Arrangements were made to borrow highly regarded "cook boys" from neighbors for the feast. Fezzes of the waiters and house boys were checked to make sure they were all the same color.

Did we attend? No. Julie, being Julie, had a festive white, *travelable* nylon dress that would dazzle the eyes of any Tung nut. I (who had even mailed home some clothes and an extra pair of shoes at Idlewild to save overweight airfare charges), had *no* dinner jacket — and even a charcoal-grey business suit would not serve properly enough. And there were no formal-dress rental outfits in Blantyre. We missed the party.

But I never missed a lunch with Sir Godfrey at the Salisbury Club. At the first one, after we returned from my up-north meetings with Wilensky and Percy Newton's Lusaka allies and black African leaders like Harry Nkumbula (head of the incipient African Mineworkers' Union in Northern Rhodesia), I reported that things seemed to be going fairly well for approval of the Federation. Huggins seemed surprised. White Rhodesians, worried and apprehensive after decades of dominance (sometimes *physical* dominance) over Mashona and Matabele tribesmen, seemed to be echoing the fears that were sending shivers through *Afrikaners* and some English-speaking South Africans above the Limpopo.

Thanks, perhaps, to Huggins' continued and intense interest, I covered the Federation referendum intensively. I went back to Northern Rhodesia when Sir Roy was so angered by British "interference" in the colony's affairs that he simultaneously resigned his Vice-Premiership and membership in the Legislative Council (equivalent to the colonial Parliament), taking all his allies with him. I was about to leave on a trip to the mines of the "copperbelt" when his secretary suggested (strongly) that I delay my departure so as not to miss the "explosion." Sure enough, he staged his theatrical resignation the next day. Julie and I were in his living room as he composed his resignation speech in the study next door, and sat and listened when he came out, ventilating anger and opposition in galluses, a collarless shirt and sloppy, unpressed trousers. It made quite a lively, vivid newsletter to Mr. Rogers.

In the end, the referendum succeeded. The "Federation of the Rhodesias and Nyasaland" was created. Huggins and, later, Wilensky, served as its Prime Ministers before Ian Smith revived *apartheid* emotions in the white electorate and planted the seeds of black rebellion that eventually produced Zimbabwe and Robert Mugabe. Julie and I moved on north to Mozambique, The Belgian Congo, Cabinda, Uganda, French West Africa, French Equatorial Africa, French Togoland and The Gold Coast. But for years thereafter I got long letters and Christmas cards from "Malvern" (no other identification, just "Malvern." Huggins, honored as "Lord Malvern," was finally given a seat in the House of Lords) and "your friend, Roy Wilensky."

Chapter 8

Trouble In Katanga

Back in 1954, if you were traveling by road in subSaharan Africa, one thing was indispensable: A copy of a thick, cloth-bound book published in 1949 by The Automobile Association of South Africa called "Trans-African Highways."

The name had little to do with reality. The only *paved* "highways" in Africa south of the Sahara Desert were in capital cities, or gold-rich South Africa. (You can read about the "strip roads" of the Rhodesias (now Zimbabwe and Zambia) in another chapter. See page 62.) North of there, in the Belgian Congo (now Zaire, or the Democratic Republic of Congo) and beyond, the strips stretched on forever — two parallel lines of gravel, asphalt, or packed dirt, far enough apart to accommodate the width of one car or truck, with tall grass in the middle and to the sides.

If a vehicle came at you from the other direction, you had to pull off to the right or left, leaving one set of wheels on the strip, and pass *carefully*. The roads could become impossible, impassable mud in rainy seasons. In dry seasons, if cars or trucks went 30 or 40 miles per hour, they could throw up lung-clogging and vision-choking clouds of dust — but the roads were so stony, rutted and rough that none but the largest trucks (or "lorries," in BritSpeak) could go that fast.

Each two facing pages of the book described a single day's travel — no more (and sometimes less, depending on difficulties). On the left-hand page was the reproduction of a hand-drawn map, and a scale of miles. On the right was an itinerary of the towns and landscape features the motorist would encounter, with marginalia — southbound reading down, northbound reading up.

That's what road travel in Africa was like back in the "good old days." This memoir chapter is about a 1954 motor trip my wife Julie and I took in Katanga Province in the old Belgian Congo, northeast from the Northern Rhodesia border toward Kampala, capital of the British colony of Uganda.

Throughout my two-year fellowship I rarely heard from Walter Rogers, ICWA's Executive Director in New York. Fax machines and email didn't yet exist, and the only way we could communicate was in writing, by air mail or occasional cablegram. Phone connections from the United States all went through each colony's European "mother country" (Britain, Belgium, Portugal, Spain, France) and were impossibly expensive, often unintelligible, and a day or night away.

So there we were in Southern Rhodesia, having explored Mozambique, the Union of South Africa, Nyasaland and Northern Rhodesia, and pondering the next step in my assignment to learn everything there was to learn about sub-Saharan Africa. A letter then arrived from Mr. Rogers, informing me that the Ford Foundation, which was funding my ICWA fellowship, was interested in assessing and evaluating higher-education opportunities for blacks in the subcontinent. Ford was paying for an exploratory trip to the region by former ICWA Africa Fellow Ned S. ("Ned") Munger, who had been sent on to get a Ph.D. in political geography at the University of Chicago and a professorship at the California Institute of Technology.

Mr. Rogers wanted all four of his Fellows to meet in Kampala, Uganda. Besides me, there was David Reed, a swashbuckling journalism Fellow from the *Chicago Daily News* who had won a two-year fellowship to Kenya, where the Mau Mau were rebelling against British colonists. Recently appointed and on their way to Central Africa were Dr. Robert W.C. Brown, a young physician studying the tradition, techniques and efficacy of traditional tribal medicine; and Robert Grey, an anthropologist studying tribal political organization. All of us except Dave Reed had accompanying wives, which violated

Mr. Rogers' 19th-Century belief that spouses hindered and complicated a Fellow's capacity to spend 24 hours a day immersed in all aspects of a foreign society. He set a meeting date a month or so later in Kampala, so the timing and the destination were decided, and we were on our way.

The day after Julie and I had crossed the border between the Northern Rhodesia "Copperbelt" and the Belgian Congo, we were in Congo's Katanga Province. We spent the first night in Kiubo Falls, "Downstream from main road," as the *Trans-African Highways* marginalium said. Two of the town's important features: "Hôtel des Chutes." "Petrol."

We utilized both, and spent the next night in Manono, "Headquarters of Géomines" (a Belgian tin-mining company). Next to the town notation, Julie neatly penciled in the financial accounting: "Geomines guest house: 200 Belgian francs. Dinner: 70 francs. Total in US$ — $7.80." Not bad. The Institute of Current World Affairs would be happy.

From Manono it was 52 miles to Piana Mwanga, just south of the "River Luvua, being crossed by a ferry," as the book said. The ferry was a small one — a welded-steel raft big enough for two cars or a single truck, although ours was the only vehicle. We were pulled across by two men using a rope attached at the ends to either bank and threaded through a pair of metal rings on the ferry. The whole thing was actually little more than a large, steel raft. Although the ferrymen were paid by the government, I tipped each one two Rhodesian cigarettes (famous, regionally, for their freshness and sweetness). They held out cupped hands, a tribal tradition symbolizing the generosity of the gift. We got broad smiles of thanks.

We drove up the north bank of the Luvua and traveled a few miles through grassy highlands toward the next town. Then, KLANG!

I mean, *KLANG!* Pebbles and small stones regularly pinged and binged against the undercarriage of the car as we drove through the grass, but this *loud, frightening* sound stopped me cold. I braked to a sudden halt. I jumped out, looked underneath. Engine oil was pouring from the bottom of the oil pan.

Engine oil! I didn't stop to think, or say anything. I jumped back into the car, reached behind the driver's seat, and pulled out the double boiler we carried to cook roadside meals at lunch time, or during overnight stops at rain-swollen streams and rivers. I leaped back under the car and stuck the bottom half of the pot under the oil stream. We had about half a potful.

I told Julie about the calamity. We were going to have to wait for help. We needed someone to tow us to the next town so we could get the car repaired. We talked. We waited. We ate our lunch of cheese, baguette and beer we'd bought that morning in Piana Mwanga. We waited. We talked some more. No one came by. No vehicle. No cyclist. We wondered how hard it would be to get a new-model British sports car repaired in a Belgian garage in the heart of a Belgian province in a remote Belgian colony in the middle of Africa. We wondered. We waited. No one came by.

We waited and talked some more. No one came. No car, no truck, no one on foot. No bus. No one on a bicycle. No animal. Nobody. Nothing. The sun began to go down. We drank some water from the canvas bag we kept hanging on the front grille of the MG. The water seeped through the canvas, and its evaporation kept the water in the bag from becoming undrinkably hot. We got out our emergency cans of soup and spaghetti and our Primus Stove. The Primus is a tiny, alcohol-fueled burner that you pump up to establish pressure. The pressure vaporizes the alcohol so you can light it. It burns with a roaring hot flame, like the flame on an American gas stove or blow torch. You can fry on it, boil water on it, heat soup and spaghetti on it. The result is not fancy and you have only one burner, but the food gets cooked.

We had our supper. No one came by. We talked about animals. This was *remote* Africa, with no towns, no houses, no huts, no villages for miles. We didn't have to worry about the prevalent antelopes, giraffes, baboons, zebras, kudu, wildebeest, and other vegetable-eating daytime critters. They wouldn't bother us. We were not about to challenge Cape Buffalo and rhinos and cause them to charge us. We were not close to the kind of shallow and deep water that's home to crocodiles or hippopotamuses.

We might, however, be seen as a potential meal or enemy by local carnivores, which probably included lions, leopards and a possible cheetah or two.

1954 MG TF Roadster (Peter's Folly), in Darmstadt, Germany, with a new oil pan, after its faithful service in Africa.

From our visits to South African and Rhodesian game reserves, we'd learned that humans inside vehicles did not seem to be proper prey to nocturnal appetites with fangs and claws. If we stayed in the car, we'd be all right.

In the first car we sensibly bought when we arrived in Southern Rhodesia in 1953, we could spend the night quite comfortably. It was a solid, normal, four-door, steel Morris Oxford sedan, with a front seat and a back, with leather upholstery, a "boot" ("trunk," in American usage) for luggage and camping gear, and high clearance. In the sports-car convertible that I now realize could (and should) have been called "Peter's Folly."

We had to spend the night sitting up in bucket seats, with the canvas roof closed (for warmth — it gets cold at night in the African high-veldt) — and to keep us non-attractive to roving carnivores.

We slept sitting up. I don't recall hearing animal sounds all night. No vehicle came by. By dawn's early light we realized that there was virtually no traffic besides ours on this "trans-African highway." Our chances of hailing any sort of passing vehicle became slimmer and slimmer. We had no one to telephone for help, and cell phones hadn't been invented. There was no visible nearby community, and no individual house or hut. What to do?

We'd have to solve the problem ourselves.

What did we have that could be of use? The MG tool kit was more complete than the equivalent in any American car. It included a jack that screwed the car up — not far, but at least seven or eight inches. We had wrenches ("spanners" in BritSpeak) that could fit any reachable nut or bolt on the wheels or the outside or underside of the car. There was a screw-driver, of course. We had "sizzle patches," rubber tire-tube patches flattened against the bottoms of small, disposable steel pans filled with some solid, flammable gel. If a tube needed patching, you placed the sizzle patch and the pan on the leak and lit the substance. It would melt the patch into the leak and make a seal.

Otherwise, we had household equipment. A few knives and forks, napkins and table cloths; kitchen spices; sheets and pillow cases; our travel bags.

Still, nothing came by. No delivery vans. No freight trucks. No bicycles. No one on foot.

With Julie at the wheel I pushed the car so the oil pan was over one of the wheel tracks in the road. I jacked up the front end of the car, inched my way underneath on my back, and looked up. The crack was there, bent in, a little over an inch long, between the protective bottom ridges of the cast-aluminum oil pan. The bottom part of the oil pan was bolted to the upper part by about 20 or 30 bolts around its edge. I inched out, got the pack of wrenches, and found one that fit the oil-pan bolts. I tugged. I could turn it. I unscrewed it and took it out.

Julie and I had "breakfast" (crackers we had for cocktail-time cheese, and water from the water bag) and consulted. My opinion was that we had to find a way to seal the crack in the oil pan. To me, that meant getting the bottom of the pan off the car, flattening out the crack as much as possible from the inside, melting a sizzle patch to the crack inside the pan, letting it cool, bolting the pan back on, pouring in the oil we'd saved, and praying that heat and internal oil pressure would press and hold the sizzle patch in place until we could reach a place where we could get more sophisticated help.

Julie listened. She asked me how sure I was sure the plan would work. I said I wasn't at all sure, but unless some vehicle or people arrived with a better plan, it was the only one I could think of. She said, "I think I'd better go for help."

We consulted *Trans-African Highways*. I measured the scale with a scrap of paper. As best as I could tell the next town, about eight or nine miles ahead, was "Kisimba." No features or facilities were mentioned in the book, but at least it deserved a circle in the line representing the "highway." To the rear, another nine or ten miles back, was the ferry with its two native ferrymen. Beyond that, another eight or nine miles or so along, was Piana Mwanga. ("Hydro-electric plant supplying power to tin foundries at Manono").

Today, Julie's suggestion would be an impossibility. Violence and thievery are everywhere in Central Africa. A car and a white skin now signify wealth, and for many impoverished blacks who live by violence and who believe the wealth is rightfully theirs, it's there to be taken.

In 1954, the opposite was true. During the entire two years Julie and I were there, we never heard an angry word addressed to us by a black African. The peace of 19th and early-20th-century Africa may have been a "peace of the graveyard," as many say today, but it was a pleasant, comfortable graveyard for whites who followed and lived by a kind of colonial "golden rule" that required white "masters" to treat their black workers and "charges" like good children.

Considering the fix we were in, then, Julie's idea of rescue was as good as mine. The rainy season was not yet upon us, but she took a raincoat and loaded her pockets with two boxes of Gold Flake cigarettes (for tips and smoking; we both smoked then), and a handful of Belgian francs. Before she left, I told her that if I got the car running, I would follow, honking the horn steadily if I passed a house or village where she might have paused. As she walked off, I still recall the bravery in that firm step and her strong self-belief I could see and sense.

When she left, I crawled back under the car. I tugged at the next bolt with the spanner, got it loose, removed it. The working space was cramped and close under there and I inched my way out. I found a couple of flat rocks, lowered the car, put them under the jack, and screwed the car up again. It was still tight, but easier working.

It took more than an hour of struggling, wrenching, and unbolting, but I finally got all the bolts out. I reached up, grasped the oil pan in both hands, and pulled down. Nothing happened.

"Maybe," I told myself, "there's some mechanism attached inside the oil pan that requires me to move it to one side or the other before it will come off."

I tugged to one side, then the other. I tugged forward, then back. No motion. No give. I thought about trying to pry the bottom off with the screw driver, then thought again. There could be some sort of cork or composition seal between the upper and lower halves of the oil pan that would never seal again if I broke it. It could make the leak far worse, maybe unrepairable. I inched out from under the car into the sunlight, sat in the driver's seat, and thought some more. At last, I went back under the car and replaced all the bolts. It was easier than removing them, and took only half an hour. Julie had been gone a couple of hours.

How to fix the leak from the outside? Some sort of compress? I imagined what it might take. One of the sizzle patches on the hole. Some sort of soft "bandage" over that. And then, pressure. Pressure that could be maintained. When the engine got warm, that might melt the patch into the hole.

I dug through Julie's suitcase and found a wire clothes hanger, and untwisted it so it was more or less straight. I pulled a table cloth out of our linens bag and walked through the grass to some small, dry shrubs. I broke off a wooden branch about half an inch thick and snapped it into pieces about five or six inches long.

I lit a match and warmed a sizzle-patch pan, loosened the patch and pressed it against the oil-pan break. I tore part of the table cloth into strips, folded the strips into long pads, and measured them against the width of the spaces between the oil pan's protective flanges. I pushed a pad against the warmed sizzle patch. Then, with a clothes hanger twisted around the exhaust pipe on one side of the engine and around a motor protrusion on the other, I began tightening the compress against the bottom of the oil pan, back and forth, back and forth, using the pliers to pull it tight.

Now I could only pray that my makeshift bandage would hold in the oil. I put away the tools and the table cloth. I poured the oil from the bottom of the double boiler into the crankcase and looked underneath. No oil leak was visible. I started the engine, eased the car into gear and began to drive. I stopped after half a mile, opened the door, dropped to my knees outside, and looked for seeping oil. Still no sign. No sign of Julie, either.

At last, as I rounded a curve, and there she was! She'd walked seven miles, I reckoned. When I stopped, I called a greeting, opened the door, dropped to the ground ... and saw a bead of oil on the compress.

"Keep on the lookout for a house or a building!" I said as she got in. "The car's running, but we're still not out of trouble." As we moved along I explained what I'd done and kept looking for a farmhouse. At last I spotted a building off to the left, up a curving lane. I drove up the lane, stopped the car in the paved courtyard of a European-looking house and dived out of the car, pot in hand. I got it under the oil pan, now streaming vital fluid, and came out to find a black African in work clothes watching my gyrations with a look of puzzled wonderment.

"Jambo," I said, remembering the Swahili word of greeting.

"Jambo," he answered.

I went on, mixing French and Swahili: "Ou est bwana?" ["Where is the boss man?"] "J'ai besoin de lui." ["I need him."]

"Bwana est mort." ["Bwana is dead."]

Thanks to Miss Baker, my French teacher at Lower Merion Senior High School, my French was pretty good in those days. From the fellow in the courtyard I learned that "Bwana," a Belgian farmer, had died a couple of months before and the family had traveled back to Belgium for the funeral. The man standing there was minding the house while they were gone.

He was not a mechanic or mechanically minded, and could not be much help with the car. I asked where the nearest farmer might be, and he offered to walk me to his home. It was going to be about an hour's walk over the grasslands. I left Julie with the car and told her I'd be back with the farmer before sunset.

I was, in the farmer's truck with the farmer. I thanked my guide, tipped him, and the farmer and I left the MG in the courtyard and went back to his house for an extremely welcome wash-up and supper with him and his wife. The farmer thought he could patch my oil pan with "dried paint" (I doubted it, but didn't say so), and he said I could get more engine oil at a rest camp for Belgian tin miners near a town called Kapona about 20 miles farther along the road.

The "rest camp," as described in *Trans-African-Highways*, sounded promising. "Géomines Guest-house," it said. "Holiday resort for employees of the Company. Petrol." The "petrol" mention sounded promising. Where there was gasoline available, there might be a mechanic.

Next morning, with some cans of dried-up barn paint in the back of the farmer's truck, Julie and I went back to try our luck with the MG. I stripped off the previous day's hanger wire and the compress, and went under the car with our Samaritan-friend. His paint was sticky, and he smeared it over the crack in the oil pan. As a final flourish, he tried to plaster it all down with a strip of nearly-dry paint from a can's surface.

He said he would follow us to the rest camp in the truck. He did, but by the time we got there our last oil was pouring out. He had done all he could for us, though, and though his dried-paint idea had been nothing like a final solution, we were in a better place than on that plateau stranded above the Luvua River.

A *much* better place! Leaving the car to drain its last remaining oil, we thanked our rescuer from our heart-bottoms. He took us to the camp manager. She turned out to be an immensely pleasant, immensely immense Belgian woman eager for company. She knew no one who could repair broken oil pans, she said, but she would put word out about our predicament. *And* she would be enchanted to have us stay in one of her cottages until we could move on.

Her tree-shaded "resort" sat atop a round, grassy hill above the Congo lowlands. It comprised a large circle of about 20 thatched bungalows with views in all directions. No tennis court or swimming pool, but we could take walks, and each bungalow had a breezy verandah with a couple of camp chairs and a tea-table overlooking the lush grassland below. Inside was a cozy sitting room, a bedroom with twin beds, and a bathroom.

Outside the bathroom, on a high metal shelf, stood a large oil drum. Every afternoon around 3 p.m., a house-boy came to the bungalow with a push-cart loaded with many tins of water and a stack of firewood. He would pour water into the drum, arrange the firewood underneath it with dry grass, and light it. He would then go to the next bungalow and do the same.

When the water was hot, he would come back and make a booming sound on the drum with a tree limb. Bath time! Julie could then take a shower and shampoo her hair if she wished, and I could use the warm water for a bath. Or we could do a vice-versa, with the remaining warm water in the drum for a rinse-off.

Then off to the main building for an aperitif or a glass of wine, dinner (steak-frites, *boeuf bourguignon* or a fricassee of chicken), and a cognac or two. We could read in the main building (they had a diesel generator) or back in the bungalow by the light of an Aladdin pressure lamp. And so to bed.

Paradise! Except for that damned oil pan. *Madame* had asked around, and the best she could come up with was a farmer who had a friend with a flatbed truck that might be big enough to carry the MG to Costermansville, a Belgian provincial capital on Lake Albert, for US$340. Three hundred forty U.S. dollars! With no alternative, we'd obviously have to pay it, but it would cause a bit of consternation for Mr. Rogers and Miss Pluntze back in New York.

When could the friend with the truck be talked to about the job? *Madame* wasn't sure. There was no telephone service in this part of the Congo, but word would get to him eventually and we surely would hear from him. I read the section of *Trans-African Highways* covering the route between us and Costermansville. It was interesting.

"This route is known as the 'Route of the Fifth Parallel'," said the book, "and crosses the range of mountains lying to the west of Lake Tanganyika sometimes called 'The Backbone of Africa'. The road has two difficult sectors, and between the turn-off to Fizi and the Lake these sectors become barely passable in wet weather." And it was the beginning of the rainy season.

I broke out my Royal portable typewriter and worked on some back newsletters to Mr. Rogers, but the waiting weighed on us and *Madame's* "library"

was all in French — not all that much fun for leisure reading. The fourth
night we were there, the dining room outer door opened and a stranger (to
us, anyway) came in. He chatted with *Madame*, and by the way they glanced
in our direction, I could tell she was talking about us and our trouble.

I thought he might be bringing word about the truck to Costermansville,
but when he came over he introduced himself to us as a neighborhood farmer.
We talked about our broken oil pan, and then he asked, "*Votre femme*" (meaning Julie), "*a-t-elle la peinture pour les ongles?*" It was a strange question full
of strange words, but when he said it again and pointed to his fingertips, I
understood he was asking whether my wife had nail polish.

She did. It happened to be "Cherries in the Snow," by Revlon, and she
had about half a bottle left at this stage in our travels. He went on to say
that what I should do was clean the bottom of the oil pan thoroughly with
gasoline, let it dry, and then paint the crack with Cherries in the Snow. (He
loved the name: *Cerises dans la neige*.) While the nail polish was still wet,
I should take an inch or two of baling twine, unravel it, and press it into the
nail polish. Again let it dry, he said, and then paint the crack and twine with
another coat of nail polish. While that was still wet, I should press another
swatch of baling twine onto the crack, the strands crosswise to the first batch.
Let it dry completely, and when *it* was dry, do it at least once more. Twice, if
there was enough nail polish left.

It didn't sound like a lasting solution, but there was a lot more logic to it
than dried paint. I bought him a couple of cognacs and we parted *avec ami-
tiés*.

Next morning, after breakfast, I pushed the MG over the mechanics' service pit the rest camp mercifully provided. From below — standing, for a
change — I scraped off the remains of the sizzle patch and dried paint and
scrubbed the oil-pan crack with sand paper gasoline. I let it dry, thoroughly.
I bought four quarts of engine oil from *Madame*. Then, a coat of Cherries
in the Snow, followed by a swatch of unraveled baling twine. I left it to dry
through lunchtime, applied more nail polish and more twine (crosswise), and
used the bath and shower ritual for drying time.

Cherries in the Snow, from a 1950s advertisement.

Before supper I used the penultimate nail polish in the bottle, with one next-to-last layer of twine. Julie and I yearned for a celebratory dry martini, but made do with glasses of Bordeaux. Steak-frites and *crèpes flambés*, demi-tasses of coffee, then back to the bungalow to pack and sleep.

After breakfast next morning I poured two quarts of oil into the crankcase. No drips. No drops. I stowed two other quarts for emergencies. We packed the car. I checked underneath. No drips. We gave *Madame* heartfelt *mercis*, started up, and headed down the hill. After five miles I checked again. No drips. No drops.

Forty-four miles to Albertville on the shore of Lake Tanganyika. No drips. (No repairs for British cars, either.) Rain. One hundred eighteen miles to Kamata. No leaks. No drips.

Trans-African Highways note: "Between Kamata and Lubondja there is a series of spectacular one-way sinuous ascents and descents with steep gradients. These are controlled by a system of sound signals." The book understated it. The road at that point was hard-packed dirt, cut into the side of tone of he so-called "Mountains of the Moon" to the west of the lake.

We would reach a barrier across the road, and stop. Ahead, the road climbed and curved upward or downward. A man holding a red-edged, triangular "*Arrêt*" sign would come to the car. "*Attendez*," he would say. "You must wait." We would, several minutes. Then a car would appear, lights on, from the other side of the barrier. The guard would open the barrier, let the car through, and tell the driver to wait. Then he would pick up a metal bar, walk over to an oil drum suspended from a beam, and hit a resounding BOOM! on the drum. From above or below would come an answering BOOM! Our BOOM told the next guard that the car he had sent our way had arrived safely. His BOOM meant, "message received and understood. Road now clear." Our guard would then say to us, "*lumières*" (headlights). We would turn ours on. He would open the barrier, hit his oil drum twice, wave us forward, and we would drive ahead, cautiously.

The mountain wall on the left, and a sometimes-sheer drop on the right, kept all senses on the alert. When we reached the next barrier, the sequence was repeated, and the next cars started on their way.

As I recall, there were four or five BOOM exchanges along the 16 miles from Kanata to Lubondja.

Then on to Uvira, at the top of Lake Tanganyika (75 miles) — Julie noted "Hotel du Lac 275 francs; 150 francs dinner." Then 88 miles to Costermansville (finally!) ... where there were NO repairs for British cars ... plus 181 miles to Rutshuru (at the Rwanda border), 167 miles to Mbarara (in Uganda), and 180 miles to Kampala, the Ugandan capital. Total miles on petrol, immaterial. Total miles on "Cherries In The Snow": 1,158! *One thousand one hundred fifty-eight!* All thanks to that farmer in Kapona ... and to Julie's nail polish!

The Book: "Leaving Lubondja the road is straight for 22 miles and then becomes very sinuous as it descends to the road junction. ... Travelling north a few miles before crossing the Mutambala River the road begins the descent of the escarpment from the summit at the turn-off to Fizi, the last three miles being a series of hairpin bends (one-way traffic only)."

BOOM! BOOM!

Chapter 9

Call Me Harry II

TIME was 34 years old and I was 26 in September 1955, when I sat down in a 25th-floor office of the old TIME-LIFE Building overlooking the skating rink in Rockefeller Center and began work as a Contributing Editor. At least that was the title. What I — and 54 young and middle-aged Contributing Editors like me — was, really, a writer.

At TIME, a writer was not simply a writer, but a *re*-writer. And not simply a re-writer, but a *creative* re-writer of "stories." From idle notions scribbled by a Senior Editor in the margins of a morning paper on a commuter train, or suggestions cabled to New York from a correspondent in Tokyo or Rio de Janeiro, or gossip repeated to Henry Robinson Luce by his wife Claire on the way home from a party, "stories" were suggested, researched and assembled, week by week, magazine section by magazine section.

As a newcomer, I was assigned to one of the least important sections of the magazine, "Hemisphere." (Which is to say, every place in North and South America and the Caribbean that was *not* in the United States. The section that dealt with the United States was called "National Affairs.")

Except for those newspaper scribbles and Claire Booth Luce's cocktail-party items, my suggestions came from TIME "bureaus" in Montreal, Toronto, Ottawa, Vancouver, Mexico City, Caracas, Buenos Aires, Rio de Janeiro and Havana. A "bureau" was headed by a "bureau chief" and staffed by full-time TIME correspondents. Every other important city and capital in the Hemi-

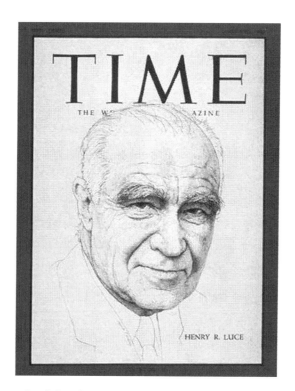

Henry R. Luce, on the March 10, 1967 cover of Time, shortly after his death.

sphere was covered by part-time correspondents ("stringers") in Yellowknife, Medicine Hat, Quebec City, Hamilton, Regina, Halifax, Prince Edward Island, Winnipeg and every major city in Latin America outside of the places we had "bureaus."

Starting with the scribbled or cabled suggestions approved by the section's Senior Editor, the Contributing Editor began to ask questions about elements of the "story." His "researcher" (a well-educated, attractive, clever, well-turned-out, womanly woman who lived, alone or with roommates, in Greenwich Village or on Manhattan's upper East and West Sides) combed through relevant books, reference works and newspaper clippings in the TIME "morgue" (library) and the city's other libraries. Together, writer and researcher composed "queries" to the original story suggester, and to any other TIME correspondent or stringer anywhere in the world who might have something interesting, relevant, amusing or titillating, to add.

What's a "stringer"? A reporter or writer, usually from some other publication, contracted to report from a place or setting where the parent publication has no regular reporter. In the *old* old days, some one measured the number of inches of column space the stringer's contributions took up, cut off an equivalent number of inches of string, and tied it onto a growing ball representing the part-timer's contributions for that week, month or year. The stringer was then paid a set amount *per inch* for his/her contribution.

A "photo researcher" sent out requests for photographs, videos, or other "art" that might illuminate the story. If a map or a chart seemed necessary or desirable, TIME's graphic designers and mapmakers went to work. If someone was available in New York or the Bo-Wash (Boston-Washington) corridor who could contribute to the story, the writer and/or researcher rode off to interview him/her. The researcher wrote up the interview and put the assembled material in a "story file."

The rest was up to the Contributing Editor. *His* assignment (there were no female Contributing Editors in those days) was not merely to write up a report and interpretation of the event and its relevance. It was to turn the report and interpretation into a compelling "story," containing all the elements of successful short-story writing. O. Henry would have made a perfect Contributing Editor at TIME.

A good TIME story required a suspenseful, interest-raising, first and second paragraph. It also needed a solid beginning, a well-constructed middle, and an unmistakable end, all put together with the rhythm and pace required of good fiction, or poetry. Touches of humor and pathos, if appropriate, were welcome. And it all should be put together with a convincing rationale, intriguing connective phrases, a climax or anti-climax, and, maybe, a final one sentence or one-word summary. Shazam!

Pulitzer-Prize-winning editorialists turned out not to have the knack. Successful and not-so-successful novelists came. And went. You either had it, or you didn't.

John McPhee had it. Paul O'Neil had it. Calvin ("Bud") Trillin had it, Kurt Vonnegut had it. Stefan Kanfer had it. Henry Grunwald had it. Brad Darrach had it. Jack Leonard had it. Harry Lee had it. Joe David Brown had it.

If you had it, or seemed as though you might get it, you went on the magazine's masthead after six months or so. From that moment on, TIME writers were required to take a "winter week" off and four other weeks of vacation a year. For what was supposed to be some vaguely menstrual misunderstanding on the part of co-founder Henry Luce, researchers got *five* weeks plus a "thirteenth week."

New Contributing Editors "floated" (filled in for established, vacationing writers) from section to section, sometimes in winter, sometimes in summer, knowing little (or, sometimes, nothing) about the basic subject matter of the Medicine Section, the Education Section, the Sport Section, the Science Section, the Art Section — even the Theater or Cinema Sections, where they could fill in as a reviewer. Bud Trillin wrote a book, "Floater", about filling in for vacationing TIME writers.

Without warning, a "yearling dinner" happened about a year after a writer had gone on the masthead. His office phone would ring and the mature, feminine voice of Mr. Luce's secretary would say something like, "Mr. Martin? Mr.

Luce wonders whether you're free for dinner on Friday, November ninth?"

As it happened, I wasn't free when my call came. My wife Julie and I were scheduled to have dinner in Peter Cooper Village in Manhattan with another new Contributing Editor, Bob Jennings, then floating in the Music section, and his very beautiful wife Mar. I stammered a bit, apologized to Mr. Luce's secretary, and asked for a rain-check.

Five or six minutes later Bob Jennings appeared at my office door. "Did you get invited to dinner with Mr. Luce?" he said, all excitement.

"Yes," I said.

"What did you say?"

"I said I couldn't make it. Julie and I are having dinner with you and Mar that night."

"I canceled the dinner!"

Omigod. I found Mr. Luce's number on the office phone list and dialed it. I told the mature, feminine voice I was Peter Martin, and I was free on the ninth after all.

"Oh, were you having dinner with Bob Jennings? You're all back on the list. The dinner's at eight at the Links Club."

"The Links Club?"

"It's at seventy-seven East seventy-seventh."

"I think I can remember that."

I haven't been back, but the Links Club was truly clubby, of a distinctly Republican persuasion. All of us yearlings arrived early. While we waited, the bartender provided martini lessons, shaking the gin and vermouth quickly in a metal shaker with chopped ice, and straining the result into straight-up glasses with stems.

"You want it extremely cold, without too much melted ice," he said

The martinis were good, and I knew that I'd arrived at the big time when I went into the men's room and found myself peeing into a urinal next to Thomas E. Dewey. He was very short.

Links Club dining tables were round. My imagination conjures up a green-felt surface, but reality probably was a white tablecloth. A lamp hung over the center and spread a central glow around the eight or nine of us around the edge of the table. Who was there? Bob Jennings, of course, and Henry Luce. Ed Jamieson, who was then floating in the Business Section and later became TIME's perennial Assistant Managing Editor. Dick Murphy, then filling in as Science writer. Marshall Loeb, writing in the Business, who'd competed with me in St. Louis at the *Globe-Democrat* ("Loeb of the Globe") on cub reporters' morning rounds, collecting relatives' photos of overnight accident and murder victims for early editions of our rival papers.

Then there was me, writing about Latin America by then in the Hemisphere Section; Roy Alexander, TIME's solidly professional and beloved Managing Editor (also a *Post-Dispatch* graduate); and Ed Cerf, the outgoing, bow-tied Assistant Managing Editor who'd interviewed and hired me and later, to the sadness of all, committed suicide.

I'm sure we all ... all except Mr. Luce, who seldom drank at parties ... had another round of martinis. To get the talk going, Mr. Luce asked us what new sections we might add to Time. Marshall Loeb suggested Agriculture, but Mr. Luce thought it smacked too much of the pre-industrial past. Ed Jamieson mentioned Aviation, and Roy Alexander (for whom aviation had been an early passion in the St. Louis of Charles Lindberg) said that TIME had tried an Aviation section that had become too predictable, and that there wasn't enough "new" going on. I proposed "Leisure," on the grounds that American vacations were getting longer (at least mine was), that people were retiring earlier, and Americans seemed to have more disposable income to spend on relaxation.

"That's why we started Sports Illustrated," barked Mr. Luce rapidly and with finality. And That was that.

From there, we began talking generally about TIME, about the personality and growth of a magazine that had begun as a quick and easy weekly news digest and was now a serious source of analysis and judgment about nearly every aspect of human activity. Mr. Luce talked about the "voice" of TIME, about his pride in the fact that when opinion and analysis were cited, it often began with the words "TIME says". As far as the tone of that voice was concerned, he said that he admired and sometimes envied the easy wit and authoritative voice of *The Economist*. He hoped that we all read it, and that we could bring something like that authority and wit to TIME. This got me going.

"Mr. Luce," I said, "back in the beginning..."

"Call me Harry," he said, rapidly, in the staccato way he threw in interjections.

"Harry," I said, "back in the 1930s, when TIME was taking shape and its reputation was growing, my father was an editor of the *Saturday Evening Post* and a lot of his close friends were working with you at TIME. Men like Dave Hulburd and Charles Wertenbaker and Pare Lorentz, and they would come to our house for parties. I was just a kid of seven or eight, but even I could sense the feeling they gave off of being involved in something important, something that *mattered*. They were working closely with you to make TIME work ... they were your companions in a great venture."

[At the time, I had not the slightest idea that "Harry" had reason to detest Wertenbaker (who happened to be one of my father's closest lifelong friends and one of my godfathers) because of the portrayal of a Luce-like character in a Wertenbaker novel based on TIME, "Death of Kings."]

I went on. "There couldn't have been more than a hundred or two hundred people involved in TIME in those days, Harry, and the sense of comradeship must have been strong. Nowadays, TIME must have close to a thousand or two thousand people putting it together every week, and you can't possibly be close to them and share that sense of purpose and accomplishment. Don't you miss that?"

"Martin," he said, abruptly and coldly, "*These* are the good old days."

End of conversation.

Chapter 10

Saving Gerald Seib

This may be my memoir, but this bit is about my good friend, Dick Dudman. In June, 1950, when I was 20 and between my Junior and Senior Years at Dartmouth, one of my father's chums and colleagues at the *Saturday Evening Post* wangled me a summer job as a copy boy at the old, un-airconditioned, hot-as-hell *St. Louis Post-Dispatch*. Ray Crowley, the *P-D's* Assistant City Editor, watched me sweat bundles of City Editions and One-Star Finals up from the Press Room, rush typewritten copy from the rewrite men to the editor's desk, then to the copy desk, and on to the composing room. He taught me to bring glass containers of his special coffee from Speck's Cafeteria ("just a speck – ha ha – of cream") next door.

A year later, traveling and singing with the Dartmouth Glee Club on its Midwest Alumni tour, I ducked out of a post-concert party in Dayton and, with an envelope full of *Daily Dartmouth* clippings, rode a midnight Pullman to St. Louis. *Mister* Crowley had just been promoted to City Editor, and I interviewed with him for a job. Result: A week after I received my Dartmouth diploma in June, 1951, I sat down at a typewriter in a back-row desk in the City Room as a reporter for the *St. Louis Post-Dispatch*.

Dick Dudman was already there. A couple of years earlier, working for the *Denver Post*, he'd won a Nieman Fellowship at Harvard, and from that had moved on to the *P-D*, then a regular on lists of "The ten best American newspapers."

Dick did well. Although Mister Crowley said during my interview that the paper would send a reporter "anywhere, any time" there was a story worth covering, the *Post-Dispatch* had no designated foreign correspondents. But Dick found stories worth covering far beyond Jefferson City and East St. Louis, and became, in effect, a one-person "corps." As for me, after a year and a half as a cityside reporter in and around St. Louis, I won an international journalism fellowship in 1953 and went off for two years to explore sub-Saharan Africa.

Back from Africa and writing about Latin America for TIME later in the 1950s, I began running into Dick at airports, usually on his way to Cuba, or Venezuela, or Asia. He covered the Viet Nam war for the *P-D*, and became instantly famous when he and Elizabeth Pond of the *Christian Science Monitor* were captured by the Viet Cong and held prisoner for more than a month. A book – "40 Days With The Enemy" – resulted.

Dick was promoted to Chief of the Post-Dispatch's Washington Bureau. When it came time to retire, Dick and his efficient, talented, smart, (and eminently lovable) wife Helen moved to Ellsworth, Maine, home of the nationally (and internationally) famous weekly *Ellsworth American*, edited by their old *Washington Post* friend, Russell Wiggins. To keep familial wits and finances sharp, they bought a local radio station as a retirement enterprise. Helen managed it.

I, meanwhile, had left TIME Incorporated, and for 28 years ran the foundation that sent me to Africa (the Institute of Current World Affairs) and a teaching organization it had spawned (the American Universities Field Staff). There was much talk in those days of a "Northern monopoly" of international reporting. I raised some money for the training of nonwestern writers and reporters in the Socialist World and the Southern Hemisphere, and started a nonprofit retirement enterprise of my own: The South-North News Service (SNNS).

The purpose of the SNNS was to train writers in what were then called the "Second" and "Third" Worlds to learn the standards and writing style of journalism in the "North," or "First World." SNNS correspondents (we identified and signed on 175 of them) would suggest and write articles about their events, issues and values, and transmit them to us in Hanover, NH, mainly by facsimile. (E-mail in those days was still a distant dream.) We would edit the articles, fact-check them, pay the writers, and distribute their writing by satellite to subscribing news organizations worldwide. We were, in effect, an educational, nonpartisan, nonpolitical mini-Reuters or mini-AP.

Based in Hanover, New Hampshire, the SNNS trained Dartmouth College students to be fact-checkers. Being in Hanover also emphasized our greatest lack: experienced, savvy, worldwise teacher-editors. To fill the gap, I recruited old friends from the *Post-Dispatch* and TIME to come to Hanover as visiting Managing Editors.

One of these was Dick Dudman. We provided our visitors with a modest car (a Chevette, if you remember how modest *they* were) a small apartment in our wonderfully ancient Wheelock House (built in 1772 by Dartmouth's founding President, Eleazar Wheelock), and a stipend small enough ($3,000 a month) to keep their retirement incomes under the amount that would make Social-Security payments taxable. To keep it that way, the maximum (and minimum) stretch of editorial work in Hanover was two or three months.

Besides re-energizing the editors' journalistic skills, the job's greatest fringe benefit was companionship. I'd known all of them personally back in our "good old days." My office in Wheelock House had been the cozy parlor of Eleazar's son John. Winter evenings, we could warm ourselves before his fireplace, sipping strong waters and improving our anecdotes.

Dick loved being back in the saddle of a news service; and we had correspondents in some unlikely places. Iran was one of these. After the deposal of the Shah in 1979 and the hostage-taking and occupation of the American Embassy by Tehran street mobs, the U.S. had no presence in Iran, official or unofficial. U.S. interests were handled at arms' length by Swiss diplomats. Our Embassy had been turned into a hostile hostel for Revolutionary Guards. American journalists could neither enter nor work in the country.

The South-North News Service was an exception. In the mid-1970s, seeking potential correspondents who could bridge the "North-South understanding gap," I queried every possible Western and quasi-Western journalism school, news organization and training program in the world for the names of Second- and Third-World journalists who had done well and then gone back to their native lands. The plan: Our trainee-correspondents would suggest stories that could interest and inform U.S. readers about their countries' issues, events, culture and values.

If the suggestions resonated with our editors, we'd give a green light, and the stories would be researched, written, faxed (or snail-mailed) to us. Our editors would go over the articles, help the correspondents get them into shape for U.S. publication (thereby teaching them U.S. grammar, style and stan- dards) and then turn them over to our Dartmouth-student fact-checkers for back-and-forth dialogue with the writers to verify accuracy. For every story that turned out well enough for us to transmit to our subscribing news or- ganizations (mostly in the United States, but in Europe and Asia as well), the correspondent received $80. Not a staggering amount by American stan- dards, but a princely sum in Zambia, Cambodia and Zamboanga. Measured by their circulations, subscribing newspapers paid from $500 to $1,500 a year to receive an article a day, plus a "Third World" tale for young readers once a week.

It was a struggle, but thanks to funding from the John D. and Catherine T. MacArthur Foundation, the Ford Foundation, the Rockefeller Foundation and the Rockefeller Brothers Fund, we raised the $385,000 we needed to get started. I traveled around the U.S. and the world seeking subscribers, and by 1987 we had signed on 17 national and international news organizations.

MacAllister College in St. Paul, Minnesota, which offers a journalism train- ing program specifically for non-U.S. students, produced an Iranian gradu- ate named Fereydon Pezeshkan, living in Tehran. I wrote to him (along with all the others) and offered him a slot as a free-lance South-North trainee. He faxed a few sample, serviceable stories and a c.v., and he was on.

"Pez," as we called him for short, was reliable but circumspect. He sug- gested no rebellious stories, nothing that would shake up the Iranian theoc- racy, but his articles did reflect the inner workings of Iran under the ayatollahs and he became a regular correspondent. Under Dick's tutelage, his writing became crisp and factual. The Iran-Iraq war was raging, and thousands of Iranian youth were being conscripted right out of high school and grammar school to form Shiite human waves to charge the machine guns of Iraqi Sunnis and go directly to martyrs' Heaven.

The war raged on, but in January 1987, the Iranians proclaimed victory. To witness the triumph, they invited more than 100 international journalists from around the Middle East to come to Iran, travel throughout the country, and interview victors and vanquished. Among these were more than a dozen Americans, including Gerald Seib, the *Wall Street Journal's* Cairo Bureau Chief. The visiting journalists were put up in Tehran hotels and escorted around the country for interviews with Iranian troops and captured Iraqis. As you might expect, the process did not produce wide-ranging, fascinating, insightful articles. After ten days, the interview window closed, and the visitors left for home.

Or, to be precise, all but one of them did. On Monday morning, February 2, 1987, Dick Dudman came in to his Wheelock House office to find a fax from Pez: "Gerald Seib, Middle East Correspondent of the *Wall Street Journal,* has been arrested in Tehran and accused of spying for the United States, Israel and Iraq. He is being held in Evyan Prison in Tehran."

What a shock! There had not been a peep about this on morning radio, nothing about it in the *New York Times*, not a line in our fine local daily *Valley News*, nor the *Boston Globe*, nor on BBC newscasts or TV.

Of course not! Their correspondents had all left Iran, and there was not a single Western correspondent who could file. A part-time reporter for the *New York Times* was with Seib when questions were raised about his passport the previous Thursday, but he could do nothing to help and was compelled to fly out on Saturday, leaving Seib behind. By Sunday, the only reporter left in Tehran with a connection to the U.S. was South-North's Fereydon Pezeshkan.

Dick edited Pez's dispatch, which included a visual description of Seib's tiny prison cell, and put it on our Associated Press satellite service exclusively for our subscribing news outlets. Digging for information, he discovered that

Seib was from the town of Hays, Iowa. He got the Seib family phone number, called, and told them about their son's arrest. He got details about Seib's life and background and sent a second-day query to Pez for continuing coverage.

What a morning! What a day! The American press is highly competitive, but it's also a vast family. When a family member gets into trouble everyone wants to help and everyone wants information. The South North News Service was the only source. Our phones began ringing nonstop.

By Tuesday, Feb. 3, the *New York Times* had pieced together the events leading up to the arrest and imprisonment. Under a headline reading U.S. JOURNALIST IS HELD BY IRAN; REASON UNCLEAR, it said, "An American journalist has been detained in Iran, the Swiss Foreign Ministry said today. The journalist, Gerald F. Seib, the Middle East correspondent for the Wall Street Journal, had spent 10 days in Iran at the invitation of the Government before a group of men seized him outside his hotel in Teheran Saturday evening. His whereabouts today were uncertain."

In that day's file from Tehran, Pez offhandedly included a phrase that he must have picked up at the Ministry of Islamic Guidance: "Seib, who is Jewish ..."

Responding by fax, Dick sent a correction: "Gerald Seib is not Jewish. He is Roman Catholic."

Back came Pez's fax: "He's not Jewish?"

"No," Dick faxed. "I talked with his family yesterday in Iowa. He's not Jewish. He was raised Roman Catholic and is Roman Catholic."

Confusion in Tehran was understandable. Seib in those days sported a full, black beard. The term "hasidic" springs to mind. His wife's maiden name, Barbara Rusewicz, was obviously Central European, but could be taken as Jewish by an unknowing Iranian.

Silence from Pez who, we found out later, was transmitting this information to the Ministry of Islamic Guidance. His next-day file began, "Because of mistakes made on both sides, Gerald Seib will be released from prison today and will fly to Europe tomorrow."

That afternoon in Hanover I got a phone call from David Stiff, a reporter at the *Wall Street Journal's* Boston bureau. "We've been hearing a lot about you down here," he said. "I've been assigned to drive up there tomorrow and see what you're all about. I can be there around six. I need driving directions and a bed for the night."

I told Dick Dudman. He glowed. He grinned. He cheered. "This is great news! It could be the making of us! *Sixty Minutes* doesn't get its story ideas from the *New York Times*. It gets them from the *Wall Street Journal*! We've got to do our normal thing when he gets here, but do it well!"

Our normal thing, of a deep New Hampshire winter evening, was to sit by the fire in my John Wheelock office, consume some seriously aged Cabot cheddar, drink a martini or two, go over the day's happenings, do some remembering of the good old days, and say good things about absent wives. (Helen was in Portland managing the family radio station; my wife Lucretia ("Lu"), Special Assistant to the President of Dartmouth, was in Boston on some mission for Jim Freedman.)

"We'll need a good fire," said Dick. "And we should drink our martinis straight up instead of on the rocks. I'll take him out to dinner, and we shouldn't book him into the Hanover Inn. Too fancy. He should be in the Occum Inn, with the clerk crammed into that alcove under the stairway and the bathrooms down the hall. He and I can talk until the fire in the office dies, and you can take him to breakfast on Main Street at Lou's the next morning. Then he can meet Ellen and Gwenda."

[Ellen Kozak and Gwenda Smith were the rest of the South-North staff. Ellen, who had been fired from a secretarial job at Gile Insurance in Hanover for what her bosses considered to be an overlong maternity leave, had turned out to be an early genius at computer manipulation, desktop publishing, office management and loving, instinctive understanding of what was happening in the minds and souls of writers many miles and cultures away. Gwenda, a smart and tough holder of an advanced degree from the University of Wales (she called herself our "resident Welsh dragon"), was a stickler for the accuracy, grammar, style and meaning of language and facts that came from the convoluted, complicated minds of Dartmouth fact-checkers, writers *and* editors.]

Fortunately, my office woodbox was out of yellow birch and maple, and I had to borrow some showy white-birch logs from an unused fireplace across the hall. They burn with amazing snap, crackle and pop. Dick, who loves community-based organizations like Rotary and Kiwanis, was still wearing the bow tie and collared shirt he'd worn to the local Rotary lunch in Hanover that day. His red-checked wool jacket and ear-flapped cap were tossed onto the floor behind his Shaker rocker.

Stiff had read his MapQuest well, and knocked at my office door a few minutes after six. The fire was crackling away and our martinis, olives gleaming, stood with the cheddar between us.

"Come in!" I called.

He came in and absorbed the scene. We stood to shake hands, and he said, "Do you do this every night?"

"Every night we can" I said.

We sat him down, poured him a diet soda (he was on duty, after all), and began talking about the drive up. At that magic moment my wife Lu burst in, back from her own trip. "I heard you on Public Radio on the Lowell By-Pass!" she said to Dick. "You were being interviewed about being captured by the Viet Cong, and how Gerald Seib must be feeling in that Iranian prison!"

"Yes," said Dick. "They called today."

Things went well that evening with Mr. Stiff, and there's nothing like a breakfast at Lou's to begin a snowy day in Hanover. Over waffles with Vermont maple syrup and home-made sausage the next morning, I explained the iffyness - and fun - of launching a Third-World news service.

His story appeared in the *Journal* the following Monday, and he got it right.

Obscure Hanover, N.H. News Agency Becomes Celebrity in Coverage of Seib

HANOVER, N.H. - Last week the world's press corps paced and fretted outside Iran's closed door while Wall Street Journal reporter Gerald F. Seib was detained in Tehran. Meanwhile, a tiny news service here seemed to be looking through the door's keyhole.

Last Tuesday, for example, while worried Journal editors and U.S. officials still were seeking word on Mr. Seib, Hanover's South-North News Service reported that he would soon be released. And on Friday he was.

South-North's reports surprised not only outsiders but its own editors as well. "I didn't know there was going to be breaking news on this job," says Richard Dudman, who edits South-North's Iran stories, which are usually features rather than hard-news stories.

Breaking the news for South-North was its man in Tehran, Fereydon Pezeshkan, a 47-year old Iranian who works only part-time for the agency. "I've been in this business from the age of 14, and like every journalist, I have my own sources," he said in a phone interview from Tehran. "They trust me because I never misquote or exaggerate what they say. And perhaps Iran wants to reflect news through South-North because it is one small window to the U.S."

To be sure, South-North reports aren't always prescient. Three days after Mr. Seib was detained, the news service reported that he would be charged and tried for espionage activities.

10.1 Obscure Agency

With its headquarters in a 214-year-old white frame house next to Dartmouth College, South-North looks like a New England bed-and-breakfast. Until last week's reports on Mr. Seib, it was an obscure Third World news service operating on a shoestring budget, one of a handful of such agencies world-wide that gather stories from part-time stringers and sell them to newspapers.

Peter Bird Martin, a former Time Inc. editor, founded South-North about a year ago - setting up shop in Hanover because he lives nearby - as a non-profit educational concern with $835,000 from the Ford Foundation, the Rockefeller Foundation and similar groups. The agency offers a kind of correspondence course to aspiring Third World reporters.

South-North recruited most of its 175 student-correspondents -including Mr. Pezeshkan - by writing to 700 foreigners who studied journalism in the

U.S. The correspondents, mostly natives of the 82 countries South-North covers, generally file features on things like drugs in Nepal and scaring off tigers in India with electrified dummies. The agency edits and returns them. "We teach by example," says Mr. Martin.

If a story is good enough, South-North makes it one of the six articles it wires each week to its 17 customers, including the Los Angeles Times, the Washington Post and the International Herald Tribune. These papers say they rarely use South-North articles intact, but have incorporated material in their own stories. "We're like a school of agriculture that sells the cheese" it makes in the classroom, says Mr. Martin.

10.2   Relaxed Pace

The pace usually is fairly relaxed, he adds, sipping a martini with Mr. Dudman before a crackling birch-wood fire in South-North's old house. Sporting a natty bow tie and a little wheel on his lapel. Mr. Dudman might pass for a retiree who belongs to the Rotary Club. In fact, he is.

But lately, the retired 68-year old St. Louis Post-Dispatch editor, who took a break from sailboat building to do a three-month stint at South-North, has been very busy. He has been getting calls as early as 5:30 a.m. from Mr. Pezeshkan and as late as 10 p.m. from U.S. reporters wanting to know what Mr. Pezeshkan said, Mr. Dudman says.

South-North's correspondents get $80 for each usable story, but Mr. Pezeshkan may get a bonus of several hundred dollars for putting South-North on the map, Mr. Martin says. South-North's editors have never met Mr. Pezeshkan, and they aren't sure why Iranian officials cooperate with him.

Educated partly in the U.S., including a year at the World Press Institute for foreign journalists in(St. Paul, Minn., Mr. Pezeshkan works for a Japanese newspaper and Britain's BBC radio besides assignments for South-North. To keep up with his three jobs, he recently took on his 19-year-old son as an assistant.

South-North editors praise Mr. Pezeshkan for being accurate and politically expedient at the same time.

10.3   A Crucial Skill

That skill is crucial for Third World journalists writing for Western publications. "We get stories, especially from African countries, with obligatory paragraphs containing reflexive, knee-jerk obeisance to the ruling party," says Mr. Martin. "And it's reflexive on my part to take those paragraphs out."

And recently, one of South-North's China correspondents mailed a story about the student demonstrations there to Hanover. But it came back, apparently intercepted by government censors, "without comment," says Mr. Martin. "He took that as a signal that he shouldn't pursue the topic."

Though South-North has become a celebrity of sorts during the past week, its struggle for recognition and credibility is far from over. "We subscribe, but we don't pay enough attention to the service to give it a fair assessment," says a spokesman for the Los Angeles Times. Adds Karin McGinn, national editor for the Seattle Post-Intelligencer: "I'm not terribly impressed with South-North. Their story ideas are good, but I think they need to be more aggressively edited."

But the Post-Intelligencer's foreign editor, Don Graydon, says South-North's coverage of Iran and South Africa has been helpful. "I'm looking for stories to back up our daily foreign coverage, and they have consistently been able to provide them" regarding Iran. He adds that the paper rarely runs South-North's articles as stand-alone stories, but sometimes inserts pieces of them in other stories.

South-North's Mr. Martin, a former editor for Time and Money magazines, hires Dartmouth students as fact-checkers, but says the service sometimes must "rely on our instincts and previous experience of reliability with our correspondents. We've all had decades of experience editing."

Nevertheless, South-North and similar services have a tough time selling their articles to Western newspapers. "American editors feel very antsy about taking stories from outside their usual channels," says Gerald Loughran, managing editor of Luxembourg-based Compass News Features, one of South-North's two or three direct competitors.

10.4   Answers to Critics

Another problem, says Mr. Loughran, is that "the Third World isn't an exciting topic" to editors in more developed nations. Both Compass and South-North were founded partly as answers to critics - the most prominent of which is the United Nations Educational, Scientific and Cultural Organization - that say little Third World news gets into Western papers.

But Compass, founded in 1984 with funding from the Aga Khan, a wealthy businessman and Moslem spiritual leader, has had little success -most of its present 30 newspaper customers are in the Third World.

South-North's Mr. Martin, 57, says one of his main goals is to provide a credible conduit through which Third World news can get into Western papers. "I'm a do-gooder," he says. Adds Mr. Dudman, a hard-bitten newsman who in 1970 was captured and held for 40 days by the Viet Cong in Cambodia: "I'm not. I want damn good stories."

To break even, Mr. Martin says South-North will need 70 subscribers -53 more than it had last week. Mr. Pezeshkan's stories have helped. Two new customers recently signed in, including the Christian Science Monitor.

"If we ever get to 70, we'll be lucky," he says. "But considering the deteriorating relations between the Third and the First worlds, there will continue to be conflicts involving old-fashioned saber-rattling. Given that, there will be other countries where Western reporters can't get in. And we'll be there."

* * * *

True to Pez's word, the Iranians released Gerald Seib on Thursday, Feb. 8 and he flew out to Germany on the 9 . Thus ended South-North's Warholian 15 minutes of celebrity. But I, Peter Martin, wondered: How did Gerald Seib feel about South-North coming to his rescue?

I got my chance a few months later, when Seib was scheduled to speak at the Harvard Club in New York City. I'm a reciprocal member, so on the appointed day I found a seat in mid-audience. His Iran misadventure has become part of his *curriculum vitae,* and the latest version says: "While living in Cairo, Seib, along with 56 other journalists, was invited to tour the Iran-Iraq warfront. On the night of January 31, 1987, he was detained by plainclothes policemen in Tehran, Iran, and taken to Evin Prison where he was accused of spying for Israel. Suddenly and inexplicably, after four days of interrogation, he was released."

At the end of the Harvard Club speech I went up to the podium to shake his hand. When it came my turn, I introduced myself: "Mr. Seib, I'm Peter Martin, editor of the South-North News Service..."

Anger suffused his voice. "You son of a *bitch!*" he spat out. "You *exploited* me!" He turned his back and said not another word.

What had happened to him? Between the lines of press reports at the time of his trouble, some details stand out. Like the rest of the outside journalists, Seib had been issued a five-day visa - too short to cover the victory lap of interviews and sightseeing, but the Ministry of Islamic Guidance said the visas would be extended. All the passports were returned, with extensions, on Thursday, Jan. 29 - all but Seib's.

Seib got several phone calls from a man who said there was some difficulty with his passport, but it had been resolved and the passport would be returned. Friday came, but no passport. He was eventually told to go to the immigration office Saturday morning for his passport because Friday was the Moslem day of worship. On Saturday he was turned away from the Ministry of Islamic Guidance in the morning without his passport, and that evening, as the rest of the foreign journalists left, he was detained. Shortly after his detention, the Iranian press reported that a "spy of the Zionist regime," posing as a journalist, had been arrested after entering Iran on a "false passport."

"Passport." "Passport." " Passport." The word was repeated time and again in the press reports of his detention and imprisonment. It occurred to me that Seib, like all professionals working regularly in the Middle East, probably had *two* passports, one for travel and work in Israel, the other for travel and work in Arab countries. The U.S. State Department, acknowledging the value of travel to both worlds, issued two passports to those who were doing it. Seib either mistakenly used the Israeli one when he arrived in Iran, or Iranians, searching his room, found it.

Mistake or not, it has had no affect on Seib's rise in the *Wall Street Journal* hierarchy. Home from Iran and Cairo in 1987, he covered the White House from the Washington Bureau and reported on diplomacy and foreign policy. In 1992 he became a news editor responsible for national political coverage from Washington and around the country. Like Dudman, he's won major journalism awards, achieved success as an international reporter, and won status as chief of the Washington bureau of a major American newspaper.

With luck, in retirement he and his wife will be able to sit with good friends over great meals and an occasional martini and re-tell great stories about his life in journalism.

Like this one.

Chapter 11

Batista and Figueres

One of the benefits of working as a writer at TIME in the 1950s was travel. If you were assigned to one of the farflung sections of the magazine on a more or less permanent basis and you didn't know much about it, you *went there* at TIME's expense for a month or more a year.

When I started as a writer, I was assigned to write in the "Hemisphere" section of the magazine, which meant that any part of North, South or Central America outside the United States was my "beat." And my *pleasure*, naturally. In the "Hemisphere" were Canada and all of Latin America. I started writing stories Canada, and did so from September of 1955 'til Christmas. In 1956 I was switched to Latin America – and the fun began.

It took a while for a new writer to learn what he was writing about. There were 21 countries and a few colonies in the territory that stretched from Hudson's Bay to the Rio Grande in Texas, across the Caribbean, and down both coasts of South America to the Straits of Magellan. Each country had a President (or a Dictator), a former President (or a former Dictator), a would-be President (or a would-be Dictator), a Vice President, important military leaders, and a flock of cabinet ministers.

We New York-based writers (there were four or five of us) had to learn their names, their political leanings, their histories, and whether they were corrupt, torturing, tinpot tyrants or democratically elected "good guys." Or a mixture of both.

Outside it all loomed the Cold War. Latin America was nominally "ours," closed off by custom and the Monroe Doctrine to influence and control by Communists, Socialists and various "Foreign Powers."

I just said "Outside it all." Amend that. *Inside* it all were "Leftists," "Socialists", "Reformers", "Rebels," "Do-gooders" and "Nice Guys." We liberal writers and researchers in the Hemisphere Section considered ourselves "Nice Guys." We called Nice-Guy politicians in Latin America 'The Democratic Left.' Mr. Luce probably called them the "Dangerous Left."

To make this all clearer, over lunch one day with one of Harry Luce's top editors later in my years at TIME, I mentioned that I had cast my first national vote for Adlai Stevenson.

"Adlai *Stevenson!*" he sneered. "Adlai *Stevenson!* He steps out of the shower to take a pee!" Obviously a wimp.

At the time, the President of Cuba was a Right-wing tyrant named Fulgencio Batista. A former sergeant in the Cuban National Guard, he was part of a so-called "Sergeants' Rebellion" in the 1930s and was installed as President of Cuba with United States support after the downfall of a previous U.S. favorite, Gerardo Machado. U.S. corporations had highly profitable investments in almost all major Cuban companies, from Woolworth's Five-and-Ten-Cent stores, to immense sugar plantations, to distilleries making Bacardi rum. Those companies felt uneasy when "friendly" Latin American political bosses were overthrown.

Over the years, Batista had become as rich and tyrannical as Machado had been, and by 1958 a group of bearded young revolutionaries called the "26th of July" Movement, led by a far-left university student named Fidel Castro, had taken to the hills of the island's Oriente Province, and was trying to overthrow him.

In Havana, the capital, *the* place to stay was the plush, posh Hotel *Nacional.* For one of my exploratory trips south, TIME had booked me a room there, and I was sharing gambling and drinking space with a group of touring Missouri businessmen looking for Latino investment opportunities. They were all over the place, particularly in the gambling casino. They all wore big badges that said, "Everything's Up to Date in Kansas City" in Spanish and English, and we chatted companionably as we played.

I was scheduled to interview President Batista while I was in the city, but the day before the interview, a group of 26th of July rebels had sneaked into town and attacked the presidential palace, trying to kill him. The attack failed. The rebels charged up the front staircase of the palace, firing their weapons, but Batista's bodyguards held them off, and killed most of them.

I received a cable from my top editors in New York, giving me a list of questions to ask Batista, but when I phoned the palace to confirm the interview, I was told that all presidential appointments had been canceled.

Ah, well, back to the blackjack tables. Talking to the Kansas Citians there, I was told that they also had an interview scheduled with the President the next day.

"It's been canceled, of course," I said.

"No," they said. "It's still on."

"You're kidding," I said. "Are you sure?"

They were. "Hey," I said. "Could you lend me one of those badges? I'd love to tag along."

"Sure. Glad to have you."

Next morning at 8 a.m., wearing my "Up-to-Date" badge, I boarded the bus at the *Nacional*. When we got to the palace, workmen were replacing the staircase marble that had been chipped and broken during the attack. In a receiving room at the top of the stairs President Batista was grinning and joking, greeting his guests. He spoke pretty good English. I was eighth or ninth in line.

"Good morning, *Señor Presidente*," I said. "But truth to tell, I'm not from Kansas City. I'm from TIME magazine, and my editors would like to know what you did and thought when those rebels came up the stairs."

Batista paused for a second, then grinned. "I did what any smart president would do. I hid in the closet."

The New York editors loved it.

On another Latin America trip I explored Central America, then a collection of "banana republics" (Guatemala, Honduras, Panama) pretty much under the control of the United Fruit Company and Pan American World Airways. Nicaragua and Costa Rica were agricultural and industrializing countries with elected governments. Nicaragua was controlled (and more-or-less "owned") by the Somoza family, descended from a friendly National Guard Non-Commissioned Officer named Anastasio ("Tacho") Somoza, who'd been installed by United States Marines sent in by the U.S. government to protect North American investments during a period of instability in the 1930s.

Costa Rica was a small, mountainous country bordering Nicaragua. It had an agricultural economy (coffee, sisal, cotton) originally developed by Sephardic Jewish exiles from Spain. It was a U.S.-controlled military dictatorship until its local tyrant was overthrown by a charismatic (but short; about five-foot-four in his stockinged feet) revolutionary leader named José ("Pepe") Figueres.

In the year of my visit, Dwight Eisenhower was President of the U.S. and Richard Nixon was Vice President. It was decided that Nixon should make a "neighborly" goodwill trip around South America.

Motorcading through Venezuela, a traditional close friend of the United States because of bounteous exports of petroleum from oilfields under Lake Maracaibo, Nixon (and the U.S. government) was surprised – make that *shocked* – when rioters spat upon, and dumped offal upon his limousine from highways overpasses around the capital, Caracas.

The State Department, the House of Representatives, the U.S. Senate, TIME magazine, and Harry Luce wanted to know: What had gone wrong? Seeking answers, Congressional leaders invited President Figueres of Costa Rica to the American Capitol to explain.

As befit a leading member of Latin America's Nice-Guy Democratic Left, Figueres had a solid answer to the question. The problem was the festering, long-standing resentment of Latin Americans, rich and poor, about U.S. exploitation of their resources and their people. He explained this in his speech to Congress. As a "Hemisphere" Contributing Editor, I was assigned to write about it for TIME.

From time immemorial, TIME writers had mastered the magic of the metaphor as a way of tackling a difficult topic. I no longer have a copy of the draft of my original opening paragraph (in those pre-computer days we used carbon-paper in our Royal typewriters to produce "cc's") but it went something like this:

> "In theater, when your show gets into trouble on the road, it's time to call in a 'play doctor.' Last week, when the U.S. show ran into trouble on the roads around Caracas, Venezuela, the House of Representatives called in a friendly play doctor – José ('Don Pepe') Figueres, President of the Central American nation of Costa Rica. In his address to Congress, he compared Latin Americans to that friendly, fuzzy, South-of-the-border beast of burden, the llama.
>
> "The llama is hard-working, patient, reliable, and uncomplaining," he said. "But when you overwork him, or overload him, or mistreat him, he doesn't kick. He doesn't bite. He spits."

The story went on in that vein, explaining that the Nixon trip was a perfect opportunity for Latinos in the street to express their long-restrained resentment of North American businesses and businessmen.

I turned the story in, and went home. Next morning the "edit" of the Assistant Managing Editor, then Otto Fuerbringer, was had landed on my desk.

It had been "edited" to read: "Yankee-baiting, Yankee-hating José (Pepe) Figueres was at it again last week." It went on to say that Figueres, a well-known tool of the Latin American Far Left and a bitter enemy of the United States, had hailed the anti-U.S. demonstration as a continent-wide signal to all his fellow leftists to take to the streets in protest against "Yankee imperialism."

The rest of the article contained phrases I vaguely recognized as part of my original story, but the "Yankee-baiting, Yankee-hating" lead paragraph negated them all, and the identification of Figueres as a Communist sympathizer was clear. I read through it two or three times, then took it down the hall to my immediate boss, Hemisphere Section Senior Editor John Walker.

John was a holdover from TIME's World War II overseas staff. His last foreign assignment was in the Moscow bureau, but alcohol was dissolving his talent and his reputation. TIME had paid for rehabilitation treatment at Payne-Whitney Hospital in New Haven and was trying to lighten his load by assigning him to the magazine's least troublesome news section.

It wasn't working. Drafts of unedited articles would pile up in his in-box in the morning. At lunchtime he would scribble "JW" at the upper right-hand corner of the top page of each draft, the usual indication that the Senior Editor had edited the story and approved.

John hadn't. He just tossed the "edits" into his out-box and buzzed for them to be carried to the copy desk and sent on to the Managing Editor. He then went off to the "Three G's", a favorite TIME restaurant across 48th Street, for his first two (or three, or whatever) lunchtime martinis. At the end of the afternoon he would come back to the TIME-LIFE Building, scribble more JW's on stories that had accumulated during lunch, and head off to the train for Port Chester in Westchester County.

Otto Fuerbringer was doing the final editing that week. It was he who'd changed the entire thrust of my portrayal of Figueres as a useful, constructive "play doctor" into condemnation of him as an anti-U.S. Communist sympathizer and manipulator.

When I'd read Otto's edit, I thought about it, furiously. Then, less furiously, I took it in to John Walker.

"Have you read this?" I said.

"Yes," he said.

"It's all wrong," I said. "He's got Figueres all wrong. We can't publish this."

"Peter," he said, "around here you win some and you lose some. You just lost one."

"But it's all wrong. This won't make Figueres look bad. It will make *us*, TIME magazine, look bad. Anyone who knows anything about Figueres will lose respect for us as a publication, as a newsmagazine. We *can't* publish this."

"Sorry. I can't do anything about it."

"Can I talk to Otto about it?"

"If you want to, go ahead."

I walked upstairs to the 26th floor and stopped at the desk of Otto's secretary. "I'm Peter Martin, a writer in the Hemisphere Section," I said. "I need to talk with Otto. Has he got a few minutes free?"

"Let me check," she said. She went into the office door behind her and came out after a few minutes. "It's okay," she said. "Go on in."

I figured that Otto was a reasonable man, and an intelligent, reasonable journalist. He had "broken in" as a reporter at the *St. Louis Post-Dispatch,* as I had. He had gone to an Ivy League college (Harvard) as I had. He was married to a St. Louis woman who had graduated from the same balanced, upright girls' school in St. Louis that my wife Julie had. He could understand my journalistic principles.

What I didn't understand was that he had decided that the best job in American journalism (as, later in our professional lives, he told me) was the Managing Editorship of TIME. He was determined to get it (he eventually did). That meant accepting and adopting the same right-wing, conservative, Republican beliefs as those breathed by that boss of all Time Inc. bosses, Henry Robinson Luce.

I sat down across from Otto at his desk and made my case about the wrongness of the Figueres story. He heard me out, patiently. He even looked amused. Then he began to talk to me, in the even-voiced tones of a professor with an ignorant scholar.

"What you don't understand," he said, is this is their technique. They come across someone from the other side, someone intelligent and open to intelligent conversation. They put on their friendliest face, talk in the most welcoming tones, accept the point of view they're hearing expressed, pronounce it reasonable and intelligent. And not just for the minute, or for the afternoon, or the evening. They do it over a cup of coffee, or a drink, or a meal. They persuade you that there are no sides, or that they're on your side, that you're in this *together*. You come away feeling that you've made your point, that you've made a friend, that you're partners in rationality."

"What they've done, is create a dupe. A useful dupe. A dupe who can be expected to accept the socialist side, or whatever. They can see reason in it, see it as a mirror image of what they already believe, and pass it on as an okay way of looking at things. That's what your friend, Don Pepe Figueres, is up to."

He put extra emphasis on "Don Pepe." He added, "They've tried it with me. I wouldn't let them get away with it. And I'm not going to let them get away with it with you."

I tried to make my case again, but for Otto, the matter was closed. As I talked, he began glancing at his watch and looking past me at the door to the corridor. His phone rang. He picked it up. He said something like, "Oh, really?" and turned back to me. "Things are happening out there," he said. "I've got to go."

I got the message. My moment was over. And the Yankee-baiting, Yankee-hating story ran the following week as he'd edited it.

Chapter 12

The Unthinkable

The Yankee-baiting, Yankee-hating article went out to four million, or five million, or six million readers of TIME, the weekly newsmagazine, that week. At Manhattan lunches, and on trips to the coffee machine, and during visits to the men's room, and to the cafeteria in the Time-Life Building, I explained its *wrong*ness to my colleagues in the Hemisphere section and to other writers and editors. They understood, of course. Their boss was also Otto Fuerbringer, and Otto was the willing shadow of Henry Luce.

The reader I was most troubled about was Jose ("Pepe") Figueres, President of Costa Rica. He would chalk it up as another political slam by lockstepping, right-wing propagandists from Up North. He would never know how and why it happened, would never know that it happened despite the protests of a North American "Contributing Editor."

I lost sleep over it. I did some personal questioning of the rationale and reasoning behind American political journalism and the values and morals of those who practiced it. After five or six days, I couldn't take it any more. I sat down at my typewriter and wrote a letter to President Jose Figueres in San Jose, Costa Rica. I mailed it. Air Mail.

Again, I don't have the carbon, but it said something like this:

"Dear President Figueres:

"Of all of TIME magazine's readers in Latin America, you are the most likely to have read last week's article about your visit to the U.S. Congress and your speech about public reaction to Richard Nixon on the highways around Caracas.

"As a writer about Latin American affairs for the magazine, I was assigned to write that article. What appeared in the magazine was not the article I wrote. What you saw was the result of editing by one of my superior editors whose views of international issues differs widely from mine.

"I made a personal appeal to that editor to change the story, to bring it closer to my original version, of which I enclose a carbon copy.

"Please accept my personal apologies for the article as it appeared in the magazine. As A.J. Liebling, a respected critic of the U.S. Press once wrote, 'Freedom of the press is guaranteed only to those who own one.'

"Yours sincerely, Peter Bird Martin"

I didn't tell anyone at TIME about the letter. Doing what I did verges on the unthinkable. As a matter of fact, it *is* the unthinkable. But I felt better after it had gone off, and I felt even better a couple of weeks later, when an air-mail letter from Costa Rica dropped into my in-box.

It was from President Figueres. "Dear Mr. Martin," it began. "I totally understand what happened in regard to your article. You can be sure that I would have preferred the original, but I have come to expect the reaction that was published in the edition of TIME that arrived in Costa Rica.

"I do not know if your work ever permits travel to Latin America, but if you can come to my country I would be pleased to receive you.

"Sincerely yours, Jose Figueres"

Talk about pleased! 1958 was a great year to be covering Latin America. One of the United States' tinpot-dictator allies, Marcos Perez Jimenez, was ousted as president of Venezuela in a bloodless "Lawyers' Coup" early that year, along with his master torturer, Pedro Estrada. (I wrote a TIME cover story about Perez Jimenez' successor, Romulo Betancourt.) Nixon's Caracas motorcade was attacked in early May, and TIME's editorial eye was already turned south. When I got Figueres' letter, an autumn trip to Central America looked good to me, and even better to the magazine's editors. I wrote back to President Figueres and began planning a trip to Mexico, Guatemala,

Nicaragua, Costa Rica and Panama. [As the old palindrome put it, A MAN! A PLAN! A CANAL! PANAMA !]

Opposites attract, and since an expense-account plane ride was open to all of Central America, I threw in visits along-the-way to Honduras and El Salvador as well. But the most compelling destinations were Costa Rica and Nicaragua. They were next-door neighbors, and rebels supported by each country invaded the other from time to time, trying to overthrow the opposite chief executives. In Nicaragua, the top dogs were President Luis Somoza and his brother, West Point-trained General Anastasio ("Tachito" – "Little Tacho") Somoza, who was in charge of the National Guard.

Their father, Anastasio ("Tacho") Somoza had been installed in the 1930s by U.S. armed forces sent in to maintain order on behalf of U.S. investors during an uprising. He turned out to be a profiteering tyrant often referred to by U.S. diplomats as an "S.O.B." From time to time, State Department officials suggested to President Franklin Roosevelt that "old Tacho" ought to be got rid of, but FDR is said to have made an understandable point: "He may be an S.O.B., but he's *our* S.O.B."

Whoever's S.O.B., in the 1930s he was shot in the stomach by an assassin during a radio broadcast, and eventually died. His sons rounded up Opposition leaders and put them in a cage, open at the top to sun and rain, in the courtyard of their hilltop mansion overlooking Lake Managua. As the brothers passed by in the morning on their way to their offices, they jeered at the prisoners, or threw things. A visit to the Somoza brothers would make a fascinating yang to my yin meeting with Pepe Figueres.

PanAm flew a kind of aerial bus route each day from Mexico City down to Panama City, stopping at each nation's capital. I won't stretch out this account with endless details of every stop, but I had friends all along the way. Our Mexico City Bureau Chief was Harvey Rosenhouse, twin brother of Robert Rosenhouse, our stringer in Guatemala City. They were born in Guatemala, had fluent Spanish, and had never been widely separated in adolescence and adulthood – witness the fact that they both were now on the Time Inc. payroll with only a borderline on a map between them.

Harvey knew everyone worth knowing in Mexico City, and brother Bob prospered as editor, publisher, advertising director, circulation manager and owner of Guatemala's principal English-language daily newspaper, the *Guatemala Sun*. Once or twice a year he made the rounds of all places in the capital and two or three other sizable Guatemalan cities where an American might think of staying or shopping or otherwise spending money. To each enterprise he sold a page, or half a page, or a quarter-page, or a column, or a half a column, of space – *advertising* space. He composed the heading, designed the ads, had them set in type, laid them out, and had them printed up on reams of type-writer paper – leaving blank spaces for the news. His overused motto might have been the same as that of my high-school paper, the *Merionite*. "All the news that fits, we print."

Each day, he made the rounds of friends whose organizations subscribed to the Associated Press or United Press, and gathered up unused English-language printouts from around their teletype machines. He scissored final paragraphs from the articles and turned the result over to a typist with an electric typewriter. She re-typed them into the blank spaces and delivered them to a job printer with a headline composed by Bob. Next morning the finished, stapled newspapers were collected by Bob and distributed for sale.

Neat. Efficient. Low-overhead. And profitable. Those were the good old days of print journalism.

After Guatemala, the next stop was the Somoza brothers' Nicaragua. Relations between the Somozas and Harry Luce's right-wing United States being what they were, I was met – warmly – at the Managua airport by the United States ambassador, Thomas ("Tommy") Whelan. I was surprised, and said so.

"TIME magazine *matters* down here," Tommy said. "And TIME writers and editors rank right up there with U.S. Ambassadors. Maybe even higher." Without a blink, I was whisked through customs and into the Ambassador's limo.

"We've been invited to a party at the President's house tonight," said Tommy, "and I've accepted for both of us. I hope it's okay with you."

It was, and the Ambassador dropped me off at the Hotel Managua. I ate dinner with a roomful of American baseball players, down for pre-season training, and watched a few of the more daring leap from the first-floor balcony into the swimming pool at the bottom of the courtyard below. They loved making splashes that sprinkled young women sitting around the edges of the pool. The women seemed to enjoy it, too.

Then, off to the Somozas' party. Their hilltop house looked like a set out of *Beau Geste,* with crenelations around the edge of the roofline and armed guards everywhere. Managua's *crème de la crème* were there, and Ambassador Whelan introduced the "TIME Editor" (I was, after all, listed on the masthead as a "Contributing Editor") to General Somoza, President Somoza and their *señoras.* General Somoza's *señora* was a New York model named Hope, whom he'd met while he was an exchange officer in training at West Point.

Hope was, to put a word to it, gorgeous. She'd decided to (or was assigned to) make the TIME editor warmly welcome, and she linked her arm in mine to introduce me to family members and local politicos. She smelled good, and expensive. (Chanel? Or was it Guerlain's "White Shoulders", which had smitten me when I danced with Jane Rogers Saturday nights at the Merion Cricket Club?) Good liquor was flowing, although I flinched a bit when I saw Haig & Haig Pinch being mixed with sweet soda as a matter of course when "Scotch and Soda" was ordered from the waiters and at the bar.

Hope and I danced until it was almost *too* warm, and then went out on a little balcony to catch our breaths. What a scene! Below us, the waves and ripples of Lake Managua shimmered in the ambient light of the little city, and beyond, across the water, the cones of dormant volcanoes silhouetted against the night sky.

"What do you think of it?" Hope asked, waving at the scenery

"It's almost too perfect," I said.

"It's a lousy town, day or night," she said, and we went back in to dance some more.

The night went on, the liquor kept pouring, and – aware that I had an interview appointment with President Luis Somoza the following morning at 10

– I told Ambassador Whelan I was ready to call it a night at about 2 a.m. Off I went, and next morning at 9:30 I was back at the palace, in the President's *sala de espera.*

I had my time-killing copy of "War and Peace" with me, and I was reading at 10:30 when a young military officer, his shoulder wrapped in several feet of braided gold, tapped my arm.

"Mr. Martin?" he said. I looked up. "Please come with me."

He led me down a couple of corridors, paused at a door, and knocked. A voice from within said something. The officer opened the door and there, seated at the presidential desk with his head resting on his arms, was President Somoza. He looked up.

"Peter," he said. "I have the most ferocious hangover. We can't talk here. Let's go to my club, where the bartender knows how to cope with these things."

We rode down in the presidential elevator, got into the presidential limo, and rode to what must have been the presidential club. The bartender mixed what seemed to be a potion of tomato juice, lemon juice, local tobasco and ice, plus some clear fluid from an unfamiliar bottle (*cachaça?* – distilled cane liquor?). He served it stirred, not blendered. The President drank it, then ordered one for me and a second for him. We drank them, slowly.

"Now," he said. "We can talk."

"Mister President," I said.

He stopped me. "Call me Luis," he said.

"Luis," I said. "I'm not going to publish this, so it's off the record. But I'd love to hear the answer. You and Tachito now have everything you could possibly want out of life. You have power, you have enough money to last the rest of your lives. You own the airline, the steamship company, cotton mills, *fincas*, the Mercedes-Benz franchise. But at the same time, you're genially detested as dictators in this country, and in many other places in Latin America.

"Now, while you can, before there's an uprising, a *golpe*, why not clear your throats, say that you have done everything you can for your country, and retire? You might not be believed at the start, but if you actually did it, and sponsored truly free elections, you could go out as remarkable historic *heroes*, at least in some minds. You might then be able to live out your lives in some sort of comfort and respectability instead of being nervous targets for rebellion and assassination."

To his credit, and – thinking back on it, to my chances of survival – he didn't explode. He looked at me almost sadly, surprised at my ignorance.

"Peter," he said. "In your literature, and in ours, is the story about riding the tiger. Once you've ridden it, you can't just stop and get off. Now, let's have a real drink."

And we had scotches and club soda.

FOOTNOTE:

Years later, President Luis had died of a heart attack and brother Tachito had taken over Nicaragua's presidency. Then came the inevitable revolution. Rebels drove Tachito's loyalists out of the capital, and he was holed up on one of the family *fincas* out in the countryside. He'd sent Hope off to Paraguay for safe-keeping under the protection of a fellow strongman, Paraguayan President Adolfo Stroessner.

I then had a powerful impulse to send Tachito a cable: "NOW? HAS THE TIME COME TO GET OUT? NOW? But I didn't have a cable address.

He was killed.

Chapter 13

Weekend With Pepe

A short PanAm Airways hop was all that separated Managua, Nicaragua, from San Jose, Costa Rica, although the capital cities were miles apart in politics and climate. Managua was humid, compressed and *Caribbean*. San Jose was crisp, clean, mountainous, and *European*. The sidewalks clicked crisply under your heels, and there was no sense of moisture when you breathed through your nose outside the San Jose Hotel.

When I got into my room, I phoned the number President Figueres had sent me. I got his secretary, told her the President had asked me to call when I got into town, and left my hotel and room number. I then did my usual thing: I went out for a walk to scout the neighborhood for interesting stores and breakfast restaurants.

When I got back it was mid-afternoon and a phone message was waiting from President Figueres.

"Mister Martin? Welcome to Costa Rica," he said. He thanked me again for my letter about his speech, asked polite questions about my plane trip, then: "Do you have weekend plans?"

It was Friday. I had no plans.

"Good," he said, when I called him back. "I'd like you to join me at my country place, *La Lucha sin Fin*, if you're free. You could see some lovely countryside, watch sisal grow, and I could show you how simple twine can become good floor covering. Can you come? I'd get you back to San Jose by

Monday morning."

What could please a journalist more than an invitation to spend a weekend with the President of an interesting country he was assigned to write about? At his country home, *La Lucha Sin Fin?* The Unending Battle? The Fight Without End? I was free, I was happy to say, and I said it.

Saturday morning came. My duffel-satchel was packed for a trip to the country, and at 9:30 the phone rang in my room. The President's car was waiting.

Figueres apologized for not driving himself, but said his security people insisted that he be driven most places to avoid being assassinated. He also apologized for the ordinariness of the car, and its dingy appearance.

"They don't want me to attract attention," he said. "They've bought three ordinary-looking cars and they rotate them. They actually spatter them with mud. On country roads the cars can't travel at high speeds because they're so heavy. We've got a lot of armor plating on the sides and underneath. Believe me, we're secure." He laughed.

"Do you ever run into trouble, Mr. President?" I asked.

"If we're going to spend the weekend calling each other Mister Martin and Mister President," he said, "we'll never get any talking done. Will Peter and Pepe do?"

"Sounds good to me," I said. "But what security precautions do you take?"

"Bulletproof underwear and bodyguards on public occasions," said Pepe. "And *special* precautions on *special* occasions.

Luis Muñoz Marin, Governor of Puerto Rico, a founding member of what we in TIME's Hemisphere Section called the "Democratic Left," a lover of Meursault wine — he ordered a bottle whenever we sat down together at lunch — and Pepe were good personal friends of one of the Section's brightest writers, Samuel Halper. Sam wrote a glowing TIME cover story in 1959 about *Muñoz's* 'bootstrapping' development of the U.S. Caribbean possession.

"Lars and I will probably be traveling together to Cuba to visit Fidel Castro before too long, and that will require a lot of security planning, believe me. Here at home, the Somoza people have sneaked across the border and shot in my direction a few times, but I was never in the car. I'm only five-foot-three, and I don't show much above the windows. I'd suggest that you don't sit too high, yourself You might make too good a target as we get closer to *La Lucha*."

The landscape outside San Jose was hilly, though not really at you'd call "mountainous." As we rode along, I asked Pepe why Costa Rica was so democratic, when dictatorships loomed all around it.

"We've been electing presidents ever since we got rid of William Walker in the eighteen-sixties," Pepe said.

"William Walker?" I said.

"You don't know about William Walker and the filibusters? And the campaign to make Nicaragua and Costa Rica southern Slave territories of the United States? Your education in American History was obviously delinquent."

As we rode and drank hot coffee from the presidential Thermos, Pepe filled some of the gaps in my Central American education. In the 1850s and 60s, as the U.S. Civil War loomed, William Walker, an American doctor and graduate of the University of Nashville (plus medical schools at Edinburgh, Heidelberg and the University of Pennsylvania) conceived the grand and grandiose idea of annexing Nicaragua and Costa Rica to the United States and creating American slave states to add to those already extant. The idea was called "freebooting," or "filibustering." An initial invasion of Nicaragua by Walker's troops had some success, but Walker and his fellow filibusters were defeated by a Costa Rican army and driven out of the country. A Costa Rican drummer boy named Juan Santamaria was killed setting fire to the filibusters' stronghold, and his memory is still celebrated with a national holiday.

Pepe was born in Spain in 1906. His father was a doctor, but Pepe grew up in Costa Rica as a restless, rebellious Socialist, self-taught in many things. He lived in Boston and New York as a young man, never earned a university degree, and in 1928 returned to Costa Rica and took to farming. He bought a small plantation where he grew *maguey*, whose fibers could be twisted into rope and strong twine for weaving into floor covering. His business prospered, and he turned to politics, then dominated by an established Old Guard of progressive-but-corrupt politicians.

Outspoken and abrasive, Figueres was exiled in 1942 for criticizing the regime on the radio but returned after a rigged presidential election, convinced that only an armed uprising could set the country straight. He organized a "Caribbean Legion" that confronted the Costa Rican Army, won a series of bloody skirmishes, and took control of the capital in 1948.

Figueres was named head of a "*Junta Fundadora*", or "Founding Council," that ran the country. Among other reforms, the junta eliminated the Army (but kept a police force), nationalized the banks, gave women and illiterates the right to vote, established a welfare system, and outlawed the Communist Party.

Pepe handed power over to an elected President in 1949 and was elected President in his own right in 1953, the year before my visit.

The tale took some telling, and by the time it was finished we passed through the entrance of *La Lucha*.

"Take a look to the right," said Pepe. "What do you see?"

"I see a long pile of dirt," I said, "with some kind of building behind."

"That's my outside-bedroom wall," said Pepe. "It looks like dirt, but it's got a high metal content. Every once in a while, Somoza's thugs slip into the country and pepper my wall with machine-gun bullets. It's a wake-up call for me and my wife, Karen, when she's here. The dirt makes a good shield, and luckily, that's as close as they get."

"Is Mrs. Figueres here now?" I said.

"No. She's up north, visiting family."

"Where up north?"

"Her family's from Copenhagen, but they've moved to the States and are naturalized citizens. They live near New York City, in Westchester County."

"Westchester! That's where I live! Where in Westchester?"

"Yorktown Heights."

"You're kidding! That's my home town! My kids go to school there! Is she up there very often?"

"When she's got Columbia University alumnae meetings or U.N. work,

José Figueres Ferrer and his second wife Karen Olsen.

that's where she stays."

"Do you go with her?"

"When I can. Maybe we can get together one of those times."

"That would be a treat! My wife and I would love it."

Pepe's people lugged my bag into the house and he showed me to a guest room.

"You'll need a rest," he said. "Then some lunch, and I'll show you around. On the ranch here, I can drive you myself."

Back in his at-home car, with himself at the wheel, the first stop on our *La Lucha* tour was the rug factory. The machines were idle, but there was plenty of evidence that the place had been up and running. Rolls of sisal carpeting were coiled outside the office and near the shipping platform. Sisal dust mites shimmered in trapped rays of sunlight.

"With your reputation as a socialist reformer," I said to him, "I'm guessing that you pay your workers well over the going rate or have you made them part-owners of the company?"

"No way," said Pepe. "Between us, Karen and I have four children. I've got two more from a previous marriage. They've all needed to be fed and educated. But you're right, I feel personal responsibility for the families of the thousand-or-so people who work for me, both on the land and here in the plant. I've built housing for them and provide health care and football fields for the kids. Milk's free from the *La Lucha* dairy."

"*La Lucha leche*," I said, digging into my vestigial Spanish. He was nice enough not to flinch at the pun.

"Besides that," he went on, "there's a community garden. But I'm a capitalist, and I aim to make a profit."

"Do you?"

"Look around. Of course I do. But so do a lot of the workers, who're more-or-less share-croppers. They can either sell their hemp to me at market prices, or to someone else, if they can get a better deal. But we're all doing pretty well."

Pepe drove me past apartment blocks for single workmen and clusters of small, concrete-block houses for workers with families. We went through a dairy barn and drove through the sisal plantations. He introduced me to some of his foremen and showed me the equipment-repair shops. When he and I had both had enough, we drove back to the ranch.

"I need a shower," he said. "And a cocktail at six. I'm a great admirer of Franklin Roosevelt. I believe he did some of his best thinking and drinking – at cocktail time."

We parted company, and I napped for 30 or 40 minutes. When I found my way to his study, a log fire was blazing away in a corner fireplace.

"That fireplace is a carry-over from my wife's Scandinavian-ness," he said. "Back in Denmark, the pride of any house in cold weather was a corner fireplace. You burned long logs, and as the ends burned, you pushed what was left in toward the corner. This saved you the trouble of getting up and throwing new dry logs on the fire all the time. And when the evening was done, you just let the fire die down. With luck, there'd be enough coals left to start a new fire the next morning with just dry grass and some kindling."

Doing honor to FDR, we drank our martinis straight up, in stemmed glasses, with biscuits and a kind of cheddar cheese from Pepe's dairy. Then to dinner, with steak from Pepe's freezer and a robust French wine.("Our Costa Rica vineyards are still immature.") We took our unfinished glasses back to the study.

"Was your revolution a *golpe* [a palace coup], or did it involve real warfare?" I asked.

"Forty-four days of real fighting," Pepe said. "It was bloody. The bloodiest fighting, they say, in this century. You don't just abolish a military establishment without resistance, particularly from an officer class used to power and good living. More than two thousand died. Look at that wall over there."

He gestured toward one of the study's paneled walls.

"What do you see?"

"I see a pair of jodphur boots. Pinned up."

"Go take a look at them. They're the boots I wore when I led the revolution."

I walked over and looked.

"Look inside them," he said. "What do you see?"

I pulled them away from the wall. "There's something in there," I said.

"Lifts," he said. "Lifts. It's hard to lead a revolution when you're five-foot-three. When I led *that* revolution, I was at least five-foot-six. Maybe even five-foot-seven, if I stood on my toes and lifted my heels."

The martinis and the wine surged. I began to sing an advertising jingle that was on the radio when I was a teenager.

> Samson, you're a funny sort,
> Your hair's too long but you're too short,
> So if Delilah you would court,
> Get Bates' Six-Footers!

Pepe burst out laughing. "Is there another verse?" he said.

"If you can stand it, there is," I said.

Folks, if you're like Mister S,
And you're just about five foot four, or less,
Step out, step up, and you'll impress,
In Bates' Six-Footers!

And I gave him the jingle's punch-line:

In a pair of one-two-three-four-five-six-footers,
Bates' Six-Footers!

It was time to go to bed.

Chapter 14

A Pet Perk

This chunk of memoir is about Mohammed Ali ... but it starts with Ali McGraw, Petula Clark and Joe Louis.

One of the pleasantest perks of a TIME Senior Editorship in the good old days was self-indulgence. When I took over the Cinema, Show Business and Theater Sections of TIME in the 1960s, one of my self-indulgences was the wonderfully hard-edged voice of Petula Clark as she sang songs like "Don't Sleep in the Subway" and "Downtown." I'm not unique in this, of course. Hundreds of thousands of other Americans, and millions of Brits before us, got shivers of pleasure from the way she sang the songs.

[And still do. TV channel-hopping in Orford, New Hampshire in 2012, during endless tributes to Year 60 of the reign of Elizabeth II, I was transfixed by the sight and sound of "Pet" Clark singing, "The lights are much brighter there, You can forget all your troubles, Forget all your cares ..." *Live*! Half a century later! Or maybe not totally *Live*. She may have been lip-syncing, and perhaps was Botoxed or plastic-surgery enhanced to a near-perfect image of the 1960s Petula. But the thrill was still there.]

Not being a Brit, but being a TIME editor new to the performing arts sections, I wondered whether we had ever published a long-form, serious interview with Ms. Clark. I consulted the magazine's archive (known around the shop as "the Morgue"). We hadn't.

We hadn't dealt seriously with Ali McGraw, either, and 1971 was a year

Petula Clark

when "Love Story" (the book) was hot and Ali McGraw was cool — playing the "cool" Radcliffe-College-type heroine of "Love Story" (the movie). With my daughter Lucy I flew to Los Angeles to get to know Ali and her then-husband, Paramount Producer Bob Evans ... and happened to notice that Petula Clark was singing, *live*, and *in person*, in Las Vegas. On the way from Beverly Hills to New York, Lucy and I stopped off at Caesar's Palace in Vegas so I could interview "Pet" (as I discovered her close friends called her) and practice my skills at the Blackjack tables.

Enter Joe Louis. Every 20 or 30 minutes (*more or less* — casino operators want gamblers to lose track of time, and allow no clocks in gambling rooms) an announcement came over Caesar's loudspeaker: "Call for Joe Louis! Telephone call for Joe Louis!" Across the room, you could see a stooped, heavyset black man rise a bit unsteadily to his feet, make his way to a side door of the casino, and disappear — presumably to take the call.

Anybody who knew anything about famous people knew that Joe Louis was broke. Dead broke. His "managers" had managed to lose or spend the hundreds of thousands of dollars he'd earned winning and defending his world heavyweight boxing championship down through the years. He owed millions in unpaid taxes to the Internal Revenue Service and, broken in mind and body, had no way to pay them.

What was he doing hanging out in a gambling casino? As I made arrangements to interview Pet, I asked about Joe Louis. It turned out that the powers-that-be (or at least the powers-that-*used-to-be*) at Caesar's Palace were performing a gambler's act of charity. There were no (repeat, *no*) phone calls coming in for the Brown Bomber. But by pretending there were, the casino management could make a show of being a place where important people gambled. And, by pretending to take the calls, the old boxer was "earning" the bed, board and walking-around money the management was providing for him. Caesar's Palace was Joe Louis' old-age home.

Nice, but sad.

I interviewed Pet, and learned things that I didn't know (and probably never would have known) about her. She was born in Epsom, England in

November 1932 and christened Petula Sally Olwen Clark.

"Petula?" Her father, Leslie ("Les"), said he made up the name, combining the monikers of two old girl friends, Pet and Ulla. Les had a yen for the theater and daughter Pet had a gift for mimicry. She sang Vera Lyn and Sophie Tucker songs for family and friends around the house — so well, that her father had her try out with a street orchestra that played tunes to lure customers into Bentall's Departmental Store in Kingston-on-Thames.

In October 1942 Pet made her radio "debut" when she attended a BBC broadcast with her father, hoping to send a message to an uncle overseas. During a German air raid, to avoid "dead air" and to distract the audience, Pet's father suggested that she stand beside a microphone and sing. She did "Mighty Lak' a Rose" to enthusiastic response — thereby launching a series of 500 wartime concerts for British troops, often with fellow kid star Julie Andrews. She became "Britain's Shirley Temple" and was such a money-maker that her father eventually bought her a bra that flattened her breasts for a series of child and adolescent films that ran until 1946.

To the everlasting (or *apparently* everlasting) dismay of her father, Pet began singing popular songs, and began traveling outside Britain. In France in 1958, she met Paris publicist Claude Wolff and fell in love with him. She became an immense hit as a yé-yé singer on the Continent, and in 1961 married Wolff. She peeled off the child-star identity (and the breast-flatteners), had two daughters, and became the Pet Clark she was meant to be. Her father was sorely displeased.

The TIME story ran in 1971, she and I became friends, and in 1972 she phoned from France to say that after all those years, she'd decided that the feud with her father had gone on too long. It was reconciliation time. Her father loved boxing, she said, and as a reunion gift she was flying him to New York for a Madison Square Garden fight between Mohammed Ali and Jerry Quarry.

(It was actually the *second* Ali-Quarry fight. The first came in Atlanta in October 1970, when Ali was trying to make a comeback after having his boxing license withdrawn because he refused to be drafted during the Vietnam war. "Ain't got nothin' against them Viet Cong," he said at the time. The fight ended in the third round, but only because of a bad cut over Quarry's eye.)

"I want my dad to have the best possible time," Pet told me. "He's never been in the States before. What would a fight enthusiast do in New York the night before an important match?"

"He'd probably take in the scene at Gallagher's restaurant," I said.

"Gallagher's?" she said.

"Yes. It's a classic New York steak house where everyone connected with sports and the fight game gathers when something big is going on at Madison Square Garden which used to be nearby. Everyone who's anyone will probably be there."

"Could you book us a table?"

"For how many?"

"Four. Claude won't be with me, but I'd love it if you and your wife could join us."

Julie couldn't, so three of us sat down at a red-checkered table cloth at Gallagher's the night before the fight. As far as I could see, no one else was sitting down, and that included all the sports writers, trainers, managers, feather merchants, doctors, publicists, gossip columnists, boxers (over-the-hill and on-the-way-up), girlfriends, camp followers, and restaurant regulars circling the room, drinks in hand, glad-handing and hallooing. I introduced Les to TIME's Sports Writer, John Phillips, and they joined the swirl. John, of course, knew many there and got to know more as the evening went on. So, as far as I could see, did Les.

Pet and I sat it out cheerfully with red wine. A waiter made it through to our table and we ordered a couple of Gallagher's famous aged steaks for Les and me (their display window was the window of the aging room, when you had to wait for a table you could kill time by watching steaks age). Oh, and a platter of those luscious fried onion rings. I couldn't do without them. Pet had a salad. Les had cheesecake for dessert.

"This has been fantastic!" Les said as Pet and I argued over the check.

"The only thing missing has been a New York shooting."

"A What?" I asked.

"A New York shooting. This is a violent city. Everyone knows that people are always getting shot on New York streets, but we haven't seen a single shooting."

"You've been watching TV and listening to the wrong rumors, Les," I said. "This is a peaceable town. I've lived and worked here for almost 20 years, and I've never even been mugged. And I certainly have never seen a shooting."

Disappointed, Les sagged a bit. Easing the moment, I said, "It's a big time in this part of town tonight. Let's go out and walk a bit."

Gallagher's was on West 53rd Street, just off Broadway. We went out past the windowful of aging steaks and turned right, down Broadway toward 42nd. A big, brightly lit record store glowed at the corner of 51st.

"Let's go in," I said. It was getting late, but a few customers hovered over the racks of records. A sales person came over.

"Where can I find Petula Clark records?" I said.

"Over this way," he said. He led us to the middle of the store and pointed to a rack.

"I was looking for *Downtown*," I said. He looked at me a bit sharply, the way New Yorkers do when they encounter an obvious nerd. He pulled out a record.

"Would you autograph this for me?" I said to Pet. The clerk looked over my shoulder. His eyes bugged.

"Are you... Aren't you?" he said.

"She is," I said.

"Hey, Charlie!" he shouted across the room to the cashier. "Petula Clark's here!"

The customers turned, looked, and not quite believing, began to move toward us. One ran to the door, opened it, and called out to no one in particular, "Petula Clark's in here!"

"Why don't you put on a Pet Clark record?" I said to the salesman. He grabbed the album out of my hand and ran to the back of the store.

In a few minutes, Pet's voice was ringing out. "The lights are much brighter there, you can forget all your troubles, forget all your cares ..." Ten or fifteen voices joined in, including mine, "... and go DOWNtown! THINGS WILL BE GREAT WHEN YOU'RE DOWNtown! EVERYTHING'S WAITING FOR YOU."

Cheers. The customers grabbed all the Petula records in the rack and the salesman ran for more. Les Clark stood beside Pet and grinned, ear to ear. The clerk handed a felt-tip to a customer, and Pet began signing. "Mark! My name's Mark!" called one. "Bonnie" yelled another. It was a crazy movie scene getting crazier. Through the window I could see more people coming. I said to Pet, "I think it's time to go." With Les and me bringing up the rear, we got out the door and crossed the street just as the light changed.

No shootings, worst luck.

Chapter 15

Bill Buckley's Buried Axiom

Back in the day when TIME magazine *mattered* and a portrait on its cover could be the capstone (or tombstone) of a brilliant (or darkened) career, a kind of intellectual and emotional umbilicus linked a TIME Senior Editor with the subject of a "cover story." Whether or not the editor had suggested the story, he was the principal connective tissue between the cover subject, the research, the interviews, the writer, the photographers, the cover artist, and the final product that appeared in millions of mailboxes and on hundreds of thousands of newsstands every week. The bond between the editor and the person on the cover could become warm and personal. Or chilly and distant. In 1967, the bond between cover-subject William F. Buckley Jr. and Senior Editor Peter Bird Martin was — at first — in the warm and personal category.

Some cover stories were "naturals," some were strokes of confective genius from the creative minds of TIME correspondents and writers. A cover story on Bill Buckley was a natural "natural." In the 1960s, Buckley became the nation's most visible, most fearsome, most likeable, most entertaining, most rapier-witted, most precocious, most theatrical, most ubiquitous, most erudite, most Conservative public figure ever to find his way into millions of American homes. His entry vehicle (his *broomstick*, some would say) was a weekly television-interview series called, "Firing Line."

With great facility, he wrote a weekly column, "On the Right," that was carried by 205 newspapers. He published *National Review*, a fortnightly mag-

Bill Buckley, Time 11/3/1967

azine of opinion that managed to make conservative thought easy to read. Even amusing. He showed off his forensic marksmanship in a weekly TV debate in which he confronted his adversaries with a polysyllabic vocabulary and an arsenal of intimidating grimaces.

As the cover story said, "When he is confronting a 'Firing Line' adversary, Buckley's secret is surprise, plus the ability to maneuver his opponent into vulnerable positions. He often hoists the man on the petard of his own argument." TV Star Robert Vaughan started naming the people he thought had conspired to commit the U.S. to the defense of Ngo Dinh Diem's regime in South Viet Nam: "Joseph Buttinger, General Edward Lansdale, Wesley Fishel, Cardinal Spellman…"

Buckley broke in: "And the Holy Ghost?"

Once a cover story was published, once its initial glow dimmed, the umbilicus was usually cut. Not so with Bill Buckley. One segment of the article commented that, "For all its championing of free enterprise, *National Review* gets precious few ads. The captains of industry it celebrates are reluctant to return the favor, largely because the magazine does not reach enough readers to suit them."

There were other reasons. Buckley was a staunch Roman Catholic. In 1964, the Ford Motor Company's Chief Executive Officer, Henry Ford II, was divorced from Anne McDonnell Ford. She was Catholic. He wasn't, but they had been married in 1940 in Southampton, Long Island, at the Roman Catholic Church of the Sacred Hearts of Jesus and Mary. In one thunderclap column in *National Review*, Buckley equated the Fords' divorce with the suicides of *Washington Post* Publisher Philip Graham and Stephen Ward, the British politician who'd been caught keeping a famous mistress, Christine Keeler.

"All were men," wrote Buckley, "wanting in the stuff of spiritual survival."

With the speed of a Mercury and the quick judgment of a Lincoln, Ford yanked all advertising from the *Review*. The TIME cover story reported this.

Since its beginnings, Time Inc. had proudly lived by the principle of "division of Church and State." That is, the money-making side of the company (advertising, or "State") was forbidden to meddle or interfere with the journalistic side ("Church"). A week after the cover story appeared, however, I got a cautious, nervous phone call from Bernie (Bernhard) Auer, the decent, nice-guy Publisher of TIME and a neighbor of mine in northern Westchester County.

"Peter," he said, "I know I shouldn't be making this call, but the Ford advertising people have been calling everyone at Time Inc. to deny the ad-cancellation story in the Buckley cover. They say it never happened. They're demanding a retraction. Otherwise, they're going to yank all Ford, Mercury and Lincoln ads from all Time Inc. publications. We're talking about major money. This could be serious."

"I don't know what we can do about this, Bernie," I said. "Buckley told me the story himself, and I believed him. But I don't have anything you might call proof. I'll see what I can do."

I phoned Buckley. I hadn't heard from him since the cover story was published, so I was a bit nervous.

"I suppose you want to know what I thought about the article," he said as soon as we were connected.

"That, of course," I said. "But another thing has come up..."

Other things were going to have to wait. Bill was ready to talk about the article. "The first time I read it," he said, "I hated it. So did Pat. The second time, I began to admire its architectural *details*. The third time, I began sensing its rhythms and pace ... its *construction*. I'm prepared to pronounce it a model exemplar of popular journalism. Pat still hates it."

("Pat" was Bill's wife, Canadian Beer Heiress and Woman-About-Manhattan Patricia Buckley. She lunched and dined everywhere, with every other important Woman-About-Town, and was in *Womens' Wear Daily* and dozens of other social-talk specialty publications in New York City.)

"What did you think of what it *said*?"

"It said amusing things in amusing ways. What I disliked about it was the buried axiom."

"The buried axiom?"

"That I'm so entertaining a writer and TV host, my conservatism can't be taken seriously."

"Did we say that?"

"Not in so many words. But at the end, you might as well have said it, and added *Quod Erat Demonstrandum*. It was axiomatic."

"I'll have to read it again to get that message. Do you want a letter to the editor?"

"No, as the article said, everything I write these days gets into print, and I don't want to give that notion further currency. But when you phoned, you mentioned something else. What's the something else?"

I told him about Ford's threat to do unto Time Inc. what it had done to *National Review.*

"Oho!" He said. "Oho! I think there's something we can do about *that.* I'll get back to you."

That afternoon he phoned again. "Are you free for lunch tomorrow?" he said. "I think we've solved Ford's ad-hoakery. Paone? One o'clock?"

Nicola Paone was Buckley's favorite Italian restaurant near his office. We'd eaten there several times during cover-story interviews.

"How'd you do it?" I said.

"You'll see, you'll see," he said. "Paone at one."

Dining with Bill was always a pleasure, and Paone's *vitel tonnato* was luscious. Predictably, Bill came to lunches primed with a fricassee of daily issues, national and international, and took delight in chuckling over excesses he found in the *New York Times* or speeches by liberal politicians.

When we met next day at Paone he gave no advance hint about a solution for the Ford advertising problem, but as lunch ended he looked toward the small tables along the side wall of the restaurant and waved a hand. A fellow in a business suit waved back, got up, came over, and sat down at our table.

Bill introduced him and explained that the *Review* was too small to have its own ad-sales staff. Instead, it contracted with an independent, outside outfit to sell advertising space. Bill said that the man who'd joined us was one of the ad salesmen — and not just *one* of the ad salesman, but *the* ad salesman who dealt with Ford. I don't recall his name; let's call him "Ed."

Bill said that Ed had negotiated the advertising contract with the Ford ad manager and they had signed it in Ed's office a few months before. Two days after the Buckley cover story was published, Ed said, the Ford man walked back into the office with an envelope in his hand.

"He sat down," said Ed, "opened the envelope, pulled out the ad contract and showed me what it was. Then, without a word, he reached for a waste basket and pulled it between his feet. He tore up the contract and, slowly, dropped the pieces in the basket. Then, still without a word, he walked out. I've written up a statement describing the whole incident and signed it before a Notary. Here it is."

He handed me a folder. "And here," he continued, handing me an envelope, "are the pieces of the contract. I pulled them out of the waste basket."

Chapter 16

Standing Pat

The Ford advertising incident cemented my friendly relations with Buckley, and we lunched and dined together fairly frequently in New York, particularly when late "closings" of his magazine and mine kept us working through the same evenings. For reasons having to do with a feud my top TIME editor, Otto Fuerbringer, was carrying on with one of Buckley's close friends, TIME-LIFE Chief of Correspondents Dick Clurman, the friendship never involved home-and-home socialization. I wished it did; Pat Buckley had a mythic reputation as one of Manhattan's premier party-givers.

One early-summer day in 1969, the phone rang on my desk.

"Peter?" Or, to put it more phonetically, "PEET-ah?" The Buckley intonation and emphasis were unmistakable. "Are you and TIME involved with Apollo Nine?"

My responsibilities had shifted. I was no longer Senior Editor of the magazine's sections on Medicine, Law, Press and Science, but was editing "Color Projects." TIME in those days was basically a black-and-white publication; reproduction of color photographs was ferociously expensive and had to be planned far in advance. It was worth it, though. The right collection of four, eight or twelve pages of color photographs could add an essential, you-are-*there* element to a major story.

The Apollo-Nine moon shot was an obvious color project, and I told Bill we were covering it. "We're doing an eight-page color spread on the shoot, to

Apollo 9 liftoff, 3/3/1969

be on the stands in that week's issue. LIFE's got all rights to the astronauts themselves and we'll be using LIFE photos here and there, but I'll be directing three exclusive TIME photographers to cover the walkup to the shoot, the Cape Canaveral scene, the blastoff from the V.I.P. stand, and the liftoff itself."

"I imagined as much. I've arranged access to the V.I.P. area for Pat and myself, but this is such a moment in the national imagination that I want more. I want to be there at the liftoff, but I want to be there with friends of perception, language and, shall we say, *taste*, for a day or two before the event. I've booked a motel at the Cape for the two days before the moonshot and I'd like you to be my guest. Will Julie be with you?"

Pat Buckley and "Beep," a King Charles Cavalier Spaniel, at home in 1976.

[This was a distinguishing Buckley touch. He had no professional or special reason to remember my wife with such particularity, but he did, with genuine warmth. When my wife first met him at a TIME magazine party, she said, on the way home, "He's truly charming. When he talked with me he focused on me completely. He wasn't looking over my shoulder for someone more interesting. It was as if there was no one else in the room."]

"No," I told Bill, "she doesn't travel with me when there's work to be done. I'll be solo."

"Then plan on staying with me and friends when duty permits. Thanks to you, I'm inviting Jim and Tom Dickey, Ted Kalem and Larry DuBois. On my behalf, I'm having Gary Wills, Rocky Converse, my brother Jim and my son Chris. Pat will be there, of course."

[James Dickey, the late South Carolina University professor, poet and novelist ("Deliverance"), became a personal Martin friend when I, fascinated by the journalistic dimension of one of his poems, "The Eye-Beaters", commissioned an article about him in TIME's Press Section. Buckley's brother Tom was a Civil War Buff and writer. Theodore Kalem was TIME's theater critic and Larry (L. Clayton) DuBois was a young TIME reporter who'd interviewed Bill extensively for the Buckley cover story. Rocky Converse was Gary Cooper's widow, and a close friend of the Buckleys.]

A good time was had by all ... as I recall. Martinis, bourbon, wine (Buckley provided cases of lovely whites) and talk flowed over and around meals that sprawled for three days across the motel dining room and Cape Canaveral. The morning of the moonshot, we all got ourselves to the V.I.P. site, where wooden grandstands and multi-level photographers' platforms had been erected with a clear view of the launch pad.

The morning turned warm — too warm for my suit coat, so I hung it from a nail on one of the photo-stand beams. The plan was for the TIME and LIFE photography teams to do their work at the site and, the minute the rocket was on its way, gather up cameras, tripods and exposed film and head for a special bus that would transport us west across Florida to the Tampa-St. Petersburg Airport and a chartered jet, fitted out as a color-photography lab, that would carry us to New York, processing film as we flew. All "normal" air traffic was banned from the Cape Kennedy airspace, and to make deadlines, not a second could be lost.

All went well. The lift-off was a triumphant burst of flame and boiling fumes, the rocket rose — slowly at first — into a photogenic, heavenly arc. It climbed, and kept climbing. We all cheered. Almost immediately, loudspeakers blared: "The TIME-LIFE bus is boarding!"

I grabbed my coat, flung my camera strap over my shoulder, and headed for the parking lot. I waited until all my photographers were accounted for, then climbed aboard the bus. I threw my coat on the overhead rack, settled into a seat and began writing notes.

Florida isn't wide, and the speed at which we were traveling made it narrower. When we pulled up at the Tampa-St. Pete airport, I plucked my coat from the overhead rack and put it on. It seemed to have shrunk. I put my hand in the side pocket and found a set of rental-car keys ... but I hadn't rented a car. In the breast pocket were a few envelopes and a rental agreement made out to ... *William F. Buckley.*

Panic! I had Bill's coat, identical in color and texture to mine, and he — back at Cape Canaveral — had my coat and a car he couldn't move, its trunk full of his and Pat's clothes. He probably also had a plane waiting, somewhere, to fly him, his wife, his relatives, and their pals, to New York.

I ran to find an airport phone, picked it up, and said something like, "This is an emergency! I'm at the airport with the TIME-LIFE bus, and I have William Buh..."

The voice at the other end finished the sentence. "William Buckley's coat! Do not move! Stay right there! NASA has sent a courier to pick it up!"

"Buh..." I said. I was about to say something like, "But I'm leaving immediately on the TIME-LIFE plane for New York!" I never got it out. I could see our photographers, with a crew of porters, trundling through a gate onto the tarmac as a motorcycle pulled to a stop in front of our bus. The rider leapt off, opened a pouch at the back of his cycle and pulled out a coat exactly like mine. He walked over to where I was waiting with Buckley's coat over my arm. He handed me mine, took Buckley's. He must have said something, but I don't remember what. Seconds later, he was roaring back across Florida.

Later that week I phoned Bill's home to apologize for the mix-up. Pat Buckley answered. "This is Peter Martin," I said. "I'm calling to ..."

"The *coat person*!" she said, her voice turning to instant dry ice.

"I want to ..."

CLICK!

In the weeks, months and years that followed, I often ran into Bill at press parties, film screenings, fashion shows, political conventions and opening nights. In friendly tones, he always asked about Larry DuBois, who'd been hired away from TIME by *Playboy* to do an Interview with none other than Hugh Hefner, but then dropped from sight. As I was, Bill was worried about Larry, but I was unable to give him any news.

I never heard another word, civil or uncivil, from Pat Buckley again.

Chapter 17

Henry Grunwald and Raquel Welch

Henry Anatole Grunwald was every inch a creative editor. He was also Viennese, American, and a lover. Born Heinz Anatol Grunwald on December 3, 1922 in Austria, Henry became a refugee from the Nazi obsession to exterminate Jewishness in 1938. He escaped from Vienna to Prague, to Paris, to Lisbon, and — in 1940 — to New York. He was 17.

Henry's editorial inches were vertical, impressive, and deserved. He, the English language and American cultural and political life were made for each other. After public high school in Hell's Kitchen in Manhattan and a B.A. at New York University, he got a job as a copy boy at TIME magazine. As he carried draft articles from a writer's office to the copy desk, he read them. And sometimes, pausing at an empty table with a pencil, he precociously — and often brilliantly — edited them.

This infuriated the original writers, but attracted the attention of his superiors. By the time I arrived at TIME in 1955 he had been promoted from "Contributing Editor" (writer) and "Associate Editor" (super writer on the brink of Senior Editorship) to become the trusted and talented Senior Editor of TIME's Arts Sections. He was recognized (and, by some, jealously resented) as an accomplished compressor of imagination, wit, language and fact into classy, thought-filled journalistic marzipan.

Henry Grunwald

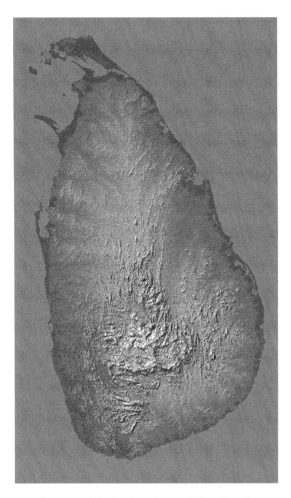

Grunwaldularly-shaped Sri Lanka

Other, more personal, circumferential inches above and below the tummy were also deserved — the result of a love of life and a life of love.

TIME writers and editors were adepts at reducing the physical character-istics of their story subjects to hyphenates. If King Mahendra of Nepal was "bean-shaped" as TIME memorably and often said, Henry was "pear-shaped." In a memoir, John Koffend, a talented TIME writer derailed to Pago Pago by divorce and ego, hit Henry below the belt in Latinate terms. He said Henry had a "surcingular chest." Henry looked, when I first met him, like Sri Lanka.

Henry's father, Alfred, was an Austrian romantic-opera librettist — a suc-cessful and well-rewarded lyricist of words for the Lehar and Strauss tunes that made Vienna the waltz-schmaltz capital of the world between the Wars. He grew up surrounded by housemaids, parties, popular entertainment, and performers. He spent hours in theater stalls and balconies melting chocolates slowly between his tongue and the roof of his mouth while watching pneumatic females twitch shapely ankles, sing love songs and swoon into the arms of baritones and tenors.

By the time Henry became Managing Editor of TIME, my father, who wrote as "Pete" Martin, had become an acknowledged American master of tape-recorded, transcribed, personal interviews with show-business stars and personalities. Three or four times a year, under the standard heading, "Pete Martin Calls On...", page after page of the *Saturday Evening Post* filled with personal conversations between Pete Martin and Bing Crosby, Pete Martin and Bob Hope, Pete Martin and Ethel Merman, Clark Gable, Jimmy Stewart, Marilyn Monroe, Zsa Zsa Gabor, Dick Powell, Hedy Lamarr, Arthur Godfrey, Alfred Hitchcock, Gary Cooper, Jack Lemmon, Danny Kaye, Groucho Marx, Grace Kelly, Shirley MacLaine, Marlon Brando, John Wayne ...

By 1969, when I'd become Senior Editor of TIME's Show Business and Cinema departments (with my name carefully listed on the masthead as Peter *Bird* Martin, to distinguish me from my far-better-known father), it was only natural that at one of the weekly one-on-one meetings where Henry and I discussed articles we were doing, or *thinking* of doing, or *wondering* about doing, Henry popped a fantastic question: "Have you ever thought of a Raquel Welch cover story?"

Cover Story! A *Cover Story*? Only people of towering fame or infamy in their fields rated portraits on the cover of the weekly newsmagazine, accompanied inside by long, detailed articles about their work, accomplishments and personalities. A Cover Story on Raquel Welch may have seemed natural to Henry. The notion was a shock to me.

"Raquel *Welch*?" I said. "Raquel *Welch*? Have you ever seen her in a movie, Henry?"

"No."

"Henry, she can't act."

Fur bikini-clad Raquel Welch in One Million Years B.C., her first movie role. Raquel had three lines of dialog, including "Me Loana ... You Tumak."

"That can't be. She's made several movies. And now she's got a leading role in Gore Vidal's *Myra Breckenridge*."

"I've seen *too many* of her movies, Henry. The only one she was any good in at all was a Stanley Donen flick called "Bedazzled", about the seven deadly sins as dreamed by a short-order cook in London. She did a cameo, as Lust. The only reason anyone besides Stanley Donen remembers her is that poster she did for *One Million Years B.C.*, wearing a couple of scraps of fur and animal skin."

"Peter, Peter. She's a *phenomenon*."

"Henry, a cover story has to *say* something. *She's* got to say something."

"She may have a lot to say. We'll never know unless we meet her. Let's do it. *Soon*."

I went back to my office, mentally sputtering.

That afternoon I phoned Pat Kingsley in California. Pat and her partner, Lois Smith, had built solid reputations as a couple of the best "personal reps" in show business. She was Raquel's press agent. I had always been straight with her, and she'd always been straight with me.

"What's going on, Peter?"

"You won't believe what Henry Grunwald's got on his mind. A Raquel Welch *cover story*."

"What's so unbelievable about that?"

"Oh, come on, Pat. You've seen as many of her movies as I have. She can't act. She can't talk. If brains were dynamite, she probably couldn't blow her nose."

"What does Henry say?"

"He says we'll never know unless we meet her."

"And?"

"He'd like to do it soon."

Aside from the time-sensitive business of writing or editing on-deadline, office hours at TIME in New York began at 10 a.m. At 10:15 the next morning the phone in my office rang. It was Pat, calling from L.A. It had to be *7:15 am* out there.

"I've talked to Raquel. She's going to be in New York next week. There's a musical, "Dames at Sea," playing in the Village. She wants to take a look at it as a possible TV vehicle for herself. Is this any good for you and Henry?"

"I'll ask."

Tuesday evening was good for Henry. As a dinner spot, he chose *Caravelle*, on West 53rd Street. *Caravelle*, they said, flew fresh string beans in from France every morning.

Tuesdays were good days for all writers and editors at TIME. Field reporting for the stories we planned to close on Saturday or Sunday hadn't come in yet from the correspondents, so re-writing and editing couldn't get done. Tuesdays (and Wednesdays) were good days for haircuts, squash games, buying shirts, picking up passports, and talking with friends over long liquid lunches at French, Italian and Swiss restaurants on the bottom and first floors of old brownstones that lined side streets from 46th to 53rd Streets west of Sixth Avenue. They were days you could get home before the kids were in bed.

Rain was spritzing as Henry and I walked north up Sixth Avenue and turned right on 53rd. Henry wore a long dark raincoat and a slouched, wide-brimmed black fedora. He looked straight out of the *Third Man*. I stayed dry under a push-button umbrella. We were in no hurry. We were early, and we expected Raquel to be late.

I figured she would have the leading elements of her famous figure more or less gift-wrapped. I was prepared not to be over-interested.

Raquel was *already there*, wrapped in knitted black. There was a bit of glitter, and it fit her well, but nothing obvious. Nothing, you might say, for *sale*. She was much smaller than I expected. Screen images are magnified images.

Fizzy water for Raquel, white Burgundy for Henry, a Tanqueray martini on the rocks for me. Conversation came easily. Henry wondered what Raquel thought of *Myra Breckenridge*. Was Gore Vidal as snotty as he seemed? Was Mae West over the hill? Was Rex Reed more than superficial? When it was time to veer away from show business we got into social trends. It was a time of Vietnam War rejection, of flower children and societal dropouts.

What did dropout time *mean*? Where was society headed? Was the rejection of success, and all that it embodied just a phase? As dinner got underway (no one ordered string beans), Raquel said: "My brother's a dropout. He and a couple of his friends have quit their jobs and moved into a tree house south of Los Angeles."

[Now, all of this happened a long time ago — *forty years* — so I can't vouch for word-by-word accuracy in these quotations. Henry Grunwald died — prematurely and *much thinner* — in 2005. That leaves Raquel. I'll be interested to hear what she's got to say, and I may report back to you. I may not.]

"I wondered what my brother was thinking," Raquel said. "Why were he and his friends doing this? I couldn't get them out of my mind. They didn't have a phone, but I got a message to them and said I wanted to spend some time with them, get to know them better. They said okay, and we picked a weekend. I would go down on a Friday afternoon, bring some provisions, spend Saturday, and leave Sunday."

I'm not sure whether Raquel even *owned* a car, but for that occasion she had a Rolls Royce, a driver and a sun roof.

"We pulled up under the tree, and the driver opened the roof," Raquel said. "He hoisted me through the opening and my brother and his friends pulled me up. Then the driver passed up the provisions."

Knowing Henry, I'm sure he envisioned her disappearing through the sun roof. She certainly had our attention.

"They didn't even have television in the tree house. So except for sleeping, we talked all through Saturday and into Sunday morning. Just before lunchtime on Sunday the driver came back. He opened the roof, and my brother lowered me down."

"And?" said Henry.

"I think they're like the Luddites of the eighteenth century," Raquel said. "The Luddites tried to stop the industrial revolution by throwing rocks and pieces of iron into the knitting machines that were destroying cottage industries like weaving, and making socks and underwear. My brother and his friends are trying to stop the technological revolution by taking themselves out of society. It's like Stop the World, I want to get off."

"The Luddites didn't succeed," Henry said.

"No," said Raquel. "And the dropouts won't, either. I don't think the Luddites were really real. They were supposed to be named after a retarded boy named Ned Ludd, who went out of his mind and broke into a house where there was a knitting machine and smashed it. After that, if a machine got smashed, people said, 'Ludd must have been here.'"

"Ludd or no Ludd," said Raquel, "the machines *were* there, and they were there to stay. I think what really got people angry was the fact that the machines fit right into the British class system. People who could afford to build them, or buy them, got rich. People who couldn't, got poor, and had to work for next to nothing in mills filled with the machines. Real social revolutionaries took advantage of this, and invented a 'King Ludd' or a 'Lord Ludd' who they said was behind a movement to put an end to the age of the machine. They even got people to go around the countryside in masks, smashing machines powered by steam."

"So your brother and his friends are Luddites?" said Henry.

"You could say that," said Raquel, "or maybe *neo*-Luddites. But they're not violent, and they certainly don't intend to smash computers and attack Army recruiters. They're more like ... like Luddites *by example.* They resist by denial and withdrawal, rather than by attacking technology directly."

"This isn't your department, Peter," Henry said to me, interrupting her, "but perhaps we ought to talk to people in the Nation Section about a cover story on Neo-Luddism."

Dinner done, the three of us went into the wet night. Raquel's rented limo was at the curb, wipers swishing.

"Can I give you a lift anywhere?" she said.

"Not me," said Henry. "You've given me a lot to think about. I'm going to walk back to the office."

"You can give *me* a lift," I said. "If I can get to Grand Central in the next half-hour, I can make the last train home."

As I settled into the back seat, Raquel turned to me. "Well," she said. "How did I do?"

My eyes widened. "You were terrific!" I said. "That stuff about the Luddites was wonderful!"

"I had my people do some research about Henry," she said. "They worked up that material. I worked it into a bit of a script."

When I walked into Henry's office the following morning, he was leaning back in his DoMore executive chair, humming a snatch of opera to himself. His fingers were interlaced on his tummy.

"That was quite an evening," he said.

"Wait 'til you hear what happened after you left," I said.

I told him.

He sat up. When I finished, he smiled a kind of I-told-you-so smile. "Well," he said. "We know she's smart. But is she sexy?"

"What are we supposed to about *that*? I said.

"That's *your* assignment," said Henry.

Chapter 18

My Erogenous Zone

Back to my office I went, back to my telephone. I dialed Pat Kingsley in Los Angeles. She — not her secretary — picked up. She obviously had her eye on Caller I.D.

"How did it go?" she asked.

"It went splendidly. Raquel mesmerized Henry and me with a comparison of today's societal dropouts to Eighteenth-Century Luddites, those people who tried to stop the Industrial Revolution in England by throwing rocks and chunks of steel into the knitting machines. There wasn't any *real* Ludd, you know …"

"I know," said Pat.

"You know everything," I said.

"True," she said. "But how did it *go* about Raquel?"

"I just left Henry's office. He said, 'We know she's smart, Peter. But is she sexy?'"

Pause. Then, from Pat: "What are we supposed to do about *that*?"

"That's exactly what *I* asked *him*."

"And what did he say?"

"He said, 'That's your assignment, Peter.'"

"Hmmm." Pause again. "Let's talk later today."

Later today came and went, and became Thursday. The phone rang.

"Obviously, you and Raquel have to get together," Pat said. "I just talked to her, and she's taping a "Tonight Show" TV segment with Johnny Carson this afternoon in the RCA Building. From there, she's going on to a little musical, "Dames at Sea", in Greenwich Village. She's thinking of it as a TV vehicle. She can sing and dance, you know, Peter. [Pregnant pause.] If you're free, you could pick her up after the taping, go see the musical with her, have some supper, and talk. She'll be finished taping by six. You could meet her in the lobby of the RCA Building."

I dropped in at Henry's office and told him about the plan.

"Sounds good to me," he said. "You know, Peter, you have the world's best job. First Jane Fonda, now Raquel Welch. I'll want a full report."

The RCA Building, NBC's headquarters known to TV-watchers as "30 Rock," was kitty-cornered from the Time-Life Building at Sixth Avenue and 50th Street, a short walk from my office. To avoid slip-ups, I got there early, and stationed myself at the lobby entrance to the NBC-Studio elevators at about 5:45. Sure enough, the doors opened a few minutes after six, and there was Raquel, dressed in blue, chatting with a guy in a business suit and escorted by a couple of Rockefeller Center guards in brown uniforms. She smiled at me, said goodbye to the suit and took my arm as the elevator doors closed.

"It's good to see you," she said, "and a real relief after all that taping. I've never been good at smart talk on demand."

In those pre-terrorism days, Rockefeller Plaza was not cut off from street traffic, and cars and taxis could drive East-West freely between 48th and 51st Streets. Limos could even park at the door of 30 Rock. The lobby of the building was also public space, and within minutes — *seconds*, it seemed — we were surrounded by women, mostly middle-aged, mostly well-dressed, and mostly white. More were on the way. They weren't quiet about it, calling, "It's her! It's Raquel Welch! Raquel! Raquel!" They waved, they shouted. They kept coming. "Raquel! Raquel! Could you please. . . !"

The crush thickened. I began to feel surrounded and, to be honest about it, scared.

"We've got to get out of here," I said to Raquel. "I'm going to just shove ahead. Hold on to me."

I pushed toward Rockefeller Plaza.

"Excuse me!" I said. And then, louder, "*Excuse me!*"

With Raquel clutching my arm, I began the most determined walk I could manage, my right shoulder pushing through the crowd. Raquel's grip began slipping, and I stopped. I put a protective arm around her shoulders.

I raised my voice to be sure she could hear me. "In football, they say, 'Always follow your interference.' I'm your interference. Hang on!"

She hung on. We kept moving. I could see the front doors about 50 feet ahead. With so many women in front of me,there was no way to use the revolving door. I veered toward one of the side doors, hit the release bar with my hip, and we exploded on to Rockefeller Plaza. A mid-sized black limo was at the edge of the sidewalk, ahead to the right.

"I hope that's your car!" I said. Raquel nodded. Women were pouring out of the building behind us. "What's the driver's name?"

"Carlos," she said.

"Carlos! Carlos! We need help!" I shouted.

The driver got out of the front seat and opened the rear door. He held it open, and I shoved my body into the opening so the pressure of the women couldn't close it. When Raquel was in — all of her — I let it get slammed shut.

"Start the motor!" I said to Carlos. "I'll go round to the other side."

The women were clutching at Raquel's door handle and hitting the window with their hands. I ran around the back of the car, opened the far-side door, jumped in, and slapped down the door lock.

"Carlos," Raquel said to the driver, "Get us out of here and park somewhere."

The limo eased forward, parting the crowd, and turned onto 48th Street. A few women pursued, but gave up as we began to move with the traffic. We crossed Sixth Avenue and Carlos pulled up next to a fire plug.

"Wow!" I said. "Does this happen all the time?"

"No, thank God," Raquel said. "They say it's pretty well known when Carson's taping a guest, and the fans gather early. It doesn't make any difference who the guest is. They want celebrity."

"Does gender matter?"

"No. I'm supposed to be a sex symbol, but in daylight it's always women."

"So, where to from here?"

"The show doesn't start 'til eight. I'd love to go somewhere for a drink, maybe somewhere near the theater?"

"I think the White Horse Tavern is fairly close."

"Carlos," she called. "Do you know where the White Horse Tavern is?"

Carlos did, and we began working our way downtown.

"Did you play football?" she said.

"I did until my knee gave out."

"Where?"

"Dartmouth."

"That's Ivy League, isn't it?"

Raquel was a California creature, with a Bolivian father and an English mother. She was born in Chicago, moved to La Jolla when she was two, grew up ungainly, but began to collect "Misses" when she was 15 — "*Miss La Jolla.*" "*Miss San Diego.*" "*Miss Maid of California.*" The sponsor of one of the contests, the *Fairest of the Fair Festival*, said later, "there were prettier girls around, but none had her figure or her drive. Most girls tremble when they go onstage. Raquel never did."

In the limo, the Raquel who never trembled began to interview *me*.

"Why Ivy League? Why Dartmouth?"

[My father went to Penn, but wanted me to go to an Ivy League college that was not in a big city.]

"Isn't the Ivy League snobbish?"

[Snobbish, but we didn't know we were snobbish.]

"Different from Yale and Harvard?"

[Very different. We had a great president, John Dickey, not much older than we, who insisted we learn all about the real world — how it came to be, how to understand it, how to write about it.]

"All-male? Four years?"

[We went to girls' schools on weekends, and girls came to Dartmouth. We necked. It was lovely.]

Raquel loved hearing that Dylan Thomas used to hang out at the White Horse. When we got downtown, I worried out loud that we were going to encounter a male scene like the female one at the RCA building. I told Raquel to wait in the car while I explored. Inside, I told the manager I was from TIME magazine, with Raquel Welch waiting outside in a limo. I was interviewing her, and needed to have a quiet drink without being mobbed by people with questions, autograph books and ballpoint pens. He said to give him five minutes.

We did. When we went back in, it was incredibly normal. Heads turned, eyes glanced, but nothing more. We sat in a booth, quietly.

"This is wonderful," Raquel said. "I'd like a gin and tonic. And do you mind if I smoke? Patrick's got a thing about my smoking. I promised to stop, but this is a special occasion."

I didn't have anything against her smoking; I smoked a pack of Larks a day myself in those days. We flicked a Bic, smoked together.

"Patrick" — Patrick Curtis — was Raquel's husband. Her *second* husband, actually. The first was a high school classmate, Jim Welch. They married a year after graduation, had two children, Damon and Tahnee. Movies, obviously, were in their genes. After three years they split. ("Inevitably," Jim Welch told a TIME correspondent later). Like Raquel, Patrick was a prizewinner. At age two he won the Adohre Milk Company's Adohreable Baby Contest and then the role of Olivia de Haviland's baby in *Gone With The Wind*. At 13 he became "Buzz" in the TV show *Leave It To Beaver*. He buzzed adoreably for six years. As an adult, he went to work as a Hollywood publicist. Patrick and Raquel met in 1964. Three weeks later, their joint venture — Curtwel enterprises — was born. Its major asset was Raquel. Raquel in bikinis, Raquel traveling through the circulatory system in *Fantastic Voyage*, Raquel wearing the skimpy wolfskin in *One Million Years B.C.* that attracted Henry Grunwald's attention.

Over the White Horse gin-and-tonic Raquel's interview of me continued.

"Why Journalism?"

[My father had such a good time as a journalist for the *Saturday Evening Post* the career was irresistible.]

"Your father's Pete Martin? Where did you start?"

[The *St. Louis Post-Dispatch.*]

"Why St. Louis? Why the *Post-Dispatch*?"

[One of my father's friends who'd worked there got me a job as copy boy, and it was one of the best papers in America.]

As *Dames at Sea* curtain time approached I paid the check and thanked the manager for the White Horse's quiet customers. Raquel kissed him on the cheek. We walked up the street, paused at the limo, and Raquel told Carlos to meet us outside the theater after the show. I was electrically conscious of walking a New York street with Raquel, but no one took special notice. She matched her step with mine and we talked about the strangeness and irony of me, the son of an unreconstructed Southerner, writing for a liberal newspaper in a racist city like St. Louis.

Dames at Sea was a parody of all those tap-dancing Busby Berkeley productions where the understudy goes out a nobody and comes back a star. Ruby arrives from Utah with nothing but tap shoes and a prayer in her heart, faints into the arms of a song writer/sailor named Dick, gets a job in the chorus of Dick's show but the theater's been *sold*. What to do? Dick helps persuade the captain of his ship to use the ship as a floating theater. The female star gets seasick, Ruby steps in, saves the show, taps out the finale, and the three leading couples decide to marry.

"I'm starved," Raquel said, as we walked to where Carlos was waiting. "Is there still such a thing as a Reuben sandwich in New York?"

"Better yet," said I. "There's still a Reuben's restaurant, uptown, near F.A.O. Schwartz."

Up we went. Now the experienced celebrity-crowd handler, I talked with the *maître d'*, told him the same story I'd used at the White Horse. Result: more Manhattan magic. Heads swiveled a bit more (we were in tourist country, after all), eyes followed, but we got a quiet banquette.

Raquel continued to talk about me.

"Was TIME all I wanted?"

[No, I'd like to try my hand at fiction. I'd started a novel in a creative-writing course at Dartmouth, read chapters aloud at weekly seminars, and got an A. Heady stuff.]

"Did I want to travel?"

[I'd had a two-year journalism fellowship in Africa, traveled by MG sports car from Cape Town through the Rhodesias and the Belgian Congo to the Gold Coast in West Africa, had adventures. Yes, I wanted more.]

The *real me* was pouring out. I wasn't with Raquel Welch, I was with a blind date at Dartmouth, and we were getting along just fine.

After cheese cake and coffee, Raquel leaned toward me, looking luscious. Her cleavage was lovely, dark and deep ... but I had promises to keep... and miles to go ...

"Am I sexy?" she said, abruptly

I stopped in mid-thought. Then, "Yes. You're sexy."

"The mind is an erogenous zone," she said. "I've been stroking yours."

The check came. I paid it.

"Carlos has got the car outside," Raquel said, "and I'm staying at the Pierre, just around the corner. Want to come up for a nightcap?"

"Raquel," I said. "If you're going to end up on the cover of TIME, the last thing I should do is come up for a nightcap. No, you get out at the hotel and ask Carlos to take me to Grand Central."

He did.

Chapter 19

THAT'S ALL VERY INTERESTING, MRS. LINCOLN, BUT HOW WAS THE PLAY?

What about the Raquel Welch cover story? The day after my exploration of Raquel Welch's sexiness I gave a full report to Henry Grunwald. He listened intently, asked questions, and at the end of my account looked at me and smiled. "We've got a cover story, Peter," he said.

As I've told this tale since then, friends have asked, "Did he believe you when you told him you said, No Thanks, to Raquel's invitation for a night-cap?"

I'm sure he did. He had been through a parallel experience earlier, when I'd assigned a writer to do a profile of Shirley MacLaine. I had an introductory lunch with her, and the writer then spent two days on the assignment, watching as she filmed a movie, "Desperate Characters," directed by my daily "Dartmouth" editor and friend, Frank Gilroy, on location in Brooklyn. The writer did the usual, reading background material provided by a TIME researcher and sharing meals with Ms. MacLaine as he interviewed.

On the morning of Day Three, my office phone rang. It was Shirley MacLaine.

"Peter?" she said. "What do I have to do to get a favorable story in your magazine?"

"What do you mean?"

"The writer made it clear last night that if I didn't go to bed with him, the story would be negative."

"Don't worry. I'll take care of it."

I went to Henry and told him about the phone call. "Do *I* fire him, or do *you?*" I said.

"I'll take care of it," said Henry.

Henry didn't fire the writer. He had a long talk with him, and so did I. The story, carefully edited by me, was balanced and positive. I never assigned that writer to another story.

I was not put in charge of the Raquel Welch cover story. I was, as they said around the office in those days, "too close to it." So was Henry, in his way. He decided that the cover illustration should not be the usual photograph, or a painted portrait. What was called for, he thought instinctively, (and brilliantly) was a *bust*, sculpted not in clay, or wood, or bronze, but in *epoxy*.

Jay Cocks, a critic in TIME's "Cinema" section, got the writing assignment. Jay was — and *is* — a perceptive and fine writer. After his TIME days he left the magazine and won a couple of Academy Awards (one for Best Adapted Screenplay, *The Age of Innocence*, and one for Best Original Screenplay, *Gangs of New York*). I knew he shared my She-Can't-Act opinion about Raquel's movies (except *Bedazzled*), so I awaited the actual story with nervous anticipation.

Timing is everything. The story ran in the issue of November 28, 1969, while Raquel's most ambitious role — Myra in the screen adaptation of Gore Vidal's *Myra Breckenridge* — was still in production, and the script was going through its *ninth* rewrite. With no movie to review, Jay never laid a critical hand on it. The story was all Raquel, all Myra, all Gore Vidal, all Jay Cocks and all Henry Grunwald.

It began by quoting Vidal and the book: "I am Myra Breckinridge, whom no man will ever possess. Clad only in garter belt and one dress shield, I held off the entire elite of the Trobriand Islanders, a race who possess no word

Raquel Welch - Time Cover - November 28, 1969. Epoxy resin sculpture by Frank Gallo now on display at National Portrait Gallery in Washington, D.C.

for 'why' or 'because.' I am the New Woman whose astonishing history is a poignant amalgam of vulgar dreams and knife-sharp realities..."

It went on with a combination of Henry and Vidal: "Few spectacles are more terrifying than the New Woman, bearing the twin torches of Desire to Succeed and Disdain for Mere Man. This quality of savage purpose was etched to its satiric extreme in Myra Breckenridge... It was Myra's unholy quest to vanquish man; she sought to blind men with her beauty, determinedly unmanning them in the way that King Kong was reduced to a mere simian whimper by beauteous Fay Wray, whom I resemble left three-quarter profile."

Then Jay Cocks: "Raquel Tejada Welch bears no resemblance to frail, delicate Fay Wray from any angle. Her attack on the male world is based on calculated carnality, on the woman as animal. The parallels between her and Vidal's carnivorous heroine are remarkable. Says Raquel, 'I understand Myra thoroughly. I've always identified with her.' Now she is bringing her sense of identification to the screen in the title role of 20th Century-Fox's forthcoming film version of Myra. Not since Cleopatra has a movie provoked so much gossip, speculation, expectation — and guerrilla war — even before going into production. As the filming staggers into its ninth week, real-life and fantasy female forces keep colliding in Raquel Welch, and the collision promises the extreme moment of her career. If she can't convincingly play the invincible, pathologically ambitious Myra, she probably can't play anyone."

What did Raquel think of the cover story? She didn't call me; I didn't call her. But about three weeks after it was published, I was making my way into a movie-preview screening room when I saw her already there. A spoken phrase my *Saturday Evening Post* writer-father used when he wanted to sound noncommittal to producers of movies he hadn't much liked sprang to mind. "*That's* what I call a movie!"

But this wouldn't do for Raquel. She saw me, waved, and came over. "I wanted to tell you how honored I was by the cover," she said warmly.

"What did you think of it?" I said.

"Actually, I never read it," she said. "Rex Reed (a Manhattan movie critic who had a bit part in the film) read me parts of it, and that was enough."

She kissed me on the cheek, and passed on into the screening room. I was — again — impressed by the way she handled it.

The Raquel-bust cover sculpture was a knockout. After being photographed for the print run of six million copies, it arrived in my office in the old TIME-LIFE Building, where it commanded (and I mean *commanded*) the room for six or seven weeks. Hollow-cheeked, gaunt, pale, staring, life-sized — if you can call something that runs only from the waist up "life-sized" — she was there to greet me mornings, to say goodbye evenings and late nights.

Then, suddenly one morning, she was gone. Gone where? My writers didn't know, my secretary didn't know, my researchers didn't know, the cleaning staff didn't know.

I didn't know — until I went to a dinner party at Henry's Grunwald's apartment on East 72nd Street about a month later. There she was, in the front hall, just inside the door. Gaunt, staring, pale, she was asking "Am I sexy?" At that point the answer had to be, "No. You're not sexy. You're Henry's trophy."

Years later, at the newly-opened portrait gallery of the Smithsonian Museum in Washington, D.C., I went around a corner on a balcony. There she was, gaunt, pale, still life-sized. Henry was dead, Harry Luce was dead, David Halberstam was dead, Bill Buckley was dead. I wasn't, but I was fast becoming part of an unremembered past.

But Raquel still lived, in the flesh as well as preserved in epoxy. At the Smithsonian, as permanent as The Spirit of St. Louis, she was there. Eternal woman, she goes on forever.

Chapter 20

Meet Otto Fuerbringer

At TIME magazine, they called him the "Iron Chancellor." Or "The Big O." Or "Otto Forefinger."

Looming a bit to the right of Barry Goldwater, or William F. Buckley, or *even* (at times) Henry Luce, Otto was the natural choice of Mr. Luce to become Managing Editor of TIME magazine in 1960 at the height of the Vietnam War. Otto believed it was the "right war, at the right time, in the right place." Tall, imperious and insistent on getting his own way, Otto "did not encourage dissent", as David Halberstam described him in a *New York Times* obituary after he died at age 97 in 2008.

Otto was also my friend, sort-of. An unlikely friend, you'd have to agree. Otto was the son and grandson of leaders of the ultra-conservative Missouri Synod of the Lutheran Church. He went to Harvard, was editor of the Harvard *Crimson*, worked as a reporter for the *St. Louis Post-Dispatch*, and married a bright, upright graduate of St. Louis's exclusive Mary Institute school before he went on to become a writer and editor for TIME.

I was the son of a Virginia Episcopal "Whiskeypalian," a popular writer for the *Saturday Evening Post* who loved high times and loved to live them. I went to Dartmouth, was an editor of the daily *Dartmouth* compus newspaper, worked as a reporter for the *St. Louis Post-Dispatch*, and married a bright, upright graduate of St. Louis's Mary Institute school before I went on to become a writer and editor for TIME.

Otto Fuerbringer in 1982, giving the forefinger.

You see a few parallels. But I was not tall, not insistent on getting my own way, and *did* encourage dissent as a senior editor at TIME and a founding editor of *Money* magazine. I was liberal, not conservative, and would probably not have lasted long at Henry Luce's Time Incorporated if I'd crossed or displeased him, which I did from time to time. But Otto protected me.

The most exposed place to write at TIME was the *Nation* section, which was staunchly — you might even say *extremely* — conservative and Republican. Henry Luce kept a close watch on it, and woe be unto him who strayed too close to liberalism.

It was occasionally suggested that I be switched from writing about Latin America to writing about the United States. For reasons never explained to me personally, Otto used his authority to keep me where I was.

One close shave came when we Latin Americanists learned about corrupt Bolivian government officials who diverted a multi-dollar U.S. aid package into some friendly banks. Only about $3 million ever came out to be spent for the original purpose. The rest disappeared into interest payments, administrative costs and side projects that benefitted the banks — and the officials themselves.

We got our correspondents to do a thorough job of investigative reporting, checked the facts, and began the process of publishing the story in TIME's Latin American edition. The edition did not circulate in the United States, but was printed in Mexico and distributed south of the border by airplane. When the Bolivia copies arrived in La Paz, the capital, a mob of government supporters went to the airport, seized the bundles and took them to the U.S. Embassy. They broke them open, soaked them with gasoline, set them afire, and started a riot in which a Bolivian passerby was killed by ricocheting bullets.

At the time, Claire Booth Luce, HRL's wife who had just served as U.S. Ambassador to Rome, had been nominated by President Eisenhower to be Ambassador to Brazil. Her confirmation was being debated in the U.S. Senate. Senator Wayne Morse of Oregon, no friend of the Luces or TIME, argued that no ambassador should be sent to Latin America if her husband's publications caused riots that killed local citizens. Claire withdrew her nomination.

Mr. Luce, who had had no idea what the story was about, and no idea that it that it was being published in *his* Latin American edition, wanted an explanation. I explained it all to Otto, and Wes was then was dispatched to the Luce home at River House in Manhattan. I got there, all nerves and worry about what was coming. I was offered a drink. I explained the story to Mr. Luce — but I could tell that he'd already heard a version from Otto.

He listened to me, asked a few questions, and then said, in the staccato way he way he often used to put an end to a conversation, "Good thing. She had enough trouble in Rome. She shouldn't have gone to Brazil anyway."

I felt a sense of Fuerbringer protection. It went both ways. Once, when I was serving as Senior Editor of TIME's "Modern Living" Section, Otto decided that he'd like to beat other publications to the Summer Punch by producing a feature article on "America's Best Summer Resorts" … *in early spring.*

Among the resorts of choice was Bailey's Beach in Newport, Rhode Island, a favorite of high and mighty New York and Boston families listed in the *Social Register*. We chose a predictably warm weekend in May to dispatch a fine photographer of female flesh to snap cover-quality shots of lovely young women in their early-season bathing suits.

He came back with several, and Otto and I looked at them projected on the color-lab wall on Tuesday morning. I particularly liked a handsome, beautifully-proportioned Wellesley student in a well-filled top and tailored bottom. "Definitely TIME style," was my judgment.

Lutheran and perhaps subconsciously Teutonic, Otto leaned toward a buxom Bailey's Beach blonde the photographer had persuaded to lean toward his Rolleiflex at water's edge one morning, her bosom nearly toppling out of her bikini, and the rising sun shining brightly and *directly* through her crotch. "That would be too raw, even for *Playboy*," I said.

"No, Peter, we're going to have fun with this," Otto said. "That's *it.*"

I tried to argue him out it on grounds of taste, of status, of our reputation, of Ivy Leagueness (Otto was from *Harvard*, after all). We jawed back and forth for a good ten minutes, but he would not be moved. The girl with the glowing crotch was his choice, and he was the Managing Editor. He ordered Charlie Jackson, the guy in charge of the lab, to ship the transparency off to Chicago, where our color photos were reduced to their four-color essentials for printing. Otto himself phoned the Bailey Beach girl to give her the good news that she was going to be in TIME magazine. On the cover!

She came in to the Time-Life Building the next morning to be interviewed, and Otto invited me to his office to meet her. I did. She was sweet and young and *terrifically* excited to be on the cover of TIME. "Have you seen the cover photo?" Otto asked.

"No," answered the sweet young thing. "But I'd love to."

"Take her down to Charlie's light room and put a duplicate up on the wall," Otto said.

We went down a flight of stairs to Charlie's realm and he put a slide in the projector. It was a big wall, and a big blow-up. And a big, sunny CROTCH. There was a gasp.

"Oh, my God!" she said. "No! Gran will disinherit us! You can't publish that! Cancel it, PLEASE!"

"I can't," I said. "Only Otto can."

On the way back up the stairs, between sobs, she told me that her parents and her brother were being supported by her grandmother, who controlled the family money. If *that* picture got on the cover of TIME, "Gran" would cut off the funds, and they would be out in the cold.

Otto was unmoved. He wouldn't budge. "You signed a release," he told her. "The presses have already started running." [The release part was true, but the cover presses wouldn't start running until Thursday. Otto was trying to convince her it was too late.] Besides, he said, "You'll be on the cover of TIME. Your grandmother will understand what an honor that is." Still sobbing, she left the office. And the building.

Next morning on my desk, the light on my direct-line squawk-box from Otto was burning. He'd tried to call me earlier, but I was out. I called him back. "I've been talking with Granny," he said. "Her son's a good friend of

Harry Luce. So's her lawyer. I've had a bit of a chat with him. Let's take another look at your Wellesley girl."

We did, and little Miss Good Taste with the tailored bottom made the cover. As we walked out of Charlie's light room, Otto stopped and shook my hand.

"Thanks," he said.

Chapter 21

LIFE — Consider the Alternative

As LIFE lay dying, Otto Fuerbringer's life and mine crossed in a more emphatic, definitive way. Mr. Luce was dead, *Newsweek* was making headway as a challenger to TIME because of its fresher, more rebellious approach to the Vietnam war, and Otto had been succeeded by the more contemporary, arts-minded, creative Henry Grunwald. With Henry as my new boss, I was Senior-Editing Time's lively-arts sections.

I had been at the magazine for more 15 years. I was eligible for a "sabbatical." A sabbatical? From a magazine job? Some of the reasons people stayed on at TIME despite tempting offers from other publications and other worlds were the imaginative fringe benefits. Want an advanced academic degree from a distinguished university? TIME would pay for it if you fulfilled the requirements and wrote your thesis while continuing your editorial job at the magazine. Mary Kelley, a Researcher for the Nation Section, earned a Ph.D. (Focus: American Womens' History) and went on to become a distinguished professor and Department Chair at the University of Michigan.

Henry Grunwald took time off from editing TIME's performing-arts sections to write a musical comedy. As I told Raquel Welch, my long-term dream (*many* journalists' dream, of course) was to write a novel. I had become fascinated by the romance and novelistic dimension of the journalism and writing career of the hero of America's war against the Vietnam War, David Halberstam ... *and* the fascination of his Polish actor wife, Ezbieta Czceweska. I needed at least a year or more to research and begin writing about it, and Henry had agreed to give me a sabbatical half-year off at full pay to begin it.

Henry found a replacement for me and I began clearing the decks for action and travel — obviously, I had to spend time in Poland. I did all my overdue expense reports. I did my U.S. income tax in advance. I packed up my office books and papers and carried them home. The time and date for my sabbatical was agreed upon by Henry and me.

The date arrived. I moved out of my TIME office and waited for word from Otto. Days went by. Weeks went by. I collected and read books about Polish history and Polish cinema. I went to Polish movies. I rebuilt the attic of my house in Yorktown Heights, New York, into an author's "garret" — laying down a 3/4-inch plywood floor over the ceiling timbers of the second floor, leaving plenty of room under the gabled roof for pacing. I installed folding stairs from the second floor into the attic space so they could be pulled up when I needed isolation, and folded down when I needed lunch, or the bathroom. I made a desk out of saw horses and more plywood spread between two metal, three-drawer filing cabinets. I bought a slide projector and borrowed all the Poland transparencies I could from the Time-Life photo collection. I practiced phonetic Polish phrases from "Say-It-in-Polish" travel books. I moved copy paper, carbon paper and an antique, black typewriter given to me by Dartmouth when I was fired from my editor's job on the college newspaper. I began outlining the novel.

Amid all this, my wife reported after breakfast one morning that Otto had phoned. I waited until lunchtime, and phoned him back.

"Well," he said, "the magazine development committee is finally going to meet next week. I've had flu, and near-pneumonia, and other problems. But now we can begin meeting."

"Not with me." I said. "I've begun my sabbatical and I'm home, writing."

"But you must have been *thinking* about new magazines," Otto said. "Couldn't you just attend some meetings for a few weeks?"

"I'm afraid not," I said. "But you must have a lot more members of the committee. Surely they can work with you."

"How about a memo?" Otto said. "Could you put some of your thinking in a memo, so we'd have a starting point for our talk?"

"I could do that," I said. "What's your office address? I can mail it to you."

"Don't you have an office in the building?"

"No. I've moved out."

I got to work. In an introduction, I embodied my earlier thinking about mass magazines *versus* special-interest magazines and then suggested 15 or 20 special-interest topics upon which a monthly magazine could focus. They included Personal and Family Health, Individual Money Management, Photography, Sex, Intelligent TV Viewing, Camping, Weight Loss, Memoir-writing, Yoga, One-Hour Meals, Cabinetry, Regional Gardening, and on and on.

I typed it out, put it in an envelope, and mailed it off to Otto. Then I pulled up my novelist's garret stairs, I began making outlines, and got to work on ... *Queen of Poland.*

Chapter 22

David and Elzbieta

Before he was a friend, David Halberstam was a powerful presence on the fringes of my professional life. In the 1960s, when I became a TIME Senior Editor, David's Vietnam War correspondence in the *New York Times* caused the John F. Kennedy Administration considerable pain.

David paid scant attention to the Saigon "Five O'Clock Follies" press conferences, where U.S. military spokesmen shone the best possible light on the day's hits and misses against the Viet Cong. He did not, as Otto put it, "hang out on the Continental Hotel Terrace in Saigon, listening to the adventures of reporters who'd been out covering the war and filing them as their own." He, and reporters like him (Neal Sheehan of United Press International and Malcolm Brown of AP), went out and did their own reporting. They wrote their own stories, and filed them, and then went out and did it again. JFK complained to *Times* Publisher Punch Sulzberger that David's reports hurt the war effort, but Punch did nothing about it.

Not so with *Times* Managing Editor Abe Rosenthal. Eager to stay on the good side of the Kennedy Administration, Abe pulled David out of Vietnam and brought him back to New York, where — in 1964 — he and Neal Sheehan were awarded Pulitzer Prizes for their Vietnam coverage. With that, as David told me, "I not only won the Pulitzer Prize. I won the *Wurlitzer* Prize. I was invited to all those Lenny Bernstein parties on the Upper East Side. I was a hero of the War against the War."

Elżbieta Czyżewska, "Queen of Poland."

David Halberstan and Elżbieta in Lazienki Park after their marriage in Warsaw, Poland, 1965.

I met David at some of those parties, and we became friends. He was a comfortable friend. We shared tales about growing up in journalism — he in the South, at the *Tennessean* in Nashville, Tennessee, I in the Midwestern equivalent of the South, at the *Post-Dispatch* in St. Louis. He had covered conflict in Central Africa, I had spent two years in subSaharan Africa on a journalism fellowship.

Also at some of those East-Side parties was Abe Rosenthal. From time to time Abe overheard a regular question about David: "What's he doing here? Why isn't he in Vietnam?"

Finally, David said, "Abe couldn't take it any more. He took me into his office and said, 'As a reward for your Pulitzer, I'm going to send you to where I won mine. Poland.'"

Poland. For the first time since 1945, when Churchill's Iron Curtain "descended across the Continent," cutting off "all the capitals of the ancient states of Central and Eastern Europe — Warsaw, Berlin, Prague, Vienna, Budapest,

Belgrade, Bucharest and Sofia" — Poland was becoming accessible. Western press organizations were opening bureaus in previously forbidden places like Warsaw and Budapest.

This was not only convenient for Abe Rosenthal; it was useful to me as the Senior Editor in charge of TIME's "color-photography projects." TIME in those days was a black-and-white publication; reproduction of color photographs with four-color separations was ferociously expensive and had to be planned far in advance. It was worth it, though. The right collection of four, eight or twelve pages of color photographs could add an essential element to a major story. It was my job to find and develop topics for "color projects."

The opening of East Europe was a natural candidate for a multi-page portfolio of color photos and an accompanying article. For the first time in 20 years TIME's readers could see what had been hidden behind the "Iron Curtain". I proposed a photographic exploration of Poland, Romania, Czechoslovakia and Hungary. I called it "The Iron Curtain Rusts", and it was accepted from the "menu" of color-project proposals I presented at a quarterly lunch with Managing Editor Fuerbringer in a private dining room atop the TIME/LIFE Building.

When one of these lunches was over and Otto had said Yes to an idea (or sometimes two or three), my fun began. It was a lot less expensive to send a writer/editor like me to the field to scout picture and story and photo possibilities than to send a professional photographer who would take photographic "notes" from rented cherry-pickers and helicopters with costly equipment and color film. I would make the initial trip, size up the story possibilities, snap some sample pictures and, essentially, write a "shooting script" for a photographer who would follow.

At the same lunch where Otto said yes to the Iron Curtain idea, he also approved a color project to contrast the "modernization" of Franco Spain with its pervasive and picturesque antiquity. I went down to my office on the 25th floor and called the Time Inc. Travel Bureau. "I need to fly to Madrid next week, spend three or four days exploring the region, then rent a car and drive to San Sebastian, Bilbao and Barcelona. I'll spend a couple of days in each place, except Barcelona, where I'll need four or five days. Then I need to fly to Warsaw for about a week, Budapest for about four days, Bucharest for three days, and Prague for about five days. I'd like to be back in New York for Thanksgiving."

I loved my job.

As the Travel people worked on visas and an itinerary, I queried European bureaus of the TIME-LIFE News Service for suggestions about sites and scenes we might want to photograph to make the Spain color spread work. We had a Madrid bureau but no East European bureau at that point, so I got David Halberstam's address at the Bristol Hotel in Warsaw from the *Times*. I cabled him about the Iron-Curtain project, and asked him to have dinner with me after I arrived.

He not only answered, he phoned. He wanted to know the idea behind the color spread. Knowing a bit about the *Times* (and about TIME, for that matter), I could tell he was doing the required check to make sure that what I was asking would not conflict with something the *Times* was doing — of might *want* to do. I told him that after all the Iron-Curtain years, we thought it would be a good idea to show readers what lay behind it.

"Warsaw's just the beginning," I said. "I'm going on to Bucharest, Budapest and Prague."

"If you want new stuff, save yourself a trip," he said. "All that's even slightly new here is the Palace of Culture, one of those wedding-cake skyscrapers modeled on Moscow University the Russians put up in captured capitals to mark their neighborhood, like a dog pissing on trees. There's one in Bucharest, too. Come take a look. I'll be happy for the company."

It was warm September when I left the States, still warm October when I finished scouting electronics factories in Barcelona. I'm not always smart about such things, but some linkage between Eastern Europe and November prompted an expense-account outlay on a Barcelona topcoat lined with a wool-blanket from the waist down — a Spanish fanny-warmer.

What followed was a comfortable Caravelle jet from Barcelona to Zurich, an unreclinable Ilyushin propjet to Warsaw, midnight highway gouging in a snowstorm by a *zloty*-mad Polish cab driver, and a bleak arrival at the immense *Europeski* Hotel in Warsaw, where all foreigners were required to stay by the Communist government.

The fanny-warmer was a blessing. Galoshes would have been, too. That early-November storm had muffled Warsaw in four inches of white fluff overnight. There was blue sky and sunshine in the morning, though, and women in babushkas pushing snow down manholes in the street. By the time I finished my first-day walkabout my Pentax was full of deceptively lovely snapshots of downtown Warsaw and my Florsheims were full of chilled wet feet. I met David for a pork and cabbage dinner and an unremarkable bottle of wine in the vast, empty, chilly dining room of the Europeski.

"Grim pickings," he said. "For tomorrow, Let's do drinks in my office and then the theater. The play's called *Po Upadku* — "After the Fall." You won't understand the Polish, but it's Arthur Miller's play about him and Marilyn Monroe and the House UnAmerican Affairs Committee. You won't need subtitles."

"I saw it in New York," I said. "I think I'll be able to track it."

"I'll get tickets. Come over to the Bristol around six."

That day I took in the virtually nonexistent remains of the Warsaw ghetto and got a cab to take me to the places east of the Vistula River where the Russians waited until the retreating Germans had finished wiping out Warsaw's resistance fighters and partisans and — literally — blowing up the city. At the Europeski I stuffed my shoes with pages from a *Herald Tribune*, jammed them under the radiator to dry out, and took a shower. I put on the shoes — warm, but far from dry — and dug out my gift jug of Beefeaters.

It was a short walk to the Bristol. The hotel looked comfortably turn-of-the-century and uncomfortably solitary, one of the few buildings the Germans didn't level because it was their headquarters.

The place was like something out of Dr. Caligari. My memory makes the lobby two stories high. An elevator platform with nearly invisible guide wires emerged from a square hole in the ceiling and settled like an immense, silent, flying platform to the floor. David came down, collected me, and we were hoisted back up through the ceiling. "Riding down in this thing," he said, "is like descending with Dante through the seven levels of hell. Now we're headed for heaven."

Heaven was a collection of dusty metal filing cabinets, desks, lamps, a much-used couch and a couple of armchairs.

"The vodka here is *awfully* good," David protested when I presented the gin. When he was being emphatic, David's baritone tended to break into italics. "If you don't mind," he said, "I'll file this." He put the Beefeaters in a wall cupboard, opened a window, and picked up a bottle of *Wybora* vodka from the space between the inside glass and the storm window. "Most reliable fridge in Warsaw," he said, and poured two glasses.

We sipped. "Ah, that whiff of licorice," he said. "The stuff of Polish memories. The play's got a touch of Poland to it as well. There's a reminiscent streak of aristocracy here, and Poles get quiet satisfaction from the belief that they're up-slope from Russians and Americans. The play's about American politics at its worst, so by reflection, the audience gets a virtue bath. They love it, and they love the woman who plays Maggie, the Marilyn Monroe part. Her name's Elżbieta Czyżewska."

He pronounced it els-BYET-uh, sheh-SHEF-skuh, and as the days went on I learned to do it too. Not until I got my hands on a program did I see how it was spelled.

"I met her," David said, "when the U.S. Information Service exhibit of the John F. Kennedy Library was being set up at the Palace of Culture. For *New York Times* reasons, I had to be there, but she passed by, late for a rehearsal. Bob de Vecchi, political officer at the Embassy, introduced us, and I interviewed her a bit. She used the interview as an excuse for being late. After that I kept running into her. She's *worth* running into. In the past year, give or take an award or two, she's won what would amount to a U.S. Academy Award, an Emmy and a Tony. She was just on the cover of the Polish equivalent of TIME. And this play has been a sensation."

"I've really gotten to know her at under-the-radar screenings of new American movies. You can't see current American films here, of course, but our embassy gets them in the diplomatic pouch. When a good one's in, word goes out. On a given evening, you go down a dark side street to the side door of an apartment complex that's seems to have nothing to do with the Embassy or the Residence. Someone lets you in, and you walk through tunnels in the basements of buildings, then through more tunnels and more basements until you finally climb some stairs or ride an elevator to the apartment of someone connected to the network. And *voilà*! There's vodka and wine and hors d'oeuvres and dark bread and salami and smoked salmon. And talk. Elżbieta's usually there, and though my Polish is still nonexistent, we get along pretty well in French and *franglais*. We've gotten to know each other, and see each other when we're off-duty."

He looked at his watch. "Time to go," he said. "It's not much of a walk, but considering the snow and the fact that you've been on those wet feet all day, let's grab a cab."

The play, the setting, the performance, the audience response, were all solid. That evening, as we stood in the theatre beating our hands together and waiting for the final curtain to re-descend, David said, "Want to go backstage and meet her? We've got time."

"You bet."

The corridor outside the dressing rooms was jammed and jubilant. Doors were open and actors popped in and out, calling to each other. The man who'd played the Arthur Miller role stepped out of one door, talking over his shoulder to someone inside the room, and gave David a hug. David spoke to him in a kind of Polish-French-English mixture, explaining who I was. The words "TIME" and "*photographe*" came through and the actor put out his hand. "*Plaisir*," he said.

"*Pour moi, aussi*," I said. "You were very good."

David asked something about Elżbieta and the actor smiled, gestured toward the room he had just left, then stuck his head in the door and called out something. He waved us in. Still in her makeup and the nightdress she had worn in the last scene. Elżbieta was sitting in front of the dressing table on a little chair turned to face a studio couch along one wall of the room.

Elżbieta jumped up, ran to David and hugged him. Enthusiastically, I noticed with some pleasure. She was blonde — not as blonde as the Marilyn wig she had worn onstage, more the blonde of honey in the comb. She was quite a bit shorter than she looked onstage. The figure was all there, though. David kissed her on both cheeks, then introduced me.

"*C'est ici Peter Martin, mon ami de TIME et New York. Peter, Elżbieta. Elżbieta, Peter.*"

Elżbieta put her arms around me and air-kissed my right ear. "*Bienvenu,*" she said. "*Est-ce que vous êtes critique aussi?*" she asked. "*J'espère que non.*"

I searched my mind for French-verb conditionals: "*Je voudrais être critique,*" I said. "*J'ecriverais une critique extatique.*"

I don't know whether she forgave my French. In English, she said, "Will you be long in Warsaw?"

I laughed. "As long as possible."

The crowd around Elżbieta and David had tidal tendencies. That evening we flowed out of the theater to a night club, the *Krokodyl*, downstairs on the rebuilt old city square. Linguistically isolated, I chatted in English with a former playwright and theatrical director whose sardonic view of Communism had left him no occupation but the closely supervised writing of children's stories and the collecting of Polish jokes.

He pointed to a pretty girl pushing apart the weather curtains at the bottom of the stairs. "See her? She's a Polish call girl."

"A Polish call girl?"

"She has no telephone."

David and I met the next evening at *Spatif*, a club and downtown gathering place for the Warsaw theatrical crowd. The food — roast goose, escorted by little crocks of mushrooms in sour cream — wiped away painful memories of the *Europeski* dining room. David came up with the name of a dry red wine, which helped.

"How'd you like the play?" David asked.

"Given the setting and the times, I'll never forget it. And that moment, the moment when Elżbieta dropped the sheet she was holding behind her and

showed her naked bottom ... That was a true stunner. You don't really hear
an audience gasp like that. It sucked all the oxygen out of the room."

"She can have that effect," David said. "I'm glad you liked her. You see,
I'm going to marry her."

"Marry her?" I said. "*Marry* her? You've got to be kidding, David."

"I'm not kidding. She's perfect. She's talented, smart, curious, intelligent,
funny and ... how to say it? Unspoiled. An actress with her credits and gifts
in New York would have run away with herself by now. But there's not an
ounce of Look at me! Look at me! in her."

"Not here, maybe, but what about New York? Here, she's Queen of Poland,
but if she marries you, and you go home, you'll be King of New York and
she'll be Queen of Nothing."

"No, Peter. She's got talent, determination, style, and stage presence. You
saw that last night. She needs English, and stage training and coaching. New
York's got those, in plenty. She's got nowhere to go but up."

"I can't believe it's as easy as all that. Looking at her, I have to say she's
physically well-equipped, but she's no Ingrid Bergman or Dominique Sanda.
And how long will all this take? Shouldn't she be deep into English lessons
already?"

"She and I are already into English. When we're alone we speak almost
nothing else. My accent may be a bit New York or broadcasty. English lessons
are available here, but the minute you sign up you're a defection suspect. The
sooner we can move on this, the better."

There was no moving him, that was plain. I could tell he did not want to
be overheard at *Spatif*, and his voice was unmistakable, so he did not raise it.
But there was determination in it. He wanted to convince me. And he wanted
to hear me to say that I was convinced.

I was together with him and them several more times before I flew off
to Bucharest, but I never felt comfortable about broaching my reservations
about marriage and a career in the U.S. When the three of us were together,
there was so much obvious longing in her that it would have been awkward to
bring up my doubts when we were alone. As far as I could tell, Elżbieta had

only been outside Poland once in her life, and then only briefly.

"Wait 'til she sees Bloomingdale's," David said somewhere in the week. "It'll be like she's died and gone to heaven."

When I thought about them as I traveled on to Bucharest, Budapest, Prague, and back to New York, I summed it up as a case of situational infatuation. To her, he smelled irresistibly of *outside*, like Meursault wine and toasted English muffins. His voice resonated with hints of encounters with Yvette Mimieux and Kurt Vonnegut, with familiarity with the innards of The Ritz Bar and the Waldorf Astoria, with remembered tastes of Porterhouse at The Palm, and *coquilles St. Jacques* at *Grand Vefour*. He was a human prize, better than any Polish Tony, and one in the eye for Polish authority that confined her to the theatrical pond of Poland and denied her the theatrical sea of Europe, England, and beyond. To him, she was the fitting reward for the prizes he'd won for telling the truth in Vietnam and getting it down on paper, for the irony of being sent to where nothing was happening to get him out of the way of reporting things that *were* happening.

And Poland's authoritarian State, worried lest this running dog of capitalism make off with the national treasure of Polish womanhood and theatre arts, increased the heat under this *ragout* of desire and unattainability by ordering them for questioning, harassing them, warning them, and doing everything in a Communist State's considerable power to keep them from getting married. The "U.B." — the Polish Secret Police — followed them when they tried to get away for a day, a weekend, even an evening. They couldn't have a quiet meal together without wondering which others in the restaurant were there to watch them. They enlisted friends to throw pursuers off the scent, and their stolen moments became even more precious as a result. Elżbieta's theater friends warned that she was jeopardizing her career. More and more frequently David was called to the Interior or Foreign Ministry to answer questions about a *Times* article — innocuous or otherwise — he'd written or was working on.

Because of its impossibility, marriage became simultaneously more desirable and certain, more difficult and elusive. Civil marriages were performed in assembly-line ceremonies in state-run establishments by appointment and prearrangement. David and Elżbieta applied for such a marriage, but permission was denied. Friends were enlisted to explore possibilities. Finally, Bob de Vecchi's Polish assistant found a marriage registrar so out-of-the-way and out-of-the-know that the names Halberstam and Czyzewska did not set off alarms.

Married they were. Harassment intensified. Elżbieta found it hard not just to get roles in plays and movies, but even to get auditions. At last, in December 1965, I spotted a short report in New York that David was being expelled from Poland for writings that denigrated the State. How? He had written, and the *Times* had published, a report that anti-Semitism lived on in Poland. Just as infuriating to his personal government watchdogs, David said, was a more-or-less light-hearted feature article saying that a touch of citrus was an essential ingredient in a traditional Polish holiday cake. Citrus was scarce, so scarce that in the weeks before Christmas, the best tip a restaurant patron could leave his waitress was the peel of his breakfast orange.

David protested, lost, packed his kit, and moved to Paris. I waited to see whether Elżbieta would follow. She could give up David and her marriage, and thereby save her career. Or not. Given the intensity of David's feelings, my bet was on Not. Sure enough, Elżbieta began the painful struggle for an Exit Visa. She was warned, and warned again, that if she left she could never again expect to act in Poland. The process of leaving was the equivalent of being skinned. Her Polish life, her Polish accomplishments and her Polish identity were peeled away. Before she could fly from Warsaw to Paris, she was *strip-searched* at the Warsaw airport.

After a Paris and south-of-France holiday to catch their breath, the Halbertstams headed for New York. As David expected, Elżbieta took naturally to Manhattan shopping, the whirl of first-and-second-nights at the theater, advance screenings of movies for magazine and newspaper critics. I joined often on suppertime walks from their East-Side apartment uptown to Elaine's, the rather crummy Second-Avenue restaurant where David and Gay Talese and Nora Ephron and Kurt Vonnegut liked to pretend they weren't celebrities and eat okay (but not great) food at rear tables near other celebrities who were also not eager to be important. On warmish evenings we'd walk back, and Elżbieta would gaily tell Nan Talese and me about her English lessons, her diction lessons, her actors' studio work, her reading and her hope-filled meetings with Joseph Papp and Josh Logan.

David was on his way up and out of the routines of reporting and writing for the Times. He had books on his mind, and was publishing long articles in prestigious and good-paying magazines conected to the "new journalism" — particularly Willy Morris's, *Harper's.* He wrote well, and intensely, and his long sentences and measured subordinate clauses established a comfortable rhythm and pace that suited their topics and attitudes.

Despite the walks and the talks, I could form no solid idea about the making of Elżbieta Czyżewska, American actress, was going. Back at their apartment one evening after a provocative dinner and theater-talk with Claire Bloom and her producer-husband, Hilly Elkins, I asked Elżbieta to lunch with me later that week. We met at the "Italian Pavilion" on 54th Street, then one of the favorite talking places for people in the publishing and magazine business.

We talked a bit about the confusions, circumlocutions and exasperations of the English language, and American ShowBiz folk. Then, my question: How's it going?

"Peter," she said, "a Polish director once told me that becoming an actress was like producing a diamond. That is, deep under the earth, you begin with three hundred thousand tons of coal. You apply pressure, heat, and luck for thousands of years. Everything has to happen at precisely the right moment. The wrong step at the wrong time can undo all the right steps, and the result can be a ruined gem, or no gem at all. But if everything is right, the result is a diamond — or an actress."

Elżbieta made the point by holding up her fingers as if she were holding a gem of impressive size. Then she dropped them. "When I left Warsaw, I became three hundred thousand tons of Polish coal."

David was not able to help, she said. He was busy leaving the *Times*, going to work for Willie Morris, writing articles and books, doing what writers changing course had to do in New York. He was rebuilding his own career at

Harpers. It became obvious to her that whatever she was going to accomplish she would have to do herself.

Her principal help were the Poles and East Europeans who had already established themselves in movies and theater in the U.S. They supported her and encouraged her. They were her *friends.* Despite her accent, they finally got her work as an understudy in Joseph Papp's "Shakespeare In The Park." That was a high point. But then, she said, with despair on her face, "the thing in California happened."

For a moment I didn't grasp what she was talking about. Then it hit me: She was talking about the Sharon Tate killings. Her Polish friends who had been helping her were the people in the circle around Director Roman Polanski. Some of her principal props had been cut down by Charles Manson's murderous gang of cultists and fanatics.

"You can't imagine what that did to me," she said. "I was lost again. I didn't know what to do." She dropped out of the Papp program, stopped her English lessons. She said she began drinking too much, drifting, doing nothing, putting on weight. "Only now have I begun thinking of work again." She was back studying her English, going to the gym with Nan Talese.

I ran into David a few days later and told him about the lunch. "What's happening to Elżbieta is novelistic," I said.

"I know," he said. "But I can't write it. I'm too close to it. *You'll* have to write it."

Despite the Halberstamian italics, the remark was made lightly. But it stuck in my mind. After college I had worked a year and a half as a reporter at the *St. Louis Post-Dispatch.* I had a two-year journalism fellowship in Africa, and had written and edited at *TIME* for a decade. Writing a novel was a natural dream for magazine writers, and Harry Luce seemed to understand. After ten years, TIME Incorporated offered writers and editors a "sabbatical" — a year off at half-pay, or six months at full pay. The objective was to recharge intellectual batteries. With a paid sabbatical you could do anything you wanted, so long as you — or the result — did not compete with any Time Inc. activity or endeavor.

"Novelistic." The term carries a notion of romance, of accomplishment, of rewarding insights into human experience strung along a thread of intriguing narrative. Without too much thought as to what the "novel" might say, or involve, both David and Elżbieta bought into the idea. David agreed to fill me in about the life and activity of a foreign correspondent in Cold-War Poland. Elżbieta would tell me about growing up as a virtual orphan in the ruins of a Warsaw leveled by the dynamite of retreating Germans, her life as a student-ward of the postwar Communist state, her education in the theatre arts as an adolescent and young adult.

By this time my color-photography spread on "The Rusting Iron Curtain" had long-since run. Harry Luce was dead, Otto Fuerbringer had moved on from TIME's managing editorship to supervise the planning of new Time Inc. magazines, and Henry Grunwald, an Austria-born, arts-oriented, liberal thinker had taken over at TIME. I went out for a drink with Henry and broached the sabbatical subject. Henry had taken his own sabbatical, years before, to write a musical comedy. When he heard why I wanted mine, he was enthusiastic. "Splendid! It's a novel pleading to get written. And Elżbieta can star in the movie version!"

David and Elżbieta were not as enthusiastic as Henry, but as friends, they understood. If Peter said he was going to write a novel based on their experience, he was going to write a novel based on their experience. Period. Bless them, they didn't ask what the novel would say, or how it would say it. But I had never lived their experience — most essentially, David's. I had worked as a writer on assignment for TIME in Latin America, but I had never been stationed permanently in an overseas bureau. I had never had to obtain credentials, find a place to live, rent office space, hire local assistants, arrange for cable and telex communications, open bank accounts, buy office equipment, negotiate expense accounts, do my own fact-checking, keep account books, maintain a news-clipping library, pay bribes, maintain a company car, arrange for medical care, buy currency on the black market — and find time for making contacts, reporting and writing. I had dodged shadowing policemen in Venezuela, Cuba and South Africa, but had never faced 24-hour, Cold-War enmity in a capital-C Communist country.

We met over coffee and drinks at their apartment, and over meals. David provided day-by-day, consequential and inconsequential details about living and working as a free-world journalist in a hostile, closed society. My "sabbatical" had begin!

Elżbieta couldn't travel with me to Poland, but she tried to describe growing up at the end of the war, piecing together bits of memory of her mother's activity as an ammunition smuggler for the Polish resistance in 1944 and, when she was five or so, being led to a foster home through the piled rubble of exploded Warsaw buildings. She promised to connect me with friends who knew the schools where she was educated and the theaters and sound-stages of Poland's film city, Lodz (pronounced "Woodch"), where she trained and worked as a performer.

In Warsaw in November '65, when we went out for tea or coffee, Elżbieta had been all generosity and smiles, as befit a major star surrounded by admiring home folk. When she paid for coffee or pastry, she had a grand habit of emptying all the metal change from her coin purse, paying no attention to how much it amounted to, and sweeping the money into a careless, gleaming pile of a tip. In Manhattan, she — and her talk — tended to be more tight-lipped. I often got the feeling that she was holding back, that reliving her life as a budding teen-ager and blossoming actress in Communist Poland was not comfortable.

David and I had fun! All in all, and off and on, our talks took about five or six weeks. Almost nonstop, his voice rumbled on (I can still hear it rumbling), broken by my laughs and questions, or by lunch, or a walk to a delicatessen, or by an afternoon coffee or beer break. If we could have muted our side talk, or gossip about friends and colleagues, we probably could have covered the same ground in a couple of weeks. But being with David was like being out for a long walk on a cool conversational afternoon. We goofed off.

Then came my note-taking travel in Poland, to the places where David and Elżbieta had courted, where she had done her first plays, where they had borrowed a wooden country cottage (and Elżbieta, much to David's horror, had shampooed her hair early one morning in a pristine valley pond) in the Mazouri lake district, to the site of the Chopin festival where they had eluded a particularly sticky government spook. In Warsaw this time I insisted on staying at the Bristol Hotel, riding that Dante-esque elevator, eating in the restaurant and coffee shop, comparing the repaired and re-faced façade of the building with the bullet- and shell-pocked stone and stucco of the unrepaired courtyard. I tried to meet with David's inquisitors and interlocutors at the Foreign and Interior ministries, but when they got wind of what I was up to their doors closed and my phone calls went unanswered.

Elżbieta's friends were much more helpful. In rented cars, they showed me the neighborhoods where she'd lived. They took me to parties hosted by Warsaw's so-called "gilded youth" — relatives and buddies of government and Party officials who seemed to be able to buy all the goodies they wanted, from *pâté*, to champagne, to bourbon, to cognac, to American cigarettes, to cocaine, to marijuana, to you-name-it. We went to improvisations, to rehearsals, to opening-night parties. After a late-night expedition to *Spatif* and a night club or two, they delighted in having me drive one of their cars so I could get stopped by a cop seeking a bribe. If one of them had been arrested while driving, the cop would talk tough, seize their i.d. and driver's license, then demand a hefty bribe to get them back. When I got stopped they would stifle laughs as I said, with a broad American accent, "What's the problem, officer? Did I go through a stop light? What's that? I'm sorry, I don't understand you. I don't speak Polish." The cop would hand me back my international driver's license, say something final and foul, and we would drive off. Safely around a corner of two, my companions would laugh like teenagers.

Then home to Yorktown Heights, NY, to write *The Queen of Poland*. I fashioned myself a garret with folding stairs I could pull up into the attic so I could be alone with my 35-milimeter slide shows, my notebooks, my books on Polish theatre and films, and my ancient typewriter. I'd write in the morning, come down for lunch, pull the stairs back up in the afternoon, and edit what I'd written two or three days before.

When I'd produced more than 200 pages of typescript, my agent, the late

John Meyer, suggested it was time to put it to a test. He asked me to prepare an outline for the entire book and put it together with the pages I'd done. He would then show it to three or four editors he knew at major publishing houses and ask them whether they thought this new author should be encouraged to keep on writing. This was an old agent's gimmick, he said. Everyone would know that he wasn't looking for a contract, or an advance. He was just getting word out that he had a new author working on a first novel, and he — and the author — wanted some indication that the author (and, of course, the book) was worth paying attention to.

John was obviously worth paying attention to. About ten days after the bundles went out, John called to say that two publishers — Viking and Lippincott — liked the book, but recognized the principal characters despite my efforts to disguise them. They weren't so much worried about lawsuits, he said. What concerned them was David's possible reaction to the book. His character seemed far from heroic, and they worried that his displeasure might cause his writing friends to boycott, or bad-mouth, the house that published it.

I phoned David. "Are we going to be famous?" he said.

"Maybe," I said. "But there's a problem. They recognize you and Elżbieta, and they're afraid that you and your friends might boycott any house that published the book."

"What can we do about it?"

"John Meyer says that what's needed is a letter from you to me, saying that you know I'm writing the book, and you approve."

"No problem," said David. "Send over a draft. I'll write the letter and send it back."

Elżbieta was on the line. "David," she said, "I think we ought to read what Peter's written."

"Elżbieta's absolutely right," I said. "You don't want to get blind-sided. I'll send over a duplicate of the bundle John sent to the publishers."

I did. I waited a couple of weeks. No letter from David. I phoned again, and Elżbieta answered.

"David's in Texas, promoting *Making of a Quagmire*," she said. "When he calls in, I'll remind him."

A week or so later, the letter arrived. Two pages. Page One was a rave. I had caught the feeling of Cold-War Warsaw perfectly. Those frigid, short, northern days, when the afternoon sun went down about 3 p.m., weak light bulbs burned a dim blue-yellow, and people gathered in chilled apartments to drink vodka and listen to John Coltrane records and wish they were somewhere else... I'd captured it, David wrote. Warsaw was almost a character in the book.

Then, on David's Page 2: "However, since it cuts so close to the personal bone, I'm afraid I cannot give it my imprimatur."

Further talk produced the same response: He couldn't, he wouldn't. And he didn't.

That did it — for John Meyer, for Lippincott, for Viking, for the novel. Cardinal Jozsef Mindszenty was living in Cold-War asylum in the U.S. Embassy in Budapest, and I used a week of my sabbatical to see whether a change of venue from Poland to Hungary might work. But no. Budapest was too warm, too friendly. Its little circus was too full of dancing bears, its cheerful restaurants too full of rack of hare and baked goose with *prieselbern*. Budapest — despite Mindszenty — couldn't substitute for Warsaw.

The Queen of Poland got taped up in a cardboard carton and stored on a closet shelf.

Time went by. I was "promoted" from Senior Editorship on Henry Grunwald's TIME, to magazine inventor with Otto Fuerbringer's Magazine Development Group. I "invented" four magazines, one of which, although initially aborted, was eventually reborn as *People*. A second, unaborted, became *Money* Magazine. It took seven years for *Money* to begin making money. When it did, Henry Grunwald (who by now was Editor-in-Chief of all Time Inc. publications and enterprises) asked me to take on a faltering TV project called *Home Box Office*. I was a print person, I told Harry, not electronic. Instead, I pursued the Executive Directorship of the small foundation that had given me a two-year journalism fellowship in subSaharan Africa in the mid-

1950s. I moved it from New York to Hanover, New Hampshire, home of my *alma mater*, Dartmouth College.

Meanwhile, David wrote on, from successful book to the ultimate successful book, *The Best and the Brightest*. His marriage to Elżbieta and his Manhattan home on Turtle Bay were inundated by a flood of Polish performing-arts exiles in the 1970s. They divorced in 1977. Elżbieta's career followed the path of frustration outlined in my book. She was allowed to return to Poland in 1968 to act in a single ... and denounced ... film. She had fleeting successes on regional European and U.S. stages, most notably in a Yale Repertory Theater production of Albert Camus's "The Possessed." But every time she came tantalizingly close to the stardom that David had dreamed for her, someone else got the role.

In New Hampshire, one February day in 1997, I got a call from the Dartmouth administrative office. David Halberstam was coming to town for a short residence as lecturer, teacher and on-campus presence, I was told, and they were looking for evening things for him to do. Tom Winship, editor of the *Boston Globe*, was also going to be in town. Would my wife and I be willing to take them out to dinner?

Certainly.

For TIME, I'd supervised an article on Winship's masterful coverage of Teddy Kennedy's role at the troubled Democratic 1968 National Convention in Chicago, and both Winship and Halberstam were born raconteurs. We got through dinner in Norwich, Vermont, just across the Connecticut River from Hanover, in great style and high good humor. My wife drove Winship back to his hotel in her car and I gave David a ride to his on-campus residence at Dartmouth. As we crossed the Connecticut-River bridge, David turned to me.

"Whatever happened to that book?"

"Come on, David. You know what happened to that book. When I couldn't change the venue to Budapest, I sealed it up and put it on a shelf in my New York apartment."

"I think you ought to get it out and finish it. Everything's changed. I have a new wife and a new life, but for Elżbieta everything's been a struggle, a downward spiral. She's had beginnings, but no endings. Your book is the only place where anyone with perception and language skill saw what she was in 1965 and put it into words. What you wrote is her best chance to be remembered for what she was."

"It's not as easy as all that, David. I haven't thought about the book for years. It's only half-done. Running my foundation is a fulltime job, and you know as well as I that you can't write novels part-time."

"Take a leave. Let someone else manage the foundation for a while. She deserves it."

"We're in the middle of choosing journalism Fellows, and there's no way I can just drop it, David. Maybe, when I retire, I'll get a chance to get back to work on it."

"That's too far off. She needs it now."

We rode up the hill from the river in silence. In front of the house where David was staying, he turned to me.

"Think about it," he said. Then he said, "Please."

It was the first time I ever heard him say the word. And the last.

There was no question about what to do. I cut through the shiny brown tape I'd wrapped around *The Queen of Poland* and began to read.

"Fictionalizing" the story, I had obscured the identities of David and Elżbieta and I'd invented a fictional me as their friend/companion.

In the following excerpt from the book I have de-fictionalized our evening at the theater in 1965. David's David, Elżbieta's Elżbieta, I'm me.

"THE QUEEN OF POLAND"

Chapter IX

Approaching the Theater of Drama across the snowy vastness of Warsaw's Parade Square was like driving onto the set of some Hollywood epic. The theater, extending from one of the corners of the wedding-cake Palace of Culture, was guarded by a heroic stone statue of a seated man and four Doric columns, each three

stories tall. Neon tubing on the frieze spelled out TEATR DRAM-
TYCZNY and turned the watery snow pale blue.

Inside, the theater was a classic European horseshoe, with two
tiers of narrow balconies around the walls. David's seats were
on the first tier, front row. "I hope you don't mind the peanut
gallery," he said, "but they didn't build the orchestra with giants
like me in mind."

The audience was well dressed; business suits and ties, with a
lot of fur collars spread over the seats behind the women. "This
theater draws a kind of literatski aristocracy," David said. "It's the
same sort of crowd you'd get for a Miller play in New York."

The cameo-shaped ceiling lights dimmed and the spots went up
on a three-level stage, with large fake rocks. "Watch for Elżbieta
Czyżewska," David whispered. "She plays Maggie. She's special."

I had seen the play the year before in New York, but time
and the language barrier played tricks on me. I remembered that
"Quentin", who represented Arthur Miller, often spoke to the audience as if it were a psychiatrist, or God. But in Polish, the pathol-
ogy of Quentin's marriage seemed endless, and so did the moral
dilemma of how much to say and what names to name before the
House Un-American Activities Committee. When Elżbieta, playing
Maggie, the Marilyn Monroe character, made her first appearance,
I was watching a play that had been stripped of meaning as well
as language. Because of this, Maggie's entrance had much more
effect on me than it had had in New York.

The dramatic necessity was to shift gears from mind to body,
from intellect to senses. Miller's script did not give an actress
much to work with: a rock and a few passersby to represent a
park, some dumb-bunny lines. A good-looking broad was picking
up a man she knew to be an ascetic intellectual, but Elżbieta re-
sisted the temptation to overplay it. The long-sleeved, high-necked
dress followed her body enough to say woman, but not enough to
shout it. The hair was blonde and loose, but not too loose.

When she sat, the unconscious crossing of the legs, a certain
lilt of the shoulders, the way she looked up at Quentin, a simplic-
ity in her voice, all said I am open, I want to give. I didn't remem-

ber the dialogue exactly something about finding a dog and buying a record but I knew that Elżbieta's performance was saying, "I don't know very much, but I like you because you know a great deal." I remembered one of her lines in English: "Could I sit with you? While you're thinking?"

The audience caught the change in mood. I could feel them settle back with an assurance that the play was beginning to happen to them. Slouched contentedly in my seat, my fingertips forming a kind of rifle sight, I focused my feelings on the lovely girl onstage. I was still like that when the lights came up at the end of the first act and the applause began.

"Terrific, no?" said David.

"Terrific, yes," said I.

In the second act, sensuality rose in Maggie like a bird to the sun. She played nymphet with Quentin, luring him, loving him, beginning to undress him with light fingers, undressing herself. Elżbieta's sense of timing, of rhythm, was perfect. Wrapped in a sheet, she walked away from the audience and toward the bed and Quentin. At the last moment the sheet dropped from her back: she was bare. The effect was spectacularly theatrical; a compulsive gasp rose from the audience.

Elżbieta never faltered. She seeded the wedding scene with doubt, nourished the weeds of ego that sprang up in the early days of the marriage, then harvested a crop of bitterness. She began to drink, to fear the world, to suspect Quentin, to feed on their love, to destroy herself. Her final, suicidal scene wrung the last bit of emotion from the audience; at the blackout there was momentary silence.

Then applause. Standing, beating my hands together, I could sense no one holding back. Curtain calls, first en masse, then individually. The applause intensified for the actor who had played Quentin, then went completely wild when Elżbieta stepped forward.

"Bravo!" I shouted. "Bravo!"

Even when the house lights went up the applause went on. Then, in that most pleasant of East European theatrical customs, the performers began applauding the audience. Not until the actors disappeared from the stage and it was certain that they were not going to return did the applause stop.

Chapter 23

The End of TIME

Before we move on, I should say a few words about TIME, its history, its ownership and its management.

Two young men, Briton Hadden and Henry Robinson Luce, whose friendship was formed at a Connecticut boarding school (Hotchkiss) and Yale University, founded TIME in the early Twentieth Century. They served in the U.S. Army together during World War I, but the war ended before they could be sent overseas. As adults, they were immersed in news and current events, but found daily news*papers* verbose, overly detailed, and boring.

Hadden's ideal publication would convey news and information in the form of *stories* that would be terse, witty and contrary. Luce's would reflect an organization that would be successful, efficiently managed, and prosperous.

Together, they wrote a prospectus, enlisted friends and classmates as writers, editors and business partners and, in 1924, launched TIME, the weekly "news*magazine*." Hadden was the scholar and editor who established TIME's brief, arrogant, and infectious literary "style." He and Luce were supposed to switch back and forth as Chief Executive, and they did for a few years. But during a flu epidemic in 1929, Haddon died of a staph infection.

When I was hired as a TIME writer in 1955, Luce was atop the whole enterprise, which included the business monthly FORTUNE, the struggling new *Sports Illustrated*, the fabulously successful news and photography weekly LIFE, and a couple of unsuccessful publishing experiments, *Architectural Fo-*

rum and *House & Home.*

But also in the '50s, along came television. And not only Television entertainment, journalism, and public-affairs programs, but TV *advertising.* It was
vibrant, compelling, *alive.* Just the thing to convince audiences to buy soup,
beer, breakfast cereal, automobiles, headache remedies, insurance, liquor . . .
just about everything. And in *moving pictures.* Speedy as Alka-Seltzer, advertisers moved their dollars from print to TV.

General-interest magazines felt it first. *Colliers* and *Liberty* went under,
Then *Look.* Then that rock-solid INSTITUTION, Norman Rockwell's (and
my father's) *Saturday Evening Post.*

Time Incorporated looked nervously over its shoulder as *LIFE's* ad revenues began to shrink.TIME was shielded by its 30-year reputation as a font
of serious, in-depth journalism, and I was then editing TIME's Science, Medicine,
Law and Press sections. Serious stuff. All of a sudden, in the eye of the ad-
revenue hurricane, corporate interest focused on Press. I had many friends
in the Press world, was well-known to editors of all sorts of newspapers and
magazines, and had a professionally famous magazine father.

Under the direction of Otto Fuerbringer, my former Managing Editor at
TIME, I went back to inventing new, monthly, special-interest magazines to
take the place of that dying, general-interest weekly giant, LIFE. I moved
into a borrowed office in what's become the *old* Time-Life Building on Sixth
Avenue and 50th Street and dropped in on Otto to ask what had happened
while I was away.

"Welcome back," he said. "Our committee never did meet. But I want you
to start four of the magazines you suggested in the memo you left when you
went off on your sabbatical."

"Four? You want me to start *four* magazines?"

In the previous chapter, I flash-forwarded outrageously – past the six-
month sabbatical from my editorial job at TIME, past the writing (and rewriting and *re*-rewriting) of my dreamed-of novel *The Queen of Poland,* all the
way forward to the deaths of the novel's inspirations, David Halberstam and
Elzbieta Czyzewska.

As you can tell, though, my sabbatical did come to an end. I came down to earth, and went back to work for Time Incorporated's New Magazine Development Committee. But after the War, in the '40s and '50s, along came television. And not only TV entertainment, journalism, and public-affairs programs, but TV *advertising.* It was vibrant, compelling, *alive.* Just the thing to convince audiences to buy soup, beer, breakfast cereal, automobiles, headache remedies, insurance, liquor ... just about everything. Speedy as Alka-Seltzer, advertisers moved their dollars from print to TV. General-interest magazines were the first to feel it. *Colliers* and *Liberty* went under, Then that rock-solid institution, Norman Rockwell's (and my father's) *Saturday Evening Post.*

Time Incorporated looked nervously over its shoulder as *Look* disappeared. I was then editing TIME's Science, Medicine, Law and Press sections, but all of a sudden the greatest of these was Press. I had many friends in the Press world, was well-known to editors of all sorts of newspapers and magazines, had a professionally famous magazine father.

Under the direction of Otto Fuerbringer, my former Managing Editor at TIME, I went back to inventing new, monthly, special-interest magazines to take the place of that dying, general-interest weekly giant, LIFE. I moved into a borrowed office in what's become the *old* Time-Life Building on Sixth Avenue and 50th Street and dropped in on Otto to ask what had happened while I was away.

"Welcome back," he said. "Our committee never did meet. But I want you to start four of the magazines you suggested in the memo you left when you went off on your sabbatical."

"Four? You want me to start *four* magazines?"

"Yes, but I want *real* magazines, not just dummies with blank type. They all have to be TIME-size, and I want real articles, by real writers, with original art work, cover design and photos. We can use old ads from TIME or *Sports Illustrated* to show how the advertising would look, but I want good, new, actual articles to show what we would be doing if we were already publishing."

"*Four* magazines?"

"Right. The one on health, the one on personal financial management, the one on photography and the one on film and television. There's a reason for the photography magazine. LIFE still has a flock of famous photographers on long-term contracts, and their salaries will go on even after the magazine folds. We might as well get some good out of their name and fame, and the money we'll have to throw at them. We can sign them on for quality picture spreads and quality advice for serious amateur photographers."

"I'm not the right editor for that one," I said. "We need an editor who knows photography and photographers. We need a retread from LIFE."

"You've got a point," said Otto. "But you edited TIME's Medicine, Science, Press, Show Business, Theater, Cinema, and TV Sections for a lot of years. Even the Music Section. You should be able to land running."

"I can run, but I can't hide," I said. "Let's do one magazine at a time. Which one do you want first?"

"Which one would take the least time?"

"Since I've been away, and since it will take me a bit of doing to get back in synch with Show Business people, I think the Health magazine could be done faster. Gil Cant (Gilbert Cant, the for-ever, rock-solid senior writer in TIME's Medicine Section) is always on top of what's new in medical practice, and he can smell fakery a mile away."

"Okay. We'll need a prospectus, and I'll find you an art director to do the initial design proposal. What'll we call it?"

"HEALTH would be the obvious favorite, but we'll need to research the availability of the title."

"I'll start the research," Otto said. "You get busy on that prospectus."

As it turned out, "Health" was already registered (as I recall) to the American Osteopathic Society. I thrashed around with several alternate titles, but ended up with "Well." Otto was not totally taken with the name, but there were precious few health-related magazine names that weren't already the copyrighted trademark of some group or other.

I struggled with the prospectus. All Time Inc. publications (LIFE, TIME,

Fortune and Sports Illustrated) had started out with a prospectus, and the health magazine was to be no exception.

"Americans have a right to good health" I began – "a right to be well." I would have italicized "well", but we didn't have computers in those days, and I was using my standard Royal typewriter.

I went on: "The phrase rings true. It beggars contradiction. It has become a cliché in the rhetoric of politicians and the texts of books on medicine and current affairs. But it is far from a reality.

"What Americans have is a potential for wellness. American physicians are the best in the world and there are more of them per 1,000 population than in such countries as Sweden or England. American hospitals endlessly seek and get the finest equipment and the most accomplished personnel. American researchers have found ways of curing or preventing diseases that have defied man for centuries, and they are ceaselessly working to find cures or preventatives for those that still remain.

"Yet in 1969 it has become a drearily familiar fact that 14 nations have better infant mortality rates than the U.S., that male adults in 18 other nations live longer than men in the U.S., that women in five nations live longer than American women. Since America is a nation where wrongs are righted, it comes as a shock that the latest World Health Organization figures show that things have gotten worse, not better. In the latest figures, recently released, the U.S. has slipped to 17th in the world in infant mortality, to 25th in male longevity, to eighth in female longevity..."

The prospectus went on from there ... 33 pages all together, if you count 12 "appendix" pages of the names of possible story-subjects for the first issues.

Beyond a prospectus, for my first issue I needed writers – the best I could find – and topics – the most interesting and compelling imaginable. I bought, and read voraciously, every magazine and newspaper dealing with health and medicine in the United States, Canada, Australia, or England. I clipped articles and made lists of writers. I hung clipboards on my office walls by topic: Food and Nutrition; Child Care and Growth; The Major Diseases (Heart, Stroke, Cancer); Aging; Sex; The Downers (Drug abuse, Alcoholism, Overeat-

ing), Geriatrics (Nursing homes, diseases of the elderly); Exercise and Rehabilitation... I had to have wooden strips installed to hold more cup hooks
and more clipboards.

I collected the phone numbers and addresses of writers about medicine and
health and began calling them for lunches and dinners. I stayed away from
people at other companies or magazines that might be interested in starting
competitive publications, or borrowing or adapting my ideas into writing that
might undercut the originality, or quality, or *idea,* of *Well.*

With in-house or out-house writers and editors of high quality I shared
some of the details of my project and search. I was particularly frank with
two medicine/health writers at the *New York Times*, Jane Brody and Lawrence
("Larry") Altman. Managing TIME's Medicine and Science Sections, I had
borrowed story ideas from them for years, and I knew they kept their eyes
and minds peeled for the same topics and subjects that Gilbert Cant (and
Jean Bergerud, our savvy Medicine-Section researcher) and I did.

Jane Brody was particularly good at spotting trends and personal-health
topics. Indeed, she had personally encountered some of the same problems
as had confronted her readers – and me, for that matter, specifically pain-
filled knees. She had investigated – and written about them – compellingly
and well.

I had many lunches and dinners with Jane and her husband, not just in
New York restaurants, but at their wonderfully restored Victorian house in
the Park Slope district of Brooklyn. I told both Jane and Larry what I was
up to, and told them that if the *Well* idea worked, I wanted them to be Senior Editors of the magazine. They liked the idea. We didn't talk salary, but
it was well known in the magazine world that Time Inc. paid top dollar.

I asked them for story ideas, and one of Jane's was particularly irresistible.
Her husband was gay, she told me. She was the family bread-winner, and he
was the house-husband who managed the home and raised their two small
sons. They wanted the boys to grow up naturally and normally, and so he had
to arrange for their living and early education in as genderless a way as possible. Doing this required imagination, and research, and skill, and he was will-

ing and ready to work with Jane to do articles – or series of articles – about it.

Jane had already written – well and thoroughlyfor the *Times* about the relatively new understanding that cervical cancer was a venereal disease, caused by a virus called Herpes 2 and spread (like gonorrhea) by sexual contact. For *Well,* she dug deeper into the implications of this discovery and predicted the development of a vaccine.

Jill Krementz, a photographer I'd worked with at TIME, knew a successful sugar broker named Dan Dyer, who'd prepared to die after two heart attacks. He couldn't walk half a mile without medication and rest; he'd wound up his financial affairs; his company had prepared his obituary. Then he heard about new open-heart surgery, studied up on it, and went through with it. He described the experience, the rehabilitation – and how he and his son won the father-son doubles championship at the Bronxville Field Club.

Jane Brody introduced me to a friend, a child psychologist and mother-of-four named Sara Stein. Sara had looked into early-learning techniques of toilet-training and reading, revised them, and put them into a practical format. We assigned a photographer to work with her and produce an eight-page, how-to, color-picture essay on how to be a relaxed, natural "super-mother."

While this was going on, I did research and some traveling. "It's an interesting time for you to visit me," said Julius Richmond, founder of the Head Start Program and a professor of Psychiatry at Harvard Medical School. "As of July 1, in addition to my responsibilities here (he was also chief psychiatrist at Children's Hospital in Boston, where I was interviewing him), I'm becoming Chair of the new Department of Preventive and Social Medicine at the Medical School, which will presumably be the department that's concerned with what you're talking about."

Elliott Richardson, then Secretary of Health, Education and Welfare, said the predictable: "It can be demonstrated that significant improvements in our health status will come about more through prevention of accidents and chronic disease than through improvements in curative medicine."

Dr. Paul Denson, chairman of Harvard's School of Community Health, understood immediately what we were up to. "Your mission," he said, "is to make it clear to your reader what good health care means to him as an individual."

"I think that one of the services that might be provided by your magazine," said Robert Ebert, dean of the Harvard Medical School, "would be to try in an editorial way to give what's needed – insight into social issues." The administrator of Mass General Hospital, John Knowles, said that "what the individual lacks is *knowing;* this is 50 percent the fault of the medical consumer and 50 percent our fault – the fault of those who provide medical service."

"*Well,*" I wrote prospectively, "must provide individuals with the knowledge they need – with the services they need – to help them cope with their own physical and emotional frailties, with the well-being of their families, with the public health of their communities and with the social health of their nation."

High-falutin' stuff, but I was writing about a health magazine to be published by *Time Incorporated.* The best short definition of "wellness" I could find was the World Health Organization's: "A state of complete physical, mental and social well-being, and not merely the absence of disease and infirmity."

You can take the boy out of Dartmouth, but you can't take Dartmouth out of the boy. Summing up, I harked back to my alma mater's Latin motto: *Vox clamantis in deserto* – A Voice Crying out in the Wilderness.

"*Well* will not be a lonely voice crying out in an unhealthy wilderness. It will be part of a growing, fundamental change in American attitudes toward medicine and health care – a change that is beginning to be known as 'The Wellness Approach.' We use the phrase as the title of the lead article in our prototype issue – the article putting forth the rationale and motivation of our magazine."

Otto top-edited the articles, an in-house designer pulled together a prototype issue, and *Well* was on its way. Or so I thought.

Chapter 24

Tarzie

When he died in September 1993 the official first name in his obituary was Varindra, but everyone called him "Tarzie." Why Tarzie? Tarzie Vittachi's father, a schoolmaster in the Sri Lanka village of Gampaha just north of Colombo, had 12 younger children. But the agility of his firstborn — Varindra — in trees in the garden and surrounding forest – won him the nickname "Tarzan." Chums quickly abbreviated this to Tarzie.

Tarzie's 1944 university degree was in economics, but he switched careers from banking to journalism in 1950. He had a gift for satire and a nose for corruption, and by 1951 his columns ("Cursory Glances" and "Bouquets and Brickbats") in the *Ceylon Daily News* won him the editorship of the newspaper and an arrest order from Prime Minister Solomon (S.W.R.D.) Bandaranaike. Before it could be served, Tarzie had flown off to Kuala Lumpur, in Malaysia, where he started the International Press Institute, and Manila, in the Philippines, where he launched the Asia Press Foundation.

Tarzie continued using his columns to chip away at arrogance and self-dealing in the Bandaranaike government. At one point, For his personal safety's sake, he was "exiled" to Britain as London editor for the Associated Newspapers of Ceylon, Ltd. "Forgiven" in 1952, he returned to Colombo at age 32 to take over the *Ceylon Observer,* the oldest English-Language newspaper in Asia and (in his words), "a stodgy journal playing second fiddle to other dailies."

Tarzie Vittachi, a journalist and executive of Unicef (1980-1988), wrote and lectured extensively about poverty in underdeveloped countries.

Bandaranaike was assassinated in 1959, and succeeded by his widow, Sirimavo. Threatening Tarzie bodily harm, her obedient subordinates chased him into airborne asylum in Britain. ("I write well at thirty-three thousand feet," he later told me). When I met him in Manhattan in early-summer 1978 Tarzie was an accomplished editor, a spell-binding story-teller, a collector of people and a collectible person himself. Small, brown, round and irresistible to women, he looked like a miniature Buddha. He spoke in straightforward, nonmysterious parables and had a gift for phraseology. Once, when asked to moderate a panel of U.N. communications people on child abuse, he looked thoughtfully over the 25 or 30 people gathered in front of him. Then he mused aloud: "Child abuse... Child abuse... Hmmm..."

Then he raised his voice: "All right. All those in favor of child abuse, raise your hand."

Eyebrows went up, but no hand.

"Good," he said. "Now we can get down to business."

At the time of our first encounter Tarzie had moved up and out of Sri Lankan journalism, was on many international boards promoting freedom of the Press, and was Director of Publications and Programs for the United Nations Fund for Population Activities, based in New York. He controlled a sizable pot of money for international conferences, writing and activities.

It was 1978. I was putting Time Incorporated behind me and had been elected Executive Director of the Institute of Current World Affairs (ICWA) and the American Universities Field Staff (AUFS). John O'Neill, a friend and seminal ICWA Trustee, had insisted that as part of the change process I *had* to meet Tarzie. I was still winding down my Senior Editorship at *Money* magazine, and Tarzie and I met in New York on a July evening in the bar of the U.N. Plaza Hotel.

As it turned out, Tarzie and I had a lot of friends in common. A 1958 book he had written about riots aimed by Sri Lanka's Sinhalese majority at the island's immigrant Tamil minority had won that year's Magsaysay Award for international leadership in Asia. The Award, named for a great postwar Philippine president, had been the brainchild of ICWA Trustee and AUFS

Albert Victor Ravenholt

Asia expert Albert Ravenholt and his wife Marjorie, who were close to John D. Rockefeller III. Tarzie knew both Ravenholts well, and had attended the prize-giving.

Willard Hanna, an AUFS professor fluent in Bahasa Indonesian and Dutch who taught Indonesian social and political history, was a good friend of a legendary anti-Soekarno Indonesian journalist named Mochtar Lubis — and so was Tarzie, who'd made a personal visit to Soekarno to try to get Lubis out of jail.

And so on, and on, and on. Names of people we both knew got dropped: Bob Semple, Foreign Editor of the *New York Times;* Harry Evans, Editor of the *Times* of London; C.K. McClatchy of California's *Bee* Papers; Frank McCulloch, a crackerjack correspondent for TIME who'd become editor of the *San Francisco Examiner;* Phil Foisie of the *International Herald Tribune;* Stan Karnow, legendary Time magazine Hong Kong Bureau Chief and writer on Vietnam ...

As ice melted around my martini olive and we found out who we had been and who we *were,* Tarzie said to me, in his no-nonsense voice: "You're coming to an international press gathering this fall. It's being funded by Jonas Salk and his Epoch B Foundation. We'll be inviting everyone who matters in international journalism. That includes you. We know *when* it will be, but we don't know *where* it will be. We need a place *near* New York but not *of* New York. We need a magical place where people will spend all day thinking, and not on the phone to their offices. We need a kind of dreamland where the unimaginable can be imagined, where nature rules instead of technology, where we can spend four or five days talking about possibilities instead of cursing the impossible. Do you know such a place?"

"You're talking about Mohonk," I said.

"Mohonk?"

"Yes, Mohonk Mountain Lodge. It's in the Catskill Mountains, about an hour and half drive north of Manhattan. It's on a plateau, high above the rest of the world. The buildings are rustic, faced in stone and the bark of sawmill logs, but the rooms are comfortable and quiet. There's a deep, cold lake at its center and the food comes from farms in the valleys below. Drink is to be had, but you don't think about it 'til the end of the day, when it's time to think about it. My foundation holds its spring and autumn meetings there. The place separates us from the world and carries us to the wild and unknown international places where our Fellows will be spending a year or two, growing into their intellectual skins, and learning."

"Expensive?" said Tarzie.

"A *bit*," I said, "but not *very*."

"Can we go there this weekend?"

"I don't know why not," I said.

That Friday Tarzie, his son Imran — then about nine or ten years old — and I were in a Mercedes Tarzie had borrowed from someone, headed up the New York Thruway toward New Paltz, west of the Hudson River. By then I knew a bit about Jonas Salk and I found out more as we drove. He was the famous inventor of a vaccine that had "conquered" poliomyelitis, the "infantile paralysis" that had killed or crippled tens of thousands — *hundreds* of thousands — of children and adults around the world for decades. Franklin Roosevelt was its most famous victim, the March of Dimes its most famous adversary. His reward had been creation of a Salk Institute on the California coast north of San Diego. He had clout and, obviously, money.

How was he connected to Tarzie? The "Third World" (aka "The Under-Developed World", "The Poor World", "The South"), was being increasingly talked about in the 1970's. Our world ("The West," "Industrialized Nations", "The Developed World", "The North", "The Rich World") was the "First World." Communist and Socialist countries (in East Europe, China, a few bits of Africa, the Middle East and Latin America) were the "Second World."

A few enlightened internationalists had taken up the cudgels on behalf of the Third World, feeling that it was a breeding ground for conflict — possibly armed conflict — between haves and have-nots, between the well-fed and the hungry, the powerful and the downtrodden. They felt that money, global attention and development help had to be focused on the have-nots, particularly in the press and the media. Tarzie was one of these engaged internationalists. He had met Jonas Salk somewhere on his normal rounds, just as I had met Tarzie. They worked together like coffee and *latte*.

As we drove, I learned quite a bit more. Salk was married to one of Pablo Picasso's favorite mistresses, Françoise Gilot, who'd become a well-bought painter in her own right. Despite the fancy Salk Institute complex, and an immense suite of Pacific-facing offices and conference rooms in a brutalist-concrete temple designed by famed architect Louis Kahn, Salk had very little to do with biological research going on there. Scientists in residence — plant scientists, specialists in aging, distinguished biologists, visiting Fellows — rarely consulted with him, considering him more an accidental hero than a working biologist, more figurehead than fountainhead.

With little to do with medical problems, Salk had turned to societal problems — particularly the population "bomb" that was exploding, particularly in the Third World. This, of course, was Tarzie's territory at the U.N. Fund for Population Activities. The well-fed, well-employed populations of the "North" were approaching stability; death rates were catching up with birth rates, and where they weren't, full employment was making up the difference. In Sweden, prosperity, low joblessness, birth control and great education had actually reversed the equation, and the population was declining.

No such progress had been made in the Third World. There, parents were having five, six, or more children to earn family food and make up for high infant- and child-mortality rates. The world population had passed 3 billion and would almost certainly go past 6 billion by the end of the century. Already, every three or four seconds, someone died of hunger in the Third World. Before the end of the 20th Century, global population would probably reach between 8 and 12 billion. Tarzie chuckled that his borrowed Mercedes could do 100 miles an hour — but nothing, he said, compared to a world birth-rate of 10,000 *babies* an hour.

We had to wake up to the crash that was surely coming, Tarzie said, and that was the reason for Salk's population conference. Salk had begun contributing all his consulting and speaking fees to an "Epoch B Foundation", and the foundation was going to pay to bring the world's leading editors together to hear his message. And, if Tarzie had anything to do about it, spread it.

We veered off the Thruway at New Paltz, drove through town, and stopped at the Mohonk gate house. We were expected; Tarzie seemed casual and off-hand, but he'd phoned ahead and booked a double for him and Imran, and a single for me. We drove up the long drive through the woods and stopped at the car-park. Our bags were taken, and among Tarzie's things I noticed the kind of flimsy, un-serious fishing pole a neglectful father picks up at a toy store before a trip to the country with a neglected urban son. We walked on to the Lodge.

"No more internal combustion engines," I said. "At Mohonk it's either foot-power or horse-power."

We met on the dock overlooking the impossibly blue lake outside the library. Happy kids were loading themselves into canoes and setting off toward the far end. Carriages clip-clopped by. We walked along the dock until it merged with a hiking trail on the left, leading upwards. The trail was smooth, paved with tanbark, and as we strolled uphill the sounds of the dock and the carriage trail faded into stillness. Trees and woods closed in on the sides of the path. Every few hundred yards, the trees on the right thinned and a rustic, covered bench jutted from the side of the trail, overlooking farms, cows and meadows far below.

After 20 or 25 minutes we veered toward one of the benches. There was plenty of support beneath us, but because of our height over the farmland below, we got the feeling that our feet were swinging in the air and we were somehow suspended over the countryside, maybe over the world.

We were quiet. Then, from Tarzie: "Joseph Smith said it. This is *the place.*"

We walked and talked for another hour. Tarzie found the entire plateau other-worldly. We met very few people. Tarzie wondered why. "A lot of them prefer horse-drawn carriages, or to ride horseback," I said. "They have completely different trails."

Over supper (braised beef, fresh string beans, corn on the cob, Finger-Lakes merlot, milk for Imran) Tarzie raved about the simple dining room, the rustic charm of the mountain lodge, the atmosphere, the farm-girl waitresses. It was as though he'd introduced *me* to Mohonk, rather than the other way around.

There was no sign of Tarzie and Imran at breakfast the next morning. I was reading the *New York Times* in the library when he and Imran came in. "It's settled," Tarzie said. "We're meeting here the second week in October."

"This year?" I said. "That's fall-foliage season, Tarzie. People reserve months ahead. The place has got to be fully booked."

"It was, and it still is," said Tarzie. "I just had a serious talk with Mr. Smiley, one of the brothers who own Mohonk. He's a good Quaker, and he came to understand how important our meeting is. He's squeezing us in."

"That's got to be some kind of miracle, Tarzie."

"Sorry to miss you at breakfast," he said. "Imran and I went fishing. We caught two fish."

"In that lake? With that tackle? That's even more a miracle."

"Imran's a very good fisherman," Tarzie said.

"So are you," I said.

Full of quiet satisfaction, we drove back to Manhattan that afternoon.

Chapter 25

Deanna Donovan, Fellow

I don't precisely recall what we talked about on the trip from New Paltz to New York, but it probably was about the change taking place in my life. Without an immensity of soul-searching, I was ending two pleasurable decades as a well-rewarded editor for national publications (TIME and *Money*), and beginning the life of a not-so-well paid director of a small foundation whose job (*calling? Responsibility?*) was to identify promising young international-affairs writers and thinkers and provide them with long (two-year) fellowships in regions and countries of the world in need of greater and deeper U.S. understanding. They needed to have, or get, the language of the part of the world they were studying, and write monthly reports of what they found going on around them. Through the Fellows and their published reports, I and their readers would learn how the world and its people worked, and struggled, and agonized, and muddled through, and sometimes succeeded. Through me, the Fellows would learn grammar, and style, and sentence rhythm, and deadlines, and the tedium and joys of thinking things through on paper.

The Director who preceded me believed that a foundation's resources were there to *spend,* and he had done this so well that the Institute of Current World Affairs' *corpus* (an appropriate term) was down from $4 million to $1.8 million. This sounds like a lot of money, but prudent budgeting required that a foundation that intended to stay in business spend only 5 percent of its capital each year — in our case, $90,000. This was supposed to cover rent, utilities, communications, staff salaries, legal costs, Trustee meetings, travel, insurance, taxes (yes, even *taxes,* on investment income), and the Fellows' living and learning costs. It didn't. My personal income, which had been around $140,000 a year at Time Inc. (including stock options and an annual bonus) had been cut to $40,000 — $20,000 from ICWA and $20,000 from the AUFS.

A loyal friend of the foundation, who owed his family's wealth to the timber industry, had become concerned about the world's dwindling forest resources and the Institute's dwindling financial resources and had provided us with a contribution to support two bare-bones, super-economy "Forest and Man" fellowships. (In those simpler days, "Man" meant "mankind" or "humankind" and had no sexist implications; today, the fellowships are called "Forest and Society" Fellowships.)

One of the first Fellows — Deanna Donovan — was studying the effect on forest resources of a Nepali Government campaign to bring peasants into the money economy by encouraging their production of items of cottage industry: dried cardamom, bricks, ceramic roof tiles, carpets, handwoven fabrics, for example. They did this despite the fact that Nepal's only energy source was fuelwood, and the government had no reliable knowledge of the impact of cottage-industry on the nation's forests. One impact was increasingly visible to the naked eye: deforestation of hills and mountainsides, landslides, and erosion of farmland.

Deanna's fellowship was to enable her to determine (and report to the government) how many measurable units of fuelwood (kilos, cubic meters) were required to produce measurable units of cottage industry (kilos of cardamom, hundreds of bricks, square meters of carpet. etc). To do this she lived in the capital, Kathmandu, during the rainy season when overland hiking was impossible, reinforcing her health with vitamins and a careful diet. During the dry season, she went "trekking" through farms and villages gathering data and experience as she watched Nepalis dry cardamom, bake roof tiles and boil carpet dyes. They were nervous about this blonde, blue-eyed person measuring and note-taking (Was this some government scheme to wring more taxes from them?) but she spoke their language and overcame their suspicions by living with them, eating their food, and — inevitably — sharing the predictable results: dysentery, diarrhea, stomach infections, mysterious fevers, gut pains and general all-around weakness. When the rains began again, she went "home" to Nirmala, her housekeeper in Kathmandu, to recover her health, write up her reports, and husband her strength and energy for the next trekking season.

Her second trekking season had ended a few weeks before my trip to Mohonk with Tarzie, and she was supposedly home with Nirmala. But I had not heard from her. In those Internetless, E-mail-less days, communication was only by typewritten letters on paper, and no letters arrived from Deanna. Telephone communication was virtually nonexistent on the far side of the Himalayas. No matter how I dialed or worked through operators, I could not get through, and U.S. Embassy diplomats, tired of listening to the tales and wails of relatives and associates of incommunicative young Americans who'd traveled to Nepal for mountain and other highs, could not — or would not — find Deanna. My right brain told me to go to Kathmandu and find out where — and how — Deanna was faring. My left brain — and the foundation bank account balance sheet — told me we did not have enough money for such a venture.

I was worried. And I told Tarzie about it. At that 10,000-a-day-birth rate he must have had a million things to do, but every five or six days he phoned to hear whether I'd heard from Deanna.

Around the time of my third or fourth "No," he asked: "Have you ever been to Sri Lanka?"

"No," I said.

"That's a serious gap in your education," said Tarzie. "There's a population conference for international parliamentarians beginning in Colombo in ten days, and the Fund for Population Activities feels strongly that an American journalist ought to be there. We'd fund your round-trip from New York and a room in Sri Lanka. And every Wednesday, there's an Air Lanka flight from Colombo to Kathmandu that comes back the same day. That could give you a week or two or three between Wednesdays to find Deanna and find out how she is. Does this sound interesting?"

"It certainly does," I said.

"You need to get a Sri Lanka visa," he said, "and one for Nepal. And while you're at it, get an India visa as well. That plane often has to lay over in India for a day or two, and if it does, you should get out of the airport for a walkabout. I'll give you a phone number for the U.N. travel office in New York. It's in the Secretariat Building. Tell them you're participating in the UNFPA conference in Colombo. They'll have your name."

"Tarzie, I don't know how to thank you."

"Thank the UN, Peter. That's why we're here."

Tarzie was right about Sri Lanka. I have a soft spot in my head and heart for former colonies where authentic and bar-sinister offspring of British aristocracies went out to take up the white man's burden and plant tea, tung nuts, tobacco, sugar or coffee. It's probably my father's fault; he grew up in chivalrous Virginia in the 1890s, and in his formative pre-manhood years absorbed and adored the bound Christmas editions of a British boys' annual called "Chatterbox." In Chatterbox, the sun never set on a British lighthouse, or on British pluck and luck. I inherited all his copies, as well as his complete collection of the works of an intrepid British foreign correspondent and glorifier of the British Empire, G.A. (George Alfred) Henty ("With Clive in India," "With Kitchener in The Soudan," "With Buller in Natal" ...)

Gloriously unreal resonances of British imperial life and attitudes thrum within me whenever I land in a former colony redolent of *lapsang soochang* tea, and where places, lakes and palaces are named "Victoria" and/or "Albert." Sri Lanka (*aka* Ceylon) is such a place.

My billet for the population conference was the Mt. Lavinia Hotel, on the Indian Ocean coast south of Colombo. My father would have loved it. Woodbladed fans swirled above the canopy bed, the bathtub was set on cloven iron legs so high you needed a short flight of steps to get in and out over the sides. The mahogany wardrobe doors shrieked in warped protest when you closed them, and the balcony overlooked a brownish sand beach that seemed to stretch for miles.

Unpacked, I went down to the pool terrace. It sat above a palm-fringed lagoon that curled in from the sea. The lagoon and the trees around it seemed uncannily familiar. Looking down for several moments, I had that out-of-body feeling of true *déjà vue*. A waiter came over as I stood there, transfixed, and asked if I would like tea.

"Not just now," I said. "But tell me: Why does this place look so famil-iar?" I pointed down to the palm trees and the lagoon.

"You've seen it at the cinema," he said. "This is where they filmed William Holden, dragging his empty canteen and dying of thirst, reaching safety in *Bridge on the River Kwai*."

"My goodness!" I said. "You're right! I see it now."

"Tea, sir?" He pointed toward the tables and chairs near the pool.

I looked. There, with teapot, cup and saucer, sat Lester Brown, head of the New York-based WorldWatch Institute. Lester had invented and founded WorldWatch to carry out in-depth research about major environmental prob-lems and publish long, substantive reports about them, one by one, month by month. He had a large, able staff of researchers and writers, funded, I think, by the Rockefeller Foundation, and was one of the heroes of the international not-for-profit world. Lester was working on a tall stack of 8x10 paper under a shady umbrella. I walked over.

"Lester!" I said. "What brings you here?"

"Probably what brings you here. The population conference. I came out with Chuck Percy."

"And what's that?" I said, pointing to the pile of paper.

"That's my chicken," he said.

"Your chicken?"

"My chicken. When I was a boy growing up in Indiana, my dog killed one of my father's chickens. To teach the dog a lesson, my father took a piece of rope and tied the chicken to the dog's neck, so he couldn't shake it off, or pull it off. The dog had to walk with it, sit with it, sleep with it, and drag it ev-erywhere as it rotted and decayed. The idea was to teach him, Never again."

He paused and looked up.

"This is my chicken, Peter," he said. "It's my manuscript about the future of the American automobile. I've been carrying it around for months, trying to get it ready for publication."

It sank in, a powerful metaphor for many undone things in my life. Ever since, when I've returned from a trip and the person I rely on asks about the article I carried off in my shoulder bag to read or edit, the answer has become predictable: "It's in my chicken."

Tarzie was right about Sri Lanka. Not having gone there was a serious gap in my global education. I was able to buy lovely sapphires (the color of the eyes of my then-fiancee Lu) just south of Colombo, to travel from lush-green Kandy tea plantations to Trincomalee (before it silted up, the bay was wide enough and deep enough to shelter the entire 19th-Century British fleet), from the famous interconnected "tanks" that provided enough trickle-down irrigation to grow rice for the entire island population in the 18th Century, to Jaffna at the northern top of the tear-drop, then trembling on the verge of ten or 20 years of rebellion by the Tamil Tigers of Eelam. But this is the stuff of a different chapter.

My most vivid memory of the flight from Colombo to Kathmandu was a swoop around Mt. Everest that the pilot threw in as a bonus. Then, landing, and there was Deanna. Her smile and bright turquoise eyes on the far side of the immigration maze were the happiest sight any foundation director could ever have.

She was all right — a bit weak, but all right. As I'd guessed, she'd gone trekking, living with peasants who were drying cardamom, weighing their output, measuring the wood they were burning as fuel, asking questions. ("You used a *baht* of wood? How big is a *baht*? Show me one. Green wood or dry wood? From what tree? May I measure? How many kilos of cardamom? Was there any waste? What do you do with it?") She'd walked from plot to plot, taking notes and photographs, measuring wood piles, eating local stews and vegetables, crouching over squat toilets, walking or riding to the next village.

As night follows day and dry seasons follow wet, she had gone home to Kathmandu and Nirmala to get over inevitable diarrhea and gut ailments. She figured she probably had dysentery, and went to the local hospital. She was right, and began treatment with antibiotics. She didn't get better, though. She got worse. She was too weak get out of bed, too weak and disoriented to write to me in Hanover, unable to do anything. Nirmala was frantic, but had no understanding of how to help.

Then, fortunately, a friend of hers who was part of a German development team stopped by. When he learned what was happening, he collected a stool specimen and mailed it off to his team's medical contact in Bangkok. Back came the response: Deanna had a second, more serious strain of amoebic dysentery, unresponsive to the medication she was taking for the first. New prescriptions were ordered, and by the time I arrived, Deanna was on the mend. She'd finally received a cable from Hanover about my travel plans, sent long after I'd left for Sri Lanka, and was at the airport to meet me.

We had a glorious week — one of those times in Nepal where the blood of sacrificed animals literally flows in the gutters, prayer wheels twirl and prayer banners flutter in Himalayan breezes. The then-ambassador was an old friend of Phil Talbot, a fellow ICWA Trustee who'd founded the American Universities Field Staff before becoming Assistant Secretary of State for the Middle East and South Asia. I used Phil's name to get Deanna and me invited to lunch at the Residence. One of his aides gave me a conversational opening by recalling tired old rumors that the Field Staff's Afghanistan expert, Louis Dupree, was actually a CIA spook. I laid that old falsehood to rest by reminding all assembled of Phil's straight-arrow reputation, and Deanna was then able to chime in with her account of being turned away like some no-account hippie when she tried to find a sympathetic medico at the Embassy. All ended cheerfully after I told the assemblage that Deanna was receiving special supplemental funding from the Rockefeller Foundation because her project was so valuable. Mr. Ambassador gave Deanna his direct-line phone number in case of future problems, and we parted friends.

Chapter 26

Mohonk

Back in the good old USA in the autumn of 1978, the Epoch B conference at Mohonk happened. From around the world came friends of Tarzie's, friends of Jonas Salk's, friends of mine.

Bob Semple (then the new Foreign Editor of the *New York Times*) was there. So were Lester Brown, Harry Evans (editor of Rupert Murdoch's latest acquisition, the *Times* of London), Jim Rose (editor of Viking Books and Britain's Westminster Press newspaper chain), Phil Foisie (editor of the International Herald Tribune), Tom Winship (editor of the *Boston Globe*), Tina Brown (girl friend of Harry Evans and glamorous and smart-as-hell editor of British *Vanity Fair*). There were editors from across Canada and the U.S., from Scandinavia, Sri Lanka, Australia, Scotland, Japan... In they came, arriving at Mohonk Monday afternoon for a party that got warmer and warmer, and drinks, and dinner, and a gathering Tuesday morning in the Mohonk library.

As Tarzie and I hoped, they were dazzled by the towering apartness of Mohonk, surrounded by hills of southern New England gone drunk with autumn color. They walked the walks, gawked the valley from the rustic gazebos, paddled the canoes, doused their pancakes with maple syrup, and fought each other over rare morning copies of the *New York Times*. Then we all gathered in the library to be welcomed by Tarzie.

Tarzie was a master of self-deprecating humor mixed with contagious caring for the world's hungry. The trouble with poverty," he said, "is, it's boring. You can get people's attention with a story that says, 'Five million four hundred thirty-two thousand six hundred ninety-six children went to bed hungry last night. Six hundred thousand of them died.'"

But then there's the problem of the second-day story. It would have to say, 'Five million four hundred forty-two thousand seven hundred eighty-four children went to bed hungry last night. Six hundred thousand of them died.' And then there's the third day: "Five million seven hundred twenty-two thousand four hundred sixty-six children went to bed hungry last night. Six hundred thousand of them died." And the fourth day. And the fifth."

"Poverty is repetitious," he said. There's no variety to it. As Elizabeth Taylor's eighth husband said on his wedding night, 'I know what to do. But I'm not sure I know how to make it interesting.'"

It's already a commonplace that the world has entered the Information Age. Like all truisms, it is true. But as with all truisms, its very glibness and pretensions to being comprehensive, hide a multitude of misrepresentations and half-truths. As a writer, a merchant of words for the past 35 years, I know the weight of words and how they can be counterfeited to undermine the value of what is communicated, and so I am deeply suspicious when big words like "world" are used. Let me ask you therefore to reflect with me on that statement: 'The world has entered the Information Age.'"

"What world? Have the share-cropping peasants in Uttar Pradesh or Kalimantan or the Karamoja in Uganda or on the border of Venezuela and Colombia entered the Information Age? Have the mothers and fathers of Asia, Africa, Latin America and the Arabic speaking people, and their young children, who make up two thirds of our planet's population entered the Information Age? Do they have access to the free flow of communications that the Western media speak of? Do they have the literacy or the material means to participate actively in that flow of communications or to even the most rudimentary technology of communication?"

Yes, some of them, the fortunate few, do. But how many? For instance, of the 400 million telephone subscribers listed in 1978 only 30 million were from the Third World. Spread the number over the populous countries of the South and we may realize how thinly distributed it is — a means of communication that people in the West have taken for granted as an essential means of existence for one hundred years. Even newspapers and other means of purveying the printed word, so familiar to us in this room, have only a very narrow outreach in the materially poor regions of the world."

On the arc stretching from Kabul to Tokyo — excluding the communist countries for that I have no figures — of the 1.4 billion people, only 92 million read a daily newspaper. And of these, 63 million are Japanese and 11 million Indians. In the whole of the rest of Asia — including Pakistan's 77 million people, Bangladesh's 90 million, Indonesia's 150 million — and the Caribbean's 46 million and so on, only 18 million daily newspapers are sold. The diffusion rate is, as you can figure, minute. And most of that readership is an urban or suburban readership."

The reasons for this thin diffusion of the printed press are not hard to find. The chief among them is that for an average customer in Bangladesh or Indonesia, it costs 5 to 7 times what it costs the average Japanese, European or North American in terms of relative income. And the reason for *that* is that 90 percent of the material means of producing a newspaper — the typesetting machines, the press, paper, ink, the delivery trucks — are imported from the industrialized countries where costs of living are much higher and where the profits earned from exports largely determine their standards of living. It is interesting to realize that 90 percent of the cost of printing a newspaper starts after the editor has handed over the copy to the printing room; the journalist is the cheapest factor of production in the whole operation."

No, ladies and gentlemen. The world has not entered the Information Age — at least, not three quarters of the people, except as passive, alienated, sentient beings whose lives are going to be profoundly affected by the technological changes that are taking place in the industrialized countries where the gadgetry and systems of collecting, storing, and selling information are advancing in capacity and quality of performance each year while most of the people of the planet gaze at them like children listening to a fast-talking and incomprehensible magician performing his tricks."

The Third World is being left far behind in the hectic race to dominate the new technology that will, without doubt, change their lives without any chance of influencing the content of communications and the use made if it by those who control it. Already the Americans have gained the dominant share of the market — estimates vary from 40 to 70 percent — and the Japanese, the West Germans and the French share the rest. Third World governments have succeeded in holding on to some rights to wave lengths through their representations at the United Nations Telecommunications Conference, but rights mean nothing when there is no power or technology to support them and to give them substance."

It is all very familiar. The same phenomenon of impotent sovereignty is evident in the debates on the rights to exploit the resources of the sea bed. *We* have the seas, but *they* have the technology and the funds to put technology to work."

It is very similar to what happened in the 17th and 18th Centuries when the nation states of the west, that had strengthened themselves with the technology of the land, and the gadgetry of shifting the burden of labor from the ox and the human shoulders to inanimate energy, were able to appropriate massive areas of the southern hemisphere that they regarded as amorphous, unorganized and passive societies awaiting the benefits of modernization. It was never openly called exploitation. Empire building and its management was claimed to be a civilizing mission. Here is a paragraph from a speech delivered by H.M. Stanley, the famous American reporter who had found Dr. Livingstone in an African village and had been welcomed as a hero by Britain's Manchester Chamber of Commerce."

'There are 50 millions of people beyond the gateway to the Congo,' Stanley said, 'and the cotton spinners of Manchester are waiting to clothe them. Birmingham foundries are glowing with the red metal that will presently be made into ironwork for them and the trinkets that shall adorn those dusky bosoms, and the ministers of Christ are zealous to bring them, the poor benighted heathen, into the Christian fold.'"

So, evidently, we were all waiting for the boons of imperialism and western technology. The British Empire was built on the simple principle of philanthropy plus 4 per cent. Now that the imperial system has been all but liquidated, it is important for us not to be overwhelmed by the second wave of technology."

In the world now being refashioned according to the computer vision of IBM, Xerox, Honeywell and Sperry-Rand, what is the place, function and future of the publisher of the printed word? Is the publishing industry doomed? Will the printed word and its myriad storehouses — books — disappear under the avalanche of processed data? Will numeracy replace literacy as we know it and will numbers and the chattering jargon of the computer overwhelm language and make it outmoded? I think not."

Is this only the wishful thinking of a practitioner of the printed word? Possibly, but then again, I think not. First I believe that some of the very advantages claimed for the new communications technology strengthen the continued need for conventional communication. The most obvious of these is that information linked to satellites can vault over all national boundaries and make a mockery of the newly minted sovereignty of developing nations."

Whether one thinks that the nation state is an outmoded concept of human development or not — and there are many indications that it well might be — the reality of the present and foreseeable future is that in the materially deprived world, nationalism shows no signs of losing its luster and force as the prime principle of social identity. Ex-colonial countries have not enjoyed their sovereignty long enough, or well enough, to be ready to yield it to the blandishments of global interdependence. Besides, more and more of us have understood that interdependence without equity is a new distortion of reality, another rhetorical effort to vindicate subservience to the needs of those who control the market-place. Interdependence can only become an acceptable relationship when it is based on a clear and substantial independence. That is as true for nations as it is between individuals. Unless our identity is secure and until we feel secure in it, we cannot submerge it in a larger commonality."

That is the need that publishers and other conventional communicators will have to continue to fulfill. The continuing story of our efforts to build our social identity, the story of people's needs and aspirations, the traditional wisdom and the ethical principles on which our human relationships are formed and the nuances of change that are taking place in our own view of our own world — the family, the village and our cities — will have to be recorded and communicated in our own languages and dialects, and stored, replicated and communicated by conventional means."

There are other reasons that make publishing of the printed word a very important and vital instrument for not only the Third World, but also the entire human world. Data and information provided and distributed by computers will provide an extremely valuable bank of certain kinds of knowledge, but this cannot replace another kind of knowledge that is not information but the substance of reflection — the stuff of the inner mind and the feelings of people. That is what will sustain the values that we all regard as the basis of our inner lives. One of those values is the democratic pluralism that the printing press made possible. The computer revolution that is now upon us may be progressive in many ways but in some important senses it takes communication back to the age before Gutenberg. It will reduce the sources of knowledge to a few disseminators."

That is why IBM preferred to leave India rather than give India the controlling share of its Indian subsidiary. It will homogenize the content of its communication to suit the demands of the market so that the nuances of meaning and colour of ideas may be blurred. It will rob us of the privacy we value as human beings, of the human right to take a thought, reflect on it in private, and reject it partially or wholly. It will reinforce the always existing tendency for messages to move irresistibly downwards from the power centers to the periphery."

That last is the real danger to development in the Third World. After many years of grappling with the problem of slow development — or actual regression in development — the lesson is beginning to be learnt: That the message from the village is at least as important as the top-down messages of the planners and administrators; that the people are experts in the art of survival; that they are the experts in poverty; that they know their needs and what can be done and not done, better than any of the doctors of philosophy from the London School of Economics ever did. This lesson is in danger of being extinguished by the essentially vertical nature of the new knowledge. It must be secured and strengthened by publishers who devote themselves to the task of bringing the message from the village to the citadels of power. But that alone is not enough. Vertical communication, top-down or bottom-up, serves one set of purposes, but popular participation in self-development can work only if there is a horizontal flow of expression between community and community. Important messages such as the possibilities offered by family planning, the lessons of hygiene and protecting the family against water-borne diseases, access to sources of cheap nutrition — a thousand lessons learned by one community need to be internally communicated to others who share the common experiences of poverty. These messages need to be printed simply and graphically, the publisher playing the role of facilitator and marketer of these lateral communications systems."

Having said what I have, it would be wrong to leave you with the impression that the new technology has no redeeming features for the Third World. On the contrary, there are opportunities for us all in that revolution; the gadgetry is rapidly becoming cheaper and more accessible so that developing countries — and the publishing industry — may have increasing access to new storehouses of knowledge. My concern is not about the technology itself but its content — the viewpoint and the values and the motivation of those who control the technology and the use they make of it. H.G. Wells made a memorable remark during World War I when airplanes were being used to drop poison gas on people: 'Man made the aeroplane, and the ape got hold of it.' That precisely is my fear. Men invented television — the most effective instrument of communication we have ever known — a medium that reaches right into our homes and has the power to transfix people and reduce them to gaping sponges of its messages. But what is it used for? Show biz. The idiotic antics of I Love Lucy, Kojak, Mission Impossible and Bugs Bunny. Every "serious" program that deals with the human reality is relegated to 'educational networks,' thus killing it by elevating it to the arid stratosphere of formal education."

"The problem for the publisher who is concerned with the Third World, therefore, is how to use the technology of the Information Age and the access to the data banks, relate it to the realities and the culture of our world in language and graphics that will communicate intelligibly and interestingly, even entertainingly, among the people whose lives are to be affected."

Exhibit A in Jonas's Epoch B show-and-tell was a standard world-population growth curve, starting at a guessed-at 100 million at the birth of Christ and growing ever-so-gradually to about 130 million at the time of Columbus. It dipped noticeably at the time of the bubonic "Black Death" of the 14th Century, but soared as science sailed into the 19th and 20th Centuries. Projections showed the number reaching 7.5 billion by the year 2000. We all knew these figures, more or less, but Jonas still got a laugh when he said, "that's billions. With a Bee."

Jonas's graphic devices to show population growth were S-shaped, "sigmoid" curves. He showed several measuring growth in closed environments — fruit flies in a bell jar, sheep in a fenced field, yeast cells in a lab culture — and pointed out that in all cases growth leveled off when the supply of nutrient (or oxygen) became insufficient to feed and sustain more fruit flies, sheep, or yeast cells. (Traveling later and interviewing scientists in Central Africa, I found the same pattern of self-leveling population growth among mountain gorillas in Rwanda and The Congo.)

Jonas went farther: "Since the planet Earth can be considered a closed system, and since the sigmoid curve reflects the operation of control and regulatory mechanisms which appear to be associated with survival of the individual or of the species, it would seem reasonable to expect that the pattern of future population growth in Man will tend to stabilize at an optimal level."

With his chalk, he continued the population curve up-up-upward on the blackboard, to what seemed to be, roughly, 15 or 20 billion. Then he flattened it out at the top.

"It is possible, of course," he said, "that an alternative pattern might resemble that of the lemmings, in which periodic catastrophe occurs with enormous loss of life. However, Man's attitude toward human life would have to alter significantly for such patterns to be endured. He is more likely to choose other ways than catastrophe for maintaining optimal numbers on the face of the earth while remaining within the limit of available resources."

With this switch from Tarzie's romantic euphemism to polysyllabic "hard" science, Jonas captured his audience. His eyes intense under dark brows, tufts of professorial gray hair above his ears, his voice resonant and sure, he was the very image of a solid, predictive scientist.

He drew a chalk line on the blackboard halfway up his sigmoid population curve at about the 9-billion level. "This is where we are about now," he said. Emphatically, he labeled the bottom half of the curve 'Epoch A'. The upper half he labeled 'Epoch B'. So firm was his stroke that the chalk shattered.

"The overriding objective of humankind in Epoch A was growth," he said. "Industrial growth, financial growth, growth in international power and prestige, military growth, population growth. Competition was the norm. Win-lose was the measure of human activity. Winners were winners, losers were losers. The emphasis was on win. The result was increasing wealth among the wealthy, increasing poverty among the poor. Wars. Damage to the environment. Threats to human survival."

"The overriding objective of humankind in Epoch B is, and will be, survival." Before the meeting Jonas had sent every participant a copy of his book, Survival of the Wisest.

He went on: Man differs from other living organisms in possessing a control and regulatory system for response to environmental and other changes. Man is able to exercise learned behavior. He also possesses individual will. He can learn to behave in ways that are anti-life as well as pro-life, anti-evolution as well as pro-evolution. In view of the greed and ideologies of Man as causes of his conflicts, his attitudes as well as his values will be put to test in the transition from Epoch A to Epoch B."

Value systems such as prevailed in Epoch A will, of necessity, have to be replaced by those appropriate for Epoch B. The profundity of the change in attitudes and values required for survival and for quality of life make it seem that what was of positive value in A may, in fact, become of negative value in B."

Medicine must change from Anti-Death to Pro-Life, from Anti-Disease to Pro-Health, from Death Control to Birth Control, from Self-Repression to Self-Expression, from External Restraint to Self-Restraint. Competition must give way to cooperation. Power must be replaced by influence. Win-Lose must give way to Double-Win or, if you will, Win-Win."

It is for these reasons that we speak of the 'Survival of the Wisest.' If Man is conscious of the processes working on him and within him, he may be able to exercise whatever measure of free will he possesses, within the possibilities of the prevailing circumstances, to change and bring his talents to bear, in influencing the direction of human evolution. His success or failure will depend equally upon errors of omission as upon errors of commission. For this reason, consciousness as well as wisdom is required for success in such an endeavor."

Jonas and Tarzie got their points across, particularly to the journalists in the crowd. After lunch that first day, playtime was declared, and we all went out to immerse ourselves in the natural joys of Mohonk. Jim Rose, who was fast becoming a good friend, suggested that we find a couple of congenial opponents and play some tennis doubles. Harry Evans and his then-girlfriend Tina Brown (eventually his wife, mother of their two children and the imaginative and sharp-edged editor-proprietor of Newsweek and the Daily Beast), thought this was a fine idea, but in honor of the occasion we should invent Epoch B tennis. Instead of Win-Lose tennis, we would play Win-Win tennis.

In Win-Win tennis, we decided, there could be no old-fashioned "winning" shots for points. Instead, any shot that an opponent couldn't return was not a "winner." It simply didn't count.

We began to play what could have become the longest game in the history of tennis. It was pattycake, pattycake, pattycake, easy shot, easy shot, easy shot ... Oops! ["Oops!" was an accidental "winning" shot]. In no time at all we lost count of the points that didn't count, and the rallies went on and on with quite a few ... Oops! It took concentration to hit the ball to a spot where your "opponent" (Scratch that – your "opposite number") could surely hit it back to a spot where you (or your "partner") could surely hit it back. And back. And back. And back... Oops!

We laughed a lot, which surely should become one of the background noises of Epoch B, and there were times when we had to call time out to breathe.

Epoch B Tennis ended — forever, probably — after eight, or ten, or twelve minutes. The climax was a smash shot, through my feet, by Tina. "Enough!" she cried. "Enough!" And we turned to good, old-fashioned, Epoch A, win-lose tennis. Tina and Harry won.

Chapter 27

Pause for ... Melanoma

My fund-raising motto: "A grant is a terrible thing to waste."

I meant it. There I was, with an idea – training Third-World journalists to write for First-World publication, and launching a wire service to get their news and views distributed and into print. The John D. and Catherine T. MacArthur Foundation *liked* the idea. I had a $100,000 exploratory MacArthur grant in the bank, and a "measly" $200,000 needed to match a second $200,000 to start the process of dealing with the problem of "North-South Communications." Total: Five hundred thousand dollars.

For reasons of memorability I reversed the usual "North-South" terminology, and called the new enterprise the "South-North News Service" – SNNS. The idea was to have the "South" – the Third World – learn to communicate with the "North" – the First World. I wrote to every foundation and funding source that had ever supported the Institute of Current World Affairs and the American Universities Field Staff, and began driving, flying and bussing in all fund-raising directions.

The Philip Graham Fund at Phil Foisie's Washington *Post* and Bob Semple's *New York Times* Fund were naturals. They each provided $10,000. Another natural was Scott McVay, the first Executive Director of the Geraldine Dodge Foundation, who had been introduced to me at a Council on Foundations meeting back in the days when Institute of Current World Affairs reports from Fellows in the field were addressed personally to me and thus began,"Dear Peter." Scott had discovered the newsletters, liked them, and had subscribed. When we met, he did a double-take at the first sound of my name.

"I *know* who you are!" he exclaimed. "You're Dear Peter!"

The Exxon Education Foundation provided $50,000. John Musser, a great friend of ICWA's founding director, did the same from his General Service Foundation. I scratched my head to think of more sources, dislodging a small scab that had healed from a previous scratching. This had happened once or twice before, and I made an appointment to have the pimple looked at the Mary Hitchcock Hospital in Hanover. It was the week after Christmas, 1981.

Two days later, I got a phone call from Dermatology. "Mister Martin? We checked that lesion on your head. It looks like melanoma."

I'd never heard the term before. "Is that serious?"

"Yes, it is. Could you come in tomorrow for a wider excision?"

I said yes, and pulled out my Webster's Intercollegiate Dictionary. It said, "a usually malignant tumor containing a dark pigment."

That was all. A lot, to be sure, but certainly not enough. I searched the Web for *Melanoma.*

There it was: "The most dangerous form of skin cancer, these cancerous growths develop when unrepaired DNA damage to skin cells (most often caused by ultraviolet radiation from sunshine or tanning beds) triggers mutations that lead the skin cells to multiply rapidly and form malignant tumors... Melanomas often resemble moles; some develop from moles. The majority of melanomas are black or brown, but they can also be skin-colored, pink, red, purple, blue or white... Melanoma kills an estimated 9,940 people in the US annually."

Yes, it *was* serious. Red, white, blue or purple, I went in for my "wider excision." It involved a surgeon going deeper under the original scab on my head, and taking more tissue from around it.

"We need to see how deeply the Melanoma has penetrated," the scalpel-man said, "and how many surrounding cells are involved. Since the original lesion is directly on the top of your head, the lymph system could carry malignant cells down either side of your neck and on to either side of your body. The head wound will be fairly wide, but you can cover it with a hat. You'll have to see an oncologist. He's Paul LeMarbre. Lives here in Hanover. He's been doing a lot of experimental work with Melanoma. We'll make an appointment for tomorrow."

LeMarbre turned out to be an open-faced, friendly fellow. He lived on Ridge Road in Hanover, two backyards away from Lu's old house on Storrs Road. His two sons, I learned, played ice hockey at Hanover High School. Nicely normal.

"What has to happen with Melanoma," he told me, "is, you have to overwhelm it with a combination of chemical compounds. You have to kill it before it spreads too far. The chemicals we've been using often don't do the job, so the Melanoma can lurk in your system and come back, stronger than ever.

"I've been trying out a new combination of chemicals," he said, "stronger on the platinum. The results have been promising. They work pretty well with breast cancer, as well. I prepared this paper for my last oncology meeting. Look it over. If it's okay with you, I'd like to use it in your case."

He handed me a sheaf of paper, stapled. I took it home and read it. I'd seen similar reports when I was Senior Editor of TIME's weekly "Medicine" section. It was studded with numbers, chemical names, percentages, dosages, outcomes, reports on "Patient A," "Patient B," etc. Most of the cases cited had ended well, or fairly well. Some hadn't. The numbers, though, were on LeMarbre's side.

I phoned him the next day. "I read your paper. It sounded good to me. With any luck, I'll be 'Patient M' on the plus side in your next report."

"I'm glad you liked it. But before we go any farther, I think you ought to have at least one second opinion. You may not know it, but your regular squash opponent at the Dartmouth Gym, Laird Meyers, was head of Oncology at Memorial Sloan Kettering before he retired and moved up here. He could point us to someone down there who's close to what's going on these days. I'll check with him."

I didn't know anything about Laird's professional background, but I knew for certain he was a good and gentle man. And a good and gentle squash opponent. The squash court is one of those places where it's entirely permissible – even expectable – to vent strong feelings when an easy shot is muffed, or missed. The S word, or even the F word, is frequently used and excused when a poorly executed sure winner becomes a painful loser and bangs loudly into the metal telltale, the squash equivalent of a tennis net.. But not with Laird. When Laird Meyers missed a sure thing, the expression that escaped his lips was a mild, self-directed, personal rebuke.

"Oh, *Laird,*" He'd say, softly to himself. "Oh, *Laird.*"

A visit to Memorial Sloan Kettering in New York City was not even much of a bother for me. The hospital, one of the world's most advanced cancer-treatment centers, was at York Avenue and East 70th Street. My Manhattan *pied a terre* apartment was at York and 72nd. An easy two-block walk.

I flew down from New Hampshire the day before my meeting at Sloan Kettering. Arrangements had been made for Paul LeMarbre to be at his telephone in Hanover an hour or half-hour after the Manhattan appointment so he could discuss my case with the Sloan Kettering specialist.

An hour before the appointment I walked down York to 70th. At the reception desk, I was told that my second-opinion person wasn't in that day. Instead, I would see a doctor named Fortner. I was sent to Dr. Fortner's office to wait. A half-hour went by. An hour. At last I was called in to Dr. Fortner's office. He had papers on his desk. There was no word of greeting, or of welcome. I sat down, and he looked up from the papers.

"Melanoma, eh?" he said. "What are they doing for you up in New Hampshire?"

I explained that plans were to remove the tumor with surgery, then begin chemotherapy.

"If you want to get sick to your stomach and die throwing up, do that," said Dr. Fortner. "If you want to live, you need to let us scalp you."

"Scalp me?" I said.

"Yes. That's what we call it. Since the tumor is on the top of your head, we have to trace the lymph system down each side of your head and neck, as far down as we can trace the melanoma. Then we have to remove it. You won't have much of a neck left, but it's your best chance of survival."

His voice and attitude were coldly professional. As I described it later to my wife, I felt like a frozen side of beef on an overhead track that had been pulled in for inspection. *Silent* inspection. I broke the silence.

"My doctor in New Hampshire is sitting by his phone, waiting to discuss my case with you," I said. "Can we call him?"

"I don't need to talk to him," said Fortner. "We've talked enough."

End of consultation. I walked back to my New York apartment, called my wife and Paul LeMarbre to give them the news, and flew home. The next day I went to Mary Hitchcock Hospital to talk things over with Paul.

"What are you going to do?" he asked.

"I'm certainly not going to get scalped," I said. "I don't like Fortner, and I like you. I'm going to stick with you."

"I like you, too," said Paul. "But this violates one of the basic rules of oncology: Don't befriend patients. Too many of them die."

We didn't dwell on the subject. I brought up the next topic.

"Before we start," I said, "I need to make something clear. This treatment has got to be kept confidential."

"Confidential?"

"Yes. You see, I'm working to raise two hundred thousand dollars for a MacArthur Foundation matching grant for a Third-World news service. I've got requests out to the Ford Foundation, the Rockefeller Foundation, and a dozen others. If word gets around that I've come down with something that could be fatal cancer, the chances of getting matching grants will probably disappear. Who'd want to make a grant to a dying man?"

"A secret cancer?" He thought a minute. "It *might* work. What we'd have to do is admit you to the hospital on Friday afternoons for your chemo. The treatment's intravenous, and each one takes a couple of days. I'd swear the staff to secrecy and you could go home Sunday afternoon. I'd try to keep it quiet."

We left it at that, and I said the same thing to another doctor, Jim Strickler, a close friend of mine and Lu's. Jim was Dean of the Dartmouth Medical School. Jim repeated what Le Marbre had said.

"A secret cancer? It's just about impossible to keep a secret in a medical school – or anywhere in a small town like Hanover, for that matter. And there's something you should know. I've already told Norman Miller."

"Norman Miller?" I said, taken more than slightly aback. Norman, an adjunct professor of family medicine and international studies at Dartmouth, was a good friend of mine and a close neighbor and even closer friend of Dean Strickler. But he was definitely a chatterer, a news-spreader. "There goes *that* secret!"

"Maybe not," said Jim. "I'll talk to him."

He did. And wonder of wonders, Norman kept the secret. So did Jim. Every third Friday, when I finished a week of office business at Main and West Wheelock Streets in Hanover, Lu delivered me to the Mary Hitchcock Hospital a few blocks north on Main. With the familiar tower of the Dartmouth's Baker Library looming outside my window, a sweet, comforting Physician's Assistant inserted entry ports for LeMarbre's cocktail of melanoma poisons in the back of my hand and taped them down. The evening National Public Radio news, local and national, came through the hospital's Public Address System and a wheeled stand loaded with hooks and bottles was rolled beside my bed. The drip, drip, drip of cancer-killing liquids began.

Ironically, when the evening news came on that first Friday, the opening segment was a local item about the death of Howie Chivers, a onetime Dartmouth Olympic skier who was managing the College Skiway. Howie had come down with Melanoma around the same time I did. He'd undergone treatment with LeMarbre's chemicals ... and died, the day before.

I never mentioned the Chivers obit to Paul LeMarbre. I didn't want to depress him – or me, for that matter. That first weekend – and every third weekend for several months thereafter – my Friday hospital dinner was served bedside. Full bottles were hung, and all through the night I came awake when a new array of bottles went up and new drip, drip, drips began. It didn't seem so bad that first week, but it seemed to take forever before Lu took me home on Sunday.

27.1 A Meeting in Menlo Park

In the weeks between Melanoma treatments, I kept up with the paperwork and phone calls needed to match that MacArthur $200,000. Some matching-grant "asks" obviously required personal visits.

One such was to the William and Flora Hewlett Foundation in Menlo Park, California. When I left Time Inc. to take over the Institute of Current World Affairs in 1977, Warren Unna, an ICWA Trustee, urged me to visit Roger Heyns, a friend of his who had just become Executive Director of the Hewlett Foundation.

Roger and I had hit it off from the start, so Hewlett was another "natural" for a matching-grant request. I sent Roger introductory material about South-North, made plans for travel, and after a couple of months of weekend hospital stays, booked plane reservations and rental cars to travel west. As I got ready to go, I had lunch with Dick Nolte, my ICWA predecessor, who'd moved to Hanover with his wife Jeanne.

"Menlo Park?" he said. "When you're out there, you should stop in and meet [NAME WITHHELD]. He's running an interesting little nonprofit. You'd probably have a lot in common. I'll send you his coordinates."

Dick did. I dropped a line to his friend and took off for California. I rented a car in San Francisco, and drove down to Menlo Park. I spent a productive and promising afternoon with Roger Heyns and his colleagues at Hewlett, and had lunch first with Dick Nolte's friend. We met and ate, significantly, on *my* travel money, at a McDonald's. He was busy creating a "Development Index" of devices and low-cost technology for Third-World organizations and individuals to enable them to tap in to First-World industrial and agricultural enterprises and "borrow" or adapt expensive techniques and applications for low-cost development projects. I ate a quarter-pounder with cheese and drank a small chocolate shake. He devoured *two* Big Macs, a salad, and a couple of containers of milk.

"This'll be my dinner," he said. And, as we got ready to part, he added, "Could we have breakfast here tomorrow morning?" I had no reason not to, and didn't have to turn the rental car in until afternoon, so I said Yes.

The next morning, over Egg McMuffins, he said to me, "I'm not supposed to tell you this, but I'm a nominator for a new program called MacArthur Prize Fellowships. Based on yesterday's talk, I'd like to nominate you for one of the fellowships. But I need your help. I have to make a convincing case for the nomination, and I need a lot more information and details about you to do it. And the only way I can get that information is from you."

I stopped eating, a plastic forkful of McSausage in midair. "Hold on a minute," I said. "Please don't do that."

"But they're wonderful fellowships," he said. "You'd get a hundred thousand dollars a year for five years, and you would not have to do or produce anything in return."

"What you don't know is that I already have a MacArthur grant of two hundred thousand dollars that I have to match to start a writing project and syndicated news service for Third-World journalists. Some grants are already coming in, but if word gets out that I've been nominated for a prize fellowship, they'll stop completely."

"Damn!" he said. "I get a thousand dollars if I submit a winning proposal for a prize fellowship, and I need the money!"

"Sorry," I said. And I meant it.

27.2   Time Out – Also, for Dick Critchfield

It took a few days, but on the flight back from Menlo Park to the East Coast, the nominee name came to me: Dick Critchfield!

The Ford and Rockefeller Foundations have immense resources, and I'm sure that these days they're tackling immense problems with those immense resources. But I remember, with great appreciation and fondness, that back in "my salid days" (the 1950s and '60s) they were willing to "think small." My 1953 journalism fellowship in subSaharan Africa, one of several funded by Ford after World War II, was one of my favorite small thoughts.

Dick Critchfield was another. *The Economist* summed him up in a combined book review/obituary in its issue of January 21, 1995. "He was a shy, friendly, busy man, the sort you came across by the score in the small-town Main Streets of his native North Dakota," the obit said. "He was also, despite his unpretended modesty ('a non-intellectual writing essentially for non-intellectuals,' he called himself), a major shaper of ideas in a subject the importance of which the world of city-dwellers is only just starting to rediscover. Critchfield spent 25 years learning, and writing about, what makes people feel they belong together – about what the word 'community' means."

A journalist who'd covered the Vietnam War for the old Washington *Star*, Dick felt that people who lived and worked in the world's villages *mattered*. He never learned their languages (he used the same interpreters in revisited villages over and over), and he traveled from favorite village to favorite village in eastern Europe, the Middle East, East Asia, Southeast Asia, Latin America, North America, subSaharan Africa, North Africa and South Asia – in short, just about every Smalltown, Everywhere.

He attracted the attention of Richard Nolte and Alan Horton, my predecessors at the Institute of Current World Affairs and the American Universities Field Staff, and they won him alternating travel/writing grants from Ford and Rockefeller. His village reports got published in The *International Herald Tribune,* The *New York Times,* The *Economist,* and many other newspapers and magazines, major and minor, around the world. He wrote occasional books – *The Golden Bowl Be Broken, Shahhat, Villages, The Villagers* . He rode in buses, Second- and Third-Class railway cars, hitchhiked in trucks and on the backs of motorcycles, and sailed as close to steerage as he could.

As successor to Nolte and Horton, I became Dick's friend and ally. He called me his "boss," but I don't think he ever had a boss.

Sometime in the 1960s the phone on my desk in Hanover, rang and Dick's soft voice was there. "Peter," he said, "Ford and Rockefeller have decided not to renew my grants, and I don't know what to do."

"What do you *want* to do?" I said.

"I want to keep on doing what I've always done," he said, "but I won't be able to afford it."

"Let me think about it," I said.

One of the main international communications problems that came up at the Mohonk Conference was what was then called the "New World Information Order." This was a shorthand reference to the fact that "Third-World" coverage in major publications in the "North" was almost exclusively provided by journalists employed by First-World News organizations – The Associated Press, United Press International, The TIME-LIFE News Service, The *New York Times* Service, *Deutsche Presse Agentur, Agence France-Presse,* Reuters, Bloomberg, The *Wall Street Journal,* The *International Herald Tribune* and a variety of other well-established news organizations.

At the final cocktail party in the tower suite at Mohonk, Jonas Salk and I celebrated the success of his conference with a self-congratulatory "man-to-man" talk. I'd had a first martini, and was dipping into my second. There's no fuel like an old fuel.

"Where next?" he said.

"How about the White House?" said I.

"Why not?" said he. "What about a topic?"

"How about the New World Information Order?"

"I heard you had some ideas about that," he said. "You know, I'm on the board of the MacArthur Foundation. Why don't you send them a proposal?"

"I will," I said.

And I did. I wrote a proposal for a $300,000 grant to launch a "South-North News Service" that would identify and train writers from the Third World (the "South," – get it?) to write in the idiom and up to the journalistic standards expected by editors and publishers of First-World news organizations up "North."

As LeMarbre's chemicals began working their way through my lymph system, the proposals for the South-North News Service began working their way through the Foundation system. I noticed no ill effects from the Melanoma treatment and chemotherapy – at first. The constant hat covering my head wound attracted attention, of course, and Judy Miller, Norman's wife, at last told me that her small children were consumed with curiosity about what lay under it. Would I take it off? I did, and when the kids saw a mere pile of gauze bandage underneath, they were satisfied.

But Paul's chemicals were killing more than just Melanoma cells. They were killing red blood cells as well, and with them the capacity of my blood to carry oxygen through my body. I began to grow more and more pale. I became nauseous, so much so that I couldn't lie flat at night without throwing up. I had to sleep sitting up.

My senses became acutely aware of other "poisons" in my environment besides LeMarbre's. When I opened a refrigerator door, I was almost blown away by the fumes of preservatives that must have been in the salami, the processed cheeses, the pickles – even my beloved Philadelphia Scrapple.

As I began to travel for fund-raising, people at such places as the Pew Memorial Trust, The Minneapolis *Star & Tribune,* The Readers' Digest Foundation, The Alicia Patterson Foundation, The *Los Angeles Times* and The Benton Foundation began to wonder about my deathly white skin. I would brightly – and, I hoped, convincingly, explain that "living in New Hampshire in the winter was like living under a rock." One good friend – a Chicago doctor named Andy Thomson who'd seen chemotherapy up close – saw through my stories, but provided $50,000 from a family trust all the same.

My shortness of breath got so bad that I couldn't climb a flight of stairs without stopping halfway (or a third of the way) to breathe. Deeply. For a long minute or two. Or three. Support for the matching grant kept coming in, though. By May, I was just $50,000 away from the $200,000 goal. Toward the middle of the month I got a phone call from Frank Karel at the Rockefeller Brothers Fund. He'd become a South-North enthusiast. "We're almost there," he said. "Let's get together at the Council on Foundations meeting in June. I may have good news."

The Council meeting was the only occasion in the year where young and mid-range grant-makers assembled to gossip, learn, eat and drink with each other. Foundation greybeards gave talks and assembled seminars. But they

never, never, never made grants or accepted petitions for grants. Or *hardly*
ever.

The Council was meeting that year in Denver – "The Mile-High City," and
therefore no place for easy breathng. I went anyway, of course, and along
about Day Three ran into Frank, who said, after remarking on my paleness,
"I'm staying at the Brown Palace Hotel. Let's meet there tomorrow, before
lunch."

"Fine," I said. "I'll meet you in the lobby about eleven-thirty."

Meet we did.

"I've booked a conference room on the mezzanine," he said. "Let's run on
up." He moved toward a flight of stairs leading up from the lobby. I looked at
the stairs. 'Running on up' would leave me panting and clinging to a handrail
about seven steps up, I figured.

"You go on," I said. "I've got to find a men's room."

I took an elevator. I found the 'Rockefeller Brothers' conference room.
Frank was the only one in it. We didn't sit down. We hugged.

"Congratulations," Frank said. "You've got the grant."

"Wow!" I said."You'll never know how relieved I am. It's been a long slog,
but now we can get going!"

27.3   Back to Critchfield ...

Home in New Hampshire, with the cogs and wheels of the South-North News
Service beginning to turn, I could switch my thoughts back to Dick Critchfield. I won't call it a feeding frenzy, but First-World/Third-World communications had become a hot international topic, and I got invited to a "Bay
Area" conference about it in San Francisco. Dick was listed prominently among
the acceptees.

My Melanoma chemotherapy made it impossible for me to go, but when
I phoned my regrets I told the conference organizer that I had a Bay-Area
friend intensely interested in Third-World issues who should go in my place.
The organizer didn't know Dick Nolte's friend but said he'd be glad to have

him at the conference, and would send an invitation.

Then I phoned the MacArthur nominator. I told him about Critchfield, and said I thought he might make an ideal MacArthur Prize Fellow. I told him that he and Critchfield would probably be at the same conference. I urged him to seek out Dick, talk with him, and get to know him during breaks in the conference routine.

"I won't tell him who you are and what you're up to," I said, "but he just might turn out to be a likely Prize-Fellowship nominee. If not, no harm's done and you can both go your merry ways. But if I'm right, you've got a likely candidate, you've got your thousand dollars, and I'll have done you and him – and maybe the world – a giant favor."

Several weeks went by. Then the phone on my Hanover desk rang again. It was Dick Critchfield.

"Peter!" he said. "You won't guess what's happened! I'm being nominated for a thing called the MacArthur Prize Fellowship! It could be the answer to all my problems!"

Dick was not only nominated for what came to be known as a "MacArthur Genius Grant." He won one of the first ones awarded, And continued traveling to and from and between the world's villages – and writing about them – until the day he died, December 10, 1963.

And the world is a better place.

Chapter 28

The Birth of South North

Still, the lessons — and message — of the Epoch B experience sank in. That evening, over drinks and dinner, Salk's survival strategy was taken apart and put together again, over and over. The term "dusky bosoms" could be heard as the red wine went around. So could "First World," "Third World" and even "Second World."

The next morning it was Lester Brown's turn to tell us all about the "Twenty-ninth Day." One of Tarzie's favorite talking partners, Lester had written a book with that title, and the title was the answer to an ancient Chinese riddle: "If water lilies grow, and cover half the remaining surface of a pond each day of a 30-day month, what is the last day any surface space remains?" Answer — The Twenty-Ninth Day! And if you apply the same time table to world resources, where are we now? What's the last day of human existence as we know it? The answer — Lester's message — The Twenty-Ninth Day! And we were living in it!

Lester, with his serious bow tie and solemn brown eyes, was good at delivering the message. It sank in.

The next morning, after another uplifting talk (by whom, I no longer remember) a rump group of us journalists gathered on the balcony outside Stan Karnow's room. "We've got the message," he said. "And we'll keep getting it, over and over. Question is, what are we going to do about it? I think it's time for us to take this thing over."

Tarzie was there. As he later told me, "That was the moment I was waiting for."

Bob Semple said, "I've been looking for something different, like this, ever since I took over the Foreign Desk at the Times. What I'd like to do, is replace the paper's Table of Contents, every day on Page Two of the paper, with articles and features about what's going on in these other worlds."

"Who's going to write them?" I said.

"It has to be someone on the staff of the New York Times," he said. "That's policy."

"Wouldn't it be better," I said, "if they were written by people from inside the Third World? People who were born there, who live there, who understand it from the inside out rather than the outside in?"

"Maybe," Bob said. "But it takes years for an outside journalist to write for the Times. They don't have the authority, the tone of voice, the experience, it takes to be trusted as Times writers. We'd have to assign staff to do the reporting, writing and fact-checking. And that might mean adding staff."

"Heaven forfend," I said.

"That's all very well for you to say," he said, "but I've got budget problems."

"So've we all," I said. "When I started at TIME, I dealt with Latin America. We had staff correspondents — Brits or Americans — in Havana, Caracas, Rio and Buenos Aires. But in every other country — and there were more than twenty other countries and colonies — we used local stringers. They had to file in English, for better or worse, and we practically had to translate what they wrote in English back into Spanish, or Creole, or Portuguese, and then re-translate it into TIME-style English. They learned by example, and by being corrected, and by being rewritten. Some of them got so good at it, we could almost run what they wrote in the magazine."

"How about fact-checking?" said Semple.

"Fact checkers are made, not born," I said. "You can train them."

"So?" said Semple.

"I think what we need is a combination Third-World news service and training program," I said. "We need to find writers in Third-World countries with a fair command of English and some understanding of what a story is. We need them to send in suggestions, the same way TIME's Latin American stringers send in suggestions. When they've got workable ideas, we should tell them to come ahead and file. And then we should advise, and get them to rewrite, and do some rewriting ourselves, and turn loose fact-checkers to make sure what they've written is not just imagination, or propaganda."

"And then?" said Karnow.

"Then we ought to pay them for their stories, and get them published."

"Christ!" said Karnow. "Give me a puff on that before you throw it away. You're talking money, you know, lots of it."

"I know," I said. "But I also know it can be done. You do, too. You've seen it done at TIME, and the Times, and Newsweek."

Jim Rose chimed in. "And the Guardian, and the Telegraph, and The Economist. But from Mohonk, you're taking off into some sort of stratosphere. The air's very thin up here."

I heard nothing more about it for the next two days, but the conference stayed airborne, and Epoch B was firmly established in the minds of all present. At the final cocktail session, all aglow, Jonas smiled his way across the room and took my arm.

"It worked!" he said. "The Mohonk magic! Where do we go next?"

"How about the White House?"

"You think you're joking, but that's not a bad idea," he said. "But I've been hearing about another of your ideas, about a nonprofit Third-World news service and training program. Karnow says it would teach Third-Worlders to write for First-World publication, and pay them for it. How would it work?"

I told him about modeling it on the TIME stringer system.

"I'd love to see a proposal for that," he said. "With a budget. Could you work one up for the MacArthur Foundation? I've just gone on the board."

"I'll give it a try," I said.

"Remember, it's the MacArthur Foundation."

I did. The M in MacArthur stood for Money and I reached for the stars.

I proposed asking every English-language university in the world with a journalism or writing program for the names and addresses of all Third-World participants who'd ever finished their studies and gone back to their home countries. These were pre-email days, so it would all have to be done with individual letters in envelopes, with stamps.

M is also for Marketing. We'd have to get compelling sample stories — ten or a dozen — from potential correspondents, pay for them, and send copies to First-World Op-Ed or Foreign Editors with personal letters explaining what we were up to. We'd have to follow up with phone calls to nudge editors into reading the samples and giving some sort of response. If there was any glimmer — even the faintest glimmer — of interest, I would have to visit the editor and be persuasive in person.

We'd have to find a way to edit and fact-check all articles and transmit them — electronically — to subscribing publications. We'd need first-class teaching editors. We'd need an accountant. We'd need office space. We'd need a librarian. We'd need a lawyer. We'd need insurance. We'd need computers. We'd need fact-checkers. We'd need ... funding.

When I added up all the needs the start-up total came to something over $300,000. Three hundred thousand dollars! I wrote a proposal and a budget and mailed them off to the John D. and Catherine T. MacArthur Foundation, Dearborn Street, Chicago.

Two weeks went by. Three weeks. About a month later, a letter came in from MacArthur. Mercifully, I don't remember exactly what it said, and I didn't keep it, but it went something like this:

"Dear Mr. Martin: We've read your proposal for an international journalism training program with great interest. You make a strong and convincing case for it, but unfortunately our resources are now fully committed and we're unable to provide the funding you need ..."

That afternoon my wife Lucretia, who worked as a Special Assistant to the President of Dartmouth College, came in to my office with a copy of a letter just received by her boss, David McLaughlin. We didn't keep it, but it went something like this:

"Dear President McLaughlin: We've read your proposal for an artist-in-residence program with great interest. You make a strong and convincing case for it, but unfortunately our resources are now fully committed and we're unable to provide the funding you need ..."

An ironic laugh was shared by all, if by "all" you mean just Lu and me. But that wasn't enough. I thought it over and decided to strike while the irony was hot.

I phoned Jonas. "I did what you said," I told him, and I read the crucial paragraph from the MacArthur letter aloud. "I didn't expect a turndown this fast, and this final."

"Peter, Peter, Peter," he said, his voice dramatically drawn out with a tone of weary impatience over my failure to understand. "Could you rewrite your proposal so it says the same thing, but in a different way?"

"I think so."

"Well, then, do it. And when you've finished, send me a copy. And then send the original to the MacArthur Foundation."

"With some kind of explanation?"

"No explanation. Just do it."

I did it. Ten days later, my office phone rang. "Mr. Martin?" said an enthusiastic young male voice. "My name's Jim Armstrong. I'm with the MacArthur Foundation in Chicago. We think there's great promise in your proposal for a third-world journalism training program. We have some questions about it, and it's not in our regular format, but we'd like to explore."

The questions were simple ones. I answered them. The format was simple, too. I re-formatted and sent the proposal back. A week later, Mr. Armstrong phoned again.

"As we see it," he said, "making the program work is a multi-stage process. First, you have to find Third-World writers interested in participating. Second, you have to find First-World editors interested in using Third-World writers, and willing to pay them for their efforts."

"You're absolutely right," I said.

"To get things under way," he said, "we'd like to start you out with a grant of a hundred thousand dollars. There'd be no strings attached. It would just be for the search process. We'd make the next two hundred thousand a matching grant. To receive it, you'd have to raise two hundred thousand dollars from other sources, other foundations. That would show that the idea resonates with other funders and with the American press."

The South-North News Service was born. And Jonas had taught me a lot about fund-raising.

Thank you, Jonas.

Chapter 29

LIFE – Consider the Alternative

The axis of my father's world — and eventually, mine — tilted drastically in the 1960s. The tilt was caused by the societal earthquake called Television — and in particular, commercial network Television.

Throughout the first half of the 20th Century, "mass" popular magazines like *Collier's, Liberty, The Saturday Evening Post, Look, LIFE, TIME and Reader's Digest* were the bedrock foundation of the general-interest periodical publishing business. Printing presses for the *Post, Country Gentleman, Jack and Jill* and *Holiday* magazines were actually inside the magnificent headquarters building of the Curtis Publishing Company, which stood amid the green grass of Independence Square in Philadelphia. The greatest of these, of course, was the *Post*, which had a weekly circulation of six million-plus. When I visited my father in the Post's editorial offices you could *feel* the presses throbbing as they printed and stapled and shipped those millions of copies — and brought in multi-millions of advertising dollars — nonstop, day and night.

In the 1960s, the throbbing slowed. Instead of reading magazines on Saturday evening — or *any* evening, for that matter — people switched to TV. And as more and more of them did that, so did advertisers of soup and headache remedies and breakfast cereals and automobiles and life insurance and soft drinks and coffee and nail polish and power tools and pressure cookers and ketchup and frozen vegetables and beer and cigarettes and gasoline and candy bars and flour and deodorants and sheets and towels and antiseptic and mouth-wash. As the advertisers went, so went the mass magazines.

They did not go quietly. LIFE was the hot photo-journalism publication that survived after *Liberty, Collier's* and *Look* folded. Under the pressure, *The Saturday Evening Post* tried a personality transplant. Telling advertisers it was becoming "The Post Influential," it announced it was going to go in for investigative journalism, muckraking, and articles on "the contemporary scene." They moved their offices from historic old Philadelphia to swinging, in-the-action Manhattan, changed the old-fashioned cover layout, severed the cover-art connection with Norman Rockwell... and *fired my father* as a too-predictable connection to the old *Post*.

Not to overstate the importance of Pete Martin. Norman Rockwell was much more iconic and symbolic. But whatever, it didn't take the magazine much longer to die. My father — and my mother — wept. At a Friday-night issue-closing supper with editors at TIME, I made some sort of "end-of an era" remark. Otto Fuerbringer, by then TIME's Assistant Managing Editor, said something like "It deserved to die."

I raised my voice. "No magazine is an island, Otto," I said, and we were on the verge of an argument. It was a verge I was often on with Otto.

"Let Peter grieve," said Senior Editor Tom Griffith, friend of everyone. Otto let it be.

Another *Post* post-mortem: Serving as Senior Editor of TIME's Press Section, I was unexpectedly invited to one of the regular noontime-Friday Managing Editors' lunches atop the TIME-LIFE Building. Present were *every* Managing Editor and Assistant Managing Editor and Publisher of *every* Time Inc. publication. There must have been 25 or 30 of us seated around the edges of a large, square table. For reasons unclear to me, a place had been saved for me next to Hedley Donovan, Time Incorporated's Editor in Chief and Henry Luce's chosen successor.

Pre-lunch drinks were ordered. Alcohol was generally chosen, but I cautiously asked for a Virgin Mary. We all ate, but Ralph Graves, then the latest Managing Editor of LIFE, ate faster than anyone. When he finished, there was a low rumble of noise beside me. It was the voice of Hedley Donovan, who could have sung the deepest second bass of any chorus of which I ever was a member.

"Let's hear from you, Ralph," rumbled Hedley.

Ralph stood up, and then began a recitation of the categories of subscribers to the defunct *Saturday Evening Post.* There were one million three hundred thousand from A counties, four hundred sixty thousand from B counties, nine hundred seventy-five thousand from A-plus metropolitan areas, two hundred nineteen thousand from Class B suburban areas, forty-nine percent had three-year subscriptions, fourteen percent had lifetime subscriptions... We could get sixteen percent of expired subscriptions for sixty-five dollars per thousand, forty seven percent of subscriptions with three months left...

These are all exemplary figures, conjured out of foggy memory of my realization that LIFE was being offered a chance to buy all the subscribers, existing, expired, and in-between, of my father's old magazine. They could be added to all the subscribers LIFE already had in these counties and urban and suburban areas. Overlapping subscribers would get special continuation offers and so on and so on and so on.

Ralph finally finished and sat down. Silence followed. Unbroken silence. I waited. No one said a word. At last I turned to Hedley.

"Are we supposed to comment on this?" I said.

"That's right, Pete," Hedley rumbled. I stood up.

"Well," I said. "This is the kind of talk that must have gone on between Ben Hibbs and Bob Fuoss and my father and all the other *Post* editors when the end was in sight in Philadelphia. They decided that growth and aggressive journalism was the only way to beat the immediacy and excitement of on-the-spot, as-it-happened, moving-pictures in the living room."

"But it wasn't. The *Post* was a journalistic dinosaur, needing a constant and increasing diet of advertising forage to survive. The forage was all being eaten by smaller, livelier animals, and there wasn't enough left to feed the dinosaurs. They were doomed to die out."

"So I say, *Don't* buy those subscribers. Don't rely on bigger numbers and sheer size to save you. You'll die of overeating first, and then starvation. Find a way to make money with the circulation you have. There are people who love *LIFE*. Raise subscription prices and the price of individual copies. Reduce circulation and production costs and cut overhead until you reach a balance point and can make a profit out of what readers *pay* for the magazine."

There was a rumble from my left.

"Well, Pete," came Hedley's voice. "There's one thing you don't realize. We've already bought 'em."

Chapter 30

The Death of Life

As it turned out, I was right. A few months later, as *LIFE* lay dying, I got a phone call from Otto Fuerbringer. He wanted to have lunch with me at his club, the Knickerbocker on Fifth Avenue. Off I went.

"I've been asked to start a new-magazine development committee," Otto said. "I want you on it. We've got a ton of money and investment tied up in *LIFE*, and we need other magazines to take its place. The committee will start meeting soon, and I want you to begin thinking about it."

I told him that since I was a Senior Editor of TIME, my boss was Henry Grunwald. I'd be glad to serve on the committee if it was okay with Henry. Also, I said, Henry had approved a six-month sabbatical for me. I didn't know when it would begin, but I didn't want committee service to conflict with the sabbatical, either.

He promised me it wouldn't, and a few days later called to say that he'd gotten Henry Grunwald's okay for my service on the New Magazine committee. The Committee would be working pretty much full-time, he said, so I should "clear my decks."

I began clearing. I did all my back expense accounts and submitted them. I made and kept doctors and dentist appointments. I did my income taxes. I played Squash. I didn't have any copy-editing responsibility, so I got home in time for suppers, to read bedtime stories to Bill and Lucy, and to convert our unfinished attic into a home office. I installed pull-up folding stairs and laid

$\frac{3}{4}$-inch plywood over the ceiling rafters of the second-floor bedrooms for the flooring of a third-floor "garret." I made a desk out of two three-drawer metal filing cabinets and another sheet of plywood, carried up copy paper, carbon paper (word processors weren't common in those days) and an ancient manual typewriter.

I thought about magazines, new and old. It was plain that magazines that depended on huge circulations to attract advertisers who sold broad-based products like toothpaste and headache remedies and corn flakes were finished. In conversation, I compared them to old Railway Express Company trucks that made more money from the ads painted on their sides than from the goods they were transporting from trains to delivery vans to homes.

What was needed, I thought, were good old-fashioned magazines with content so attractive and useful to the reader that people would pay money to buy single copies, or subscriptions. "General interest" magazines couldn't do it. The magazines had to appeal to a reader's "special interest." — to his (or her) love of skiing, or photography, or cabinetry, or sex, or investing, or personal health. They would need to avoid the costs of publishing millions of copies once a week, and come out by the hundreds of thousands once a month. They would need specialized ad-sales staffs thoroughly knowledgable about wine, or health insurance, or gardening, or overnight camping.

I ate lunches and dinners with writers and editors with narrow editorial focuses and got them to help me think through the complications and intricacies of pinpoint publication. The talk fascinated me — and quite a few of them. I made notes, and wrote memos to myself and waited. A month went by. Otto got sick, and then was well again. Another month went by. And another. At last, a week before my sabbatical was scheduled to begin, I got a call from Otto.

"Sorry for the delay," he said. "We begin meeting next week."

"Not with me," I said. "My sabbatical begins then."

"But surely, you've been thinking about new magazines. Could you give me a memo?"

"I can, and I will. But after that, I'm pulling the stairs up into the attic behind me, and writing."

I wrote a long memo, summing up my thoughts and suggesting topics for fifteen or twenty "special-interest" magazines. I put it in the inter-office mail, went home, and began to write a novel based on the love, marriage and adventures of David Halberstam and his Polish actress-wife, Elzbieta Czewewska.

Even though we "launched" the magazine during the recession of 1972, *Money* subscriptions sold well, and subscribers renewed enthusiastically. Newsstand sales, however, when mentioned by the Time Inc. powers-that-were at all, were described as "disappointing." For a company that sold copies of LIFE, TIME, and *Sports Illustrated* by the millions, sales of individual copies of *Money* by news vendors might be — and *were* — described in the elevators of the Time-Life Building as "not worth the trouble."

In New York, at least, Mafia biggies controlled the newsstands, and prominent, upfront display positions cost more than our "startup" budget allowed. Also, our early covers were expository, not exclamatory. They did not feature famous bosoms, or famous faces, or famous disasters. They featured *words*. Words. And not even famous words. They were practical, dry-as-dust words that described the investment and budget-saving advice to be found in the articles inside.

The cover of our first issue, dated October 1972, contained 89 (count 'em! — and I just did! — 89!) words: "The promises — and pitfalls — of real estate tax shelters"; "Something will have to be done about the erratic prices of prescription drugs"; "Many working wives labor under the impression that their salaries can add greatly to family fortunes..."

Solid. Serious. But not the kind of stuff to catch the attention of passersby and persuade them to dig in their pockets or pocket books for 75 cents to pop for a magazine. Bill Rukeyser had been "kidnapped" from a promising career as a FORTUNE word-editor to serve as Managing Editor of *Money*, but his strength was financial ideas and strategies, not newsstand sales. But *I* — I had been plucked out of a TIME Senior Editorship dealing with famous Show-Biz and Cinematic people to plan new magazines to replace the then-fading LIFE. One of my inventions was *Money*, and as a "reward" (I think), I was given a *Money* Senior Editorship to help Bill develop the magazine.

In many ways, it was fun. Where else could you get a chance to start a new publication from scratch, with someone else's money? Our pockets were not bottomless, but Time Inc. did not want another flop, and we could afford anything we thought would help. We launched a popular feature called "One Man's (or "One Woman's or "One Family's) Finances" to exemplify how individuals could manage their financial lives with the help of a team of specially recruited professional advisors. I started a light-hearted up-front feature (like the *New* Yorker's "Talk of the Town") called "Current Accounts" to get the reader into the magazine painlessly, with short, engaging anecdotes about human use and misuse of money. My daughter Lucy thought up a title ("*Money* Helps") for a continuing series of short blasts of advice for individuals with complicated financial problems.

We did well. Circulation grew. Advertising revenues grew. Subscriptions grew. With decreasing distress, Bill could report progress to the Time Inc. Board of Directors about just about everything ... everything, that is, but newsstand sales.

Over platters of sushi at our favorite Japanese restaurant, Bill asked. "What can we do about it?"

We talked. Before those TIME Senior Editorships of the Cinema and Show Business Sections, I was in charge of color-photography portfolios. After John F. Kennedy's assassination, I was asked by the managing editor to keep my mind, ear and eye peeled for any ideas that could lead to a Jackie cover photograph. She was the National Widow, and every time she made the cover, newsstand sales hit new highs.

"We've got to find a way to put Jackie on the cover," I told Bill as I plucked a bit of Bluefin Tuna from the platter. "Or famous people like her."

"Of course," said Bill. "But how? Stories about their money management and budgeting don't come up very often. Even if they did, it would be hard to give them any kind of personal flavor."

"How about a special *One Widow's Finances*, getting Jackie to talk with us and our advisers about coping with life, with the costs and rewards of rais-

Jackie Kennedy weds Aristotle Onassis in 1968.

ing Caroline and John-John, and at the same time serving as a national inspirational symbol?"

"Worth a try," said Bill. "But I'll bet an extra order of sushi she won't go for it."

I didn't take the bet; we always had extra orders of sushi anyway. Back at the office I phoned Tish Baldridge, Jackie's forever secretary, and suggested an article about Mrs. Onassis' finances that could be "an inspiration to young American widows."

There was a silent moment while Ms. Baldridge absorbed this. Then a burst of laughter.

"Nice try, Mr. Martin," she said. "But you might as well ask her to talk about her sex life."

"Well, *that's* not a bad idea, either." There were mutual chuckles, and we signed off.

Bill's next question: "What do we do now?"

"I think we can tackle Jackie's finances anyway. She didn't have any personal income after her editing jobs at Viking and Doubleday in the seventies. And when Kennedy was assassinated, her entire financial life became a matter of wills and trusts that had to be reported, dollar by dollar by dollar, to state, city and federal tax people. All of that would have to be on the public record. Except for what she may have inherited under Greek law when Onassis died in 1975, she lived on U.S. income from trusts set up for her and the children by the Kennedys and Onassis."

"Can we find this all out legally?"

"I think so. It'll take a lot of legwork in Massachusetts, New York, New Jersey, Washington, and maybe Greece, but we've got a lot of legs at Time Incorporated, thank goodness."

"Maybe she inherited a lot of money we don't know about, not from Kennedy and Onassis, but from the Bouvier side of the family. They called her father 'Black Jack' Bouvier, and he had a seat on the New York Stock Exchange in the roaring Twenties. And her mother was some kind of heiress."

"We'll see. Want to go ahead with this?"

"It's worth a try. I think Val would be the best pick for head reporter."

Valerie Gerry, a reporter at TIME and Newsweek before she came to *Money*, was a godsend. She quickly sifted through the trickle-down fortunes of the Lees (Jackie's mother was Janet Norton Lee, "heiress" to a New York real estate and banking "fortune") and the Bouviers. She found that the Depression had not been kind to either family.

Black Jack Bouvier was not a lucky gambler, on or off the stock market; he won the nickname because he liked girls the way he liked cards at the table — 21 or under. In 1934, when Jacqueline was five and sister Lee was one, Bouvier spent $38,894.81 to maintain his family, two household servants and a chauffeur, a stable of seven horses, a "cottage" in East Hampton, NY, and a duplex on Park Avenue. Those, obviously, were the Bouvier version of Harry Luce's "good old days."

The first large chunk of money Jackie could call her own was an inheritance of $80,000 (plus a "picture of Arabian horses by Schreyer") left to her by Black Jack, who died in 1957. Sizing up her assets with Val Gerry and the team of expert advisers we recruited to analyze Jackie's finances, we assumed that the inherited money was invested. In those days, though, Jackie was busy buying paintings, antiques and clothes, so she may have spent it. She was also *selling* paintings; she unloaded the Schreyer in 1958 for $900.

Senator — and President — John Kennedy's complaints about his wife's extravagance became legendary. In a memoir, one of her personal secretaries

(Mary Gallagher) said that in 1961 Jackie spent just over $40,000 on clothes. On the thrift side of the ledger, she sent her used garments to Encore, a New York re-sellit house. Her total expenditures for 1961 were $105,446.14, said Ms. Gallagher, and rose to $121,461.61 in 1962. The President was then giving his salary to charity and living on his family income, but his wife was spending money faster than it was coming in. "Isn't there a Shoppers Anonymous?" he asked.

This light-hearted complaint darkened, of course, when her husband was assassinated in 1963. In 1961 Kennedy reported that the value of a trust created for him by his father, Joseph P. Kennedy, was $10 million. In May 1962, when he turned 45, half of the principal was transferred from the trust to his personal holdings. Taxes pared the $5 million considerably. In February 1965, when Senator Edward Kennedy filed a post-assassination inventory of his brother's estate for inheritance-tax purposes, its total value was $1,844,369.

Under the President's will, the estate was divided into two equal portions. One portion was put in trust for Jackie, and the other was divided into two equal trusts for Caroline and John Jr. In addition to the trust, the will gave Jackie and the children an eleven-room, five-bath "summer cottage" in Hyannis Port, MA.

Before Dallas, the Kennedys built a sprawling house in Virginia hunt country. Jackie sold it in 1964 for $200,000 and (eventually) bought a $200,000, 15-room cooperative apartment on the 15th floor of 1040 Fifth Avenue in Manhattan.

After President Kennedy was killed, his widow became more than ever an object of intense public curiosity, sympathy and attention, witness my instruction from the managing editor of TIME. She had Secret-Service protection, but her trust income of between $130,000 and $150,000 a year was nowhere near enough to pay the taxes and maintenance on her New York and Hyannis homes, *and* provide education for the children, *and* provide personal and family safety, *and* clothing, *and* travel, *and* ....

Little wonder that the privacy and luxury afforded by the wealth of Aristotle Onassis were attractive to her. Onassis had been offering Jackie comfort and seclusion ever since he first met her with her husband at a cocktail party for Winston Churchill aboard his yacht Christina in the summer of 1959. When her two-day-old son died in 1963, Onassis took her on a recuperative cruise, along with sister Lee Radziwill and Mr. and Mrs. Franklin D. Roosevelt Jr. When Kennedy was assassinated, Onassis immediately flew to Washington, and during Mrs. Kennedy's widowhood he visited her at the house she rented in the countryside near Peapack, N.J.

Onassis, however, was not one to let caring and infatuation run away with business sense. Widows of Greeks are entitled to one-fourth of their husbands' estates if there is no will, or the will is declared invalid. After Jackie accepted his proposal, but before they were married, he had an agreement drawn up under which she gave up her rights to 25 percent of his billion-dollar shipping, real-estate and airline empire. She signed it in the U.S., and it was notarized.

Rumors about the contents of the agreement ran the gamut from separate sleeping quarters to immense payments in case of divorce, but Onassis' will made it clear that its main provision was a trust fund of tax-exempt securities that provided Jackie with a tax-free income of $100,000 a year.

There were other, tangible benefits to being Mrs. Onassis. "Would you like to see what Ari gave me?" Jackie asked the wedding party aboard the Christina anchored at Skorpios. After she asked the question, "it was quiet as a tomb," according to Ari's sister Artemis. "Jackie went below and when she returned she was wearing a new diamond ring — so heavy, my God, I don't know how she could hold her hand up — and a bracelet, a necklace, and two absolutely incredible ear pendants made of diamonds and rubies — rubies maybe as big as strawberries."

That was only the beginning. The first year of their marriage, Onassis spent some $5 million on jewels for his wife — including a 40-carat diamond appraised at $1 million by a New York jeweler, for her 40th birthday; an $800,000 strand of pearls from Mikimoto in Japan; 30 diamond and gold bracelets worth an average of $2,300, one for her breakfast tray every two weeks; a $1 million pair of emerald and diamond earrings from Van Cleef & Arpels for their first anniversary.

Added to the items she received while she was married to John Kennedy, the jewels she got during her marriage to Onassis brought the total retail value of the major pieces in her collection to well over $7 million.

During Onassis' lifetime, all his wife's living expenses — apartment maintenance, staff, limousines, beauty care, bodyguards, utilities, clothes — were paid by his New York secretary. All this bill-paying, added to her travel and living expenses in Paris, Athens and elsewhere, came to a total of over $450,000 a year.

$450,000! Quite an Outgo! How did it compare with her income? When we initiated the "One Family's Finances" series in the first issue of *Money*, we selected an advisory panel of two or three financial professionals with particular expertise in the investment and business interests of the family or individual featured in the article. We did the same for the widow Onassis.

For comment and advice in the fields of tax planning and tax law, we called on Jules Ritholz and Edward Tannenbaum of the New York firm of Kostelanetz, Ritholz & Mulderig. For investment analysis and guidance, we consulted with senior vice president Raymond F. DeVoe Jr. and vice president John E. Reid III of the brokerage firm of Spencer Trask & Co. Ray DeVoe, like me a Dartmouth graduate, had a particular insight into the social milieu that surrounded Jackie in her New York "coming-out" years. He was on the list of acceptable debutante escorts and had obviously avoided the dreaded "NSIT" ("Not Safe In Taxis") asterisk beside his name. From time to time he'd been assigned to take Jackie to debutante parties, and see her home.

Onassis's will, written "by hand from beginning to end on my private Lear aircraft from Acapulco to New York, on the day of Thursday, between the hours of 4 p.m. and 10 p.m. of the 3rd of the month of January in the year 1974," made it plain that although he was willing to underwrite his wife's caprices in life, he was not about to saddle his heirs with them.

After ordering his executors to set up a charitable foundation in a tax haven like Lichtenstein and to merge his corporations into two holding companies controlled by the foundation, his will set up a pecking order of payments for his heirs, including the foundation, to follow.

From the revenues of his enterprises, they were first to pay the operating expenses of his companies. Second, they were to pay installments on the debts of his companies. Third, they were to make an annual payment of $250,000 to his daughter Christina, an annual payment of $100,000 to Jacqueline and annual payments of $25,000 a year apiece to her children until they were 21. (Caroline was then 17; John Jr. was 14.) At that point, Jacqueline was to begin receiving $150,000 a year.

The will made it clear that Onassis was restricting his wife to a life-long income of $150,000 a year because he had "already attended in life" to her. Farther down in the list of payments lurked the faint possibility of more income for the widow Onassis. After various annual sums are paid to sisters, cousins, business associates and the Alexander Onassis Foundation (a minimum of $1 million a year) and after 50% to 60% of the Onassis companies' profits are reinvested, and after 10% of the profits are put aside for a reserve — then 2% of any remaining profits are to be divided among the permanent board members, one of whom is "my wife Jacqueline."

Among the will's mixed blessings for Christina and Jacqueline were the yacht and the island of Skorpios, which, "should my daughter and wife so desire, they may retain for their own use" — if they could afford the upkeep. Helpfully, Onassis listed the annual maintenance of the yacht at $500,000, of the island at $100,000. If daughter and wife decided not to keep the yacht and island, they could not sell them, but had to offer the island to the Greek government as a resort for the chief of state or for the employees of Olympic Airlines, and donate the yacht to the government for the chief of state's use. Before they gave away the yacht, Christina and Jacqueline were to have their pick of its art and furnishings — three-fourths for the daughter, one-fourth for the wife. This could have been a considerable boon. The paintings, antiques and other artworks, including an El Greco, ancient jeweled Buddha and several priceless icons, were conservatively estimated to be worth $25 million.

Onassis clearly expected that Jackie might challenge the will, and several of its provisions were designed to fend her off. The most specific said that "if she or her inheritors claim part of my inheritance over and above the afore-

mentioned annual income, I order the executors of my will and my other inheritors to deny her such a right through all lawful means at the expense of
my inheritance. Should she be entitled to such a share by final court decision not allowing contestation by any legal means, I limit her to one-eighth of
the inherited estate, to be received from the hereditary share of my daughter
Christina."

Where did this leave Jackie in 1978, the year we tackled the problem of
evaluating the financial pluses and minuses of her status as double widow, national symbol and mother of two school-age children?

In calculating her income, we had the details of the wills of John Bouvier,
John F. Kennedy and Aristotle Onassis. Sources close to the Onassis family
in Athens told our researchers that Ms. Onassis was considering an offer of an
additional $100,000 a year in return for not challenging Ari's will. Estimated
incomes from the Bouvier inheritance and the Kennedy trust represented the
6.5% investment trusts were generally paying in those days.

We knew that Jackie was allowed to file a joint income tax return for two
years after her husband's death. The real estate taxes she paid in New Jersey
and Massachusetts were based on public records. Other figures were based on
Jackie's known living, spending and travel habits. We decided that she would
probably not sell her jewelry, art or real estate to balance the books.

INCOME:

Tax-exempt income from trust established by Onassis	$100,000
Fully taxable income under Onassis' will	100,000
Possible payment from Onassis estate for not contesting will	100,000
Tax-exempt income from John F. Kennedy trust	37,050
Tax-exempt income from Bouvier inheritance	4,160
TOTAL	$341,210

OUTGO:

Income taxes	$100,200
Staff & servants (at least six full-time, plus temporaries)	85,000
Home decoration and renovation	50,000
Clothes	30,000
Fifth Avenue apartment maintenance fee	30,000
Food and household expenses	25,000
Air fares	10,000
Art acquisitions	10,000
Entertainment (theater tickets, meals out, parties)	10,000
Insurance	7,500
Utilities	7,000
Real estate taxes	5,700
Hairdressing and beauty care	4,500
Gifts	2,500
Contributions	2,000
Maintenance of pony Macaroni	1,200
Magazines and books	500
Uninsured medical and dental costs	500
TOTAL	$381,600

Jackie was spending $40,390 more than she was receiving!

Imagine the New York tabloid headlines:

JACKIE IN THE RED! OUTSPENDS INCOME BY $40 GRAND!

JOHN-JOHN, CAROLINE INHERITANCES THREATENED!

ONASSIS SLAMS DOOR ON JACKIE LAWSUIT!

Bill Rukeyser's headline on my article was much more restrained:

"The Pleasant Problems of Jacqueline Onassis."

How did Jackie react? We never heard, and never will. Tish Baldrige?

Ditto. How did magazine newsstand buyers respond? A modest uptick.

Much more meaningful to me, at least, was the response of the Cunard

Line, operator of the *Queen Elizabeth II*, then the monarch of passenger ships, making luxury summertime transatlantic crossings between New York and Europe. When the phone on my desk rang, the voice at the other end was all upper-middle Britannic butter and toffee.

"Mr. Martin? This is Justin Smithers, [Not his real name. which I forget.] I'm Passenger Relations Vice President at Cunard. To attract the right sort of travelers, we're sponsoring a 'Festival of Life' this summer aboard the QE-Two. On each voyage over and back, we're offering individual talks by two lecturers in the main auditorium. We've signed on John Guare, the play-wright,[1] as one of the lecturers for one of the voyages, and we'd like you to be the other, talking about Jacqueline Onassis' finances. In return, we'd offer first-class passage over and back for two people, or a single first-class cabin plus two thousand dollars."

I was between marriages at the time, and chose Option One. As a result, and as a good *Money* reporter, I can open your eyes to a dining world I'd never before dreamed of. Going first class on the QE-Two (and now, I presume, on the new *Queen Mary*), you chose your dinner dishes at lunchtime. The first-class menu was splendid, but that was only the beginning. I quickly learned that when ordering dinner, you didn't have to limit yourself to items on the printed menu; you could have *anything you wanted.* Breast of duck? (How do you like it cooked?) Rack of lamb? (Rare? One rack? More?) *Foie de veau seignant?* Veal *ravigote?* (*Certainement!*)

Another thing to remember: Tips — handsome tips — are *de rigeur* on ships like the QE-Two and the *Queen Mary.* How to pay them? For *Money* magazine, I'd edited a story on *Playing Winning Blackjack,* and it worked! Unlike John Bouvier, I sidled off to the QE-Two's casino after dinner and dancing in one of the night clubs, and stayed under twenty-one enough to reward my waiters, the captain, the deck steward and the cabin steward — not lavishly, but well.

At sea ... and on the newsstand ... there's no such thing as a free launch.

---

[1]He wrote *House of Blue Leaves, Six Degrees of Separation,* and *Landscape of the Body.*

Chapter 31

Mohammed Ali

So where does Mohammed Ali fit in to all of this? He's actually part of *two* memoir chunks, the Petula Clark chunk and the Jackie Onassis chunk.

Putting Jackie on the cover of *Money* did produce a quick jump in newsstand sales, but no noticeable long-term improvement. We needed to keep the pot boiling, the trend trending, and newsstand sales sailing. The unspoken question around the office: Who do we do next? And how?

The answer came from an unexpected source, a man named Howard Bingham. In his Wikipedia writeup, Bingham described himself as "the biographer of Muhammad Ali and a professional photographer." He was also a hungry photographer. Shortly after we published the Jackie Onassis cover, our Assistant Design Director, Robert ("Doc") Dougherty, stopped me on the way to the men's room one spring morning in 1977 and asked whether I was interested in interviewing Ali.

Earlier that year someone shooting for the Guinness Book of Records had claimed that Ali, with 12 months of boxing purses worth $14.8 million and an estimated additional couple of million from endorsements and TV appearances, was the best-paid man in America.

He certainly was one of the most famous men in America — in the world, for that matter. I told Doc, "Sure."

"Well," Doc said, "there's this black photographer, Howard Bingham, who's a friend of Ali's. Bingham would like to get some of his photographs in a na-

Mohammed Ali in 1977, as photographed by Michael Brennan.

tional magazine, and he's offered to sneak you into Ali's apartment here in New York for an interview, introduce you, and take pictures of the interview."

"Sneak?" I said. "*Sneak*? What odds have you got that the pictures won't show me crumpled in a corner, a trickle of blood at the corner of my mouth, and Howard Bingham counting me out?"

"Howard's sure it will work," Doc said. "Anyway, Ali wouldn't hit a guy just for asking for an interview." Pause. "Would he?"

I carried the offer to Managing Editor Bill Rukeyser. "If you're game, it doesn't sound like a bad idea," said Bill.

I was game. Besides, Ali wouldn't hit a guy just for asking for an interview, would he?

The details: Early some morning when Ali was in town, I would show up in the lobby of the Hampshire House on Central Park South, where the Champion had an apartment. Bingham would meet me there at 7 or 8 a.m., escort me up to the apartment in a service elevator, and deposit me in Ali's living room. There I could wait until Ali got up and came out of the bedroom. I could then introduce myself, explain why I was there, and do the interview. When all was done, Ali would pose with me for photographs, Bingham would snap them. And I would leave with my scoop.

Simple.

Along about the third week in May, we got the call. Ali was going to be in town on Thursday, May 26, and Bingham was ready to meet me at 7 a.m. at

Hampshire House on Central Park South. In those days I had a small apartment on East 72nd Street, between First Avenue and the East River. At that hour on a Thursday, I could catch a cab easily and be on Central Park South in half an hour.

I got up at 5:30, turned on the TV, showered, shaved, dressed carefully, put on a dignified necktie. You are what you pretend to be, says Kurt Vonnegut, and after all, I was calling on Mohammed Ali as a *national magazine editor*. I watched the morning TV news out of the corner of my eye. The big local news was a man, tediously climbing the South Tower of the World Trade Center. On the *outside*.

The climber, they said, was a toy maker who'd visited the building quietly, at night, a year before. He'd made careful measurements of the window-washer tracks that ran up all 110 stories of the building, then the third tallest structure on earth. He had devised special clamps that would fit on the tracks and lock into place when they were pulled down by his body weight. He'd gone secretly to the building four or five times at night to test his equipment.

As he was climbing that Thursday morning, a crowd had gathered at the base of the building. Some men held a safety net. An ambulance was parked below. Men with bullhorns kept the pavement below the climber clear. Police had begged the man to stop, to come down. He had kept climbing. Two officers, one a suicide expert, were lowered down the side of the building in a window-washing basket to try to persuade him to stop. He swung away from them so they could not grab him. Helicopters hovered overhead.

It was like a scene from *King Kong*, but I couldn't dally. I had my own rendezvous with destiny on Central Park South. I got there at 6:40. Bingham was there, nervously waiting in the lobby

"I just came down through the apartment," he said. "Ali's asleep, but his people are already gathering in the living room."

"His people?" I said.

"Yeah," Bingham said. "A boxing champ always has a lot of people — trainers, sparring partners, managers, assistant managers, friends, doctors, friends of friends, friends of managers, go-fers — people who want to be near a champion, who want other people to know they're close with the champion."

"Photographers too," I said, to add a light touch.

"I'm the only photographer there," said Bingham, seriously. "We've been close forever. We practically grew up together."

"Does Ali know I'm coming?" I said. "Does he know I want to interview him?"

"I told him," he said, "but I'm not sure it got through. When he sees you, he'll probably remember."

I checked the TIME-LIFE shoulder bag holding my tape recorder and extra tapes. It didn't say TIME-LIFE in English. It said, *TEMPUS VITA DISPORTATI ILLUSTRATI.* Latin. Clever. My watch said it was a few minutes after 7.

We went through the lobby, down some stairs, along a corridor. Bingham pressed a button, an elevator door opened. Up we went, and came out into what was obviously the service area of a large apartment. There was a kitchen to our left. Through a door or two — details are hazy now — and we were in what was plainly the living room of Ali's apartment. It was a large, square-ish room, with chairs — many chairs — lined up around the walls. A television set stood in a corner, the picture on, no sound. I could see the Spider Man, still climbing, climbing. When the camera backed away you could see he was about a quarter of the way up.

Many men, all men, all Afro-American men, sat in the chairs around the walls. Bingham walked me to an empty chair, nodded, said nothing, disappeared. I put my *TEMPUS VITA* bag under the chair. The men paid no attention. They didn't just not look at me. They didn't *notice* me. Heads didn't turn. They talked softly, softly. I wasn't there. They weren't watching the TV. They kept their voices low, presumably not wanting to disturb the Champ. It was awfully quiet. On the TV screen, Spider Man seemed to be halfway up.

We were waiting for Mohammed. We were all waiting for Mohammed. I looked at my watch. The TV screen stayed quietly on, but no one looked at it. I did. I thought about pulling the *New York Times* out of my *TEMPUS*

VITA bag, but I didn't. The Spider Man was still climbing, climbing. 7:20. A few more black men came in, sat, talked quietly. 7:35.

7:40. I wished I'd brought a book. I'd never felt so invisible. Here I was, one white man among many black man, and *I* was the invisible man, not Ralph Ellison. How the world turns. 8:05. The door rattled once. Then again. It opened, and Mohammed Ali came in from what was obviously the bedroom. He was bare-chested, wearing only a pair of grey pants, slip-on shoes. Voices spoke up. "Mornin'." "Sleep okay?" "Mornin', Roger." Everyone perked up. Ali spoke to one or two at a time.

I must have been as obvious as a bar of soap in a coal scuttle, but Ali paid no attention. He may have glanced my way, but I didn't notice. He didn't notice. Was he *ever* going to see me? He saw the television screen, and the climber, climbing, climbing. He stopped and stared.

"Whut's *that?*" he said, loudly.

No one answered. No one had been watching. My opportunity.

"That's the man who's climbing the World Trade Center," I said, just as loudly.

"Doin' *whut?*" said Ali.

"Climbing the World Trade Center," I said.

"What's he doing that for?"

"I guess because it's *there*," I said.

That did it. Ali couldn't ignore me after that. He came over to see who I was. I introduced myself.

"I'm Peter Martin," I said. "I'm the *Money* magazine editor Howard Bingham's been talking to you about. I was in Las Vegas a while back, and saw Joe Louis shilling for a gambling casino. My editors want to know whether you're going to end up old and broke, like Joe Louis."

He stared at me. Then he said, loudly, angrily,

"Ain't gonna be *no* Joe Louis! Ain' gonna be *NO* Joe Louis!"

"He was robbed blind by crooked managers." I said. "They never paid income tax on his purses. He owes the government hundreds of thousands of dollars. Caesar's Palace gives him a room and food to pretend he's being paged for phone calls. But there aren't any phone calls. He's broke and broken, a sick old man!"

"Ain' gonna be *NO* Joe Louis!"

"How are you managing your money?" I said. "You got rid of those Kentucky businessmen you had before Sonny Liston, and joined the Nation of Islam. You made Elijah Muhammed's son your manager. How's he turning out?"

Ali pulled out the chair next to mine and sat down. I pulled the tape recorder out of the TIME-LIFE bag and pressed the Record button.

Ali said, "How can a little old black boxer who don't talk good, read contracts and know whut he's doin'? Even people who go to school don't know the tax laws. Even they get confused. So the boxer hires lawyers and people to handle things for him. He says, 'I have $1 million here. That's $500,000 after taxes."

Ali: "*They* say, 'Don't pay that tax. You don't have to pay the government all that money.' So he gives them the money, and they set up an office with *Negroes* in it so things look good." Ali didn't italicize *Negroes* as strongly as I have. He italicized it only conversationally, so I would know what he was getting at. But when he did, I knew he was leveling; we were going to have a good interview.

"And 99 percent of them are dishonest," he said. "They pay themselves, and use the money. And when they disagree, they don't say, 'George, this man handles this for you and he's doing poorly.' They say, 'George, it's terrible. You're broke.' When it comes time to pay taxes, there's no more money. And then the boxer goes to court and he ends up owing the government half a million dollars."

I asked, "Did something like that happen with you and the Louisville Management Group?"

"No, no, the deal they gave me was good. They put fifteen percent of all my earnings in a trust, which is there right now. They paid all my training fees, expenses, sparring partners. They weren't hungry, they didn't need the money. Now, I'll tell you something. Boxers don't all get robbed. Sixty percent of their money they spend on rising."

Rising? I didn't understand his use of the word. But as he went on, it became clear. *Rising* meant *rising status.* Coming up in the world. Being able to afford things you could never afford before. Buying things just because you wanted them.

He explained. "I bought a farm up in Michigan. It cost me $400,000 with 88 acres, and it don't earn me a quarter[1]. That's for rising. I got a training camp in Pennsylvania with log cabins, houses all over. It's cool there in that old log cabin up on the hill. Got my own gym, got my own kitchen, rec room — a little village. And I love it. I bought it. Five hundred thousand for that.

"So there I've got almost a million in two projects that don't make a quarter. To get that million, I had to get about three million. Of the three million, the government takes about half, and I give away about half a million. There goes two million. And my second wife — I gave her a two million settlement. So for me to give her two million, I have to get six million."

"That's what happens. I like nice cars. I wanted a Rolls Royce, and why not? It cost $42,000 to buy it. See a pretty Cadillac Eldorado, don't want to ride in the Rolls every day, buy the Eldorado. Cost me fifteen grand. I do a lot of traveling on the road, go from city to city, don't want to ride with two, three people. I want a beautiful mobile home. So I bought a Greyhound bus. Cost me around $170,000, finally."

"Now, say I didn't have a divorce suit. Say I didn't buy these things, just kept a nice apartment or a nice little modest house, bought me a Ford and drove the Ford until it fell over. I'd save two, three million dollars. But, see, I did get the divorce. I see things I want, I like them. The Rolls Royce is pretty. It's heavy, it drives nice. I want that. In the mobile home, we can cook in it, you can watch the movies, it's got six beds, it's got a bathroom, shower, it's got lounges. It's like an airplane, cockpit and all. Can't beat it."

"I give to charity, right? I gave an old folks' home in New York City $100,000.

---

[1] In 1975 Ali purchased an estate in Berrien Springs, Michigan, once owned by Louis "Lefty" Campagna, a bodyguard of Chicago mobster Al Capone.

I gave $1 million to hospitals, gave $30,000 for furniture. See, you want to take care of your mother, your father, your brother, your sister, charities and all like that. So you put a lot of money into things that don't make a quarter. They're not like investments."

I asked Ali: What *do* you invest in?

"There are people in the world who specialize in looking for people with money to make deals. They're convincing, and they really make you believe they've got it. I learned. I've been in everything. Oil, real estate, import-export — all these deals people just want your money to do the deal. They were looking out for their own pockets. There are no good deals! Best thing is tax-free municipal bonds. Put them up and don't touch them. If a man can get himself, oh, five million clear, why do you want to make money? You've *got* money. Some of the tax-free bonds are making what, six percent? What's that a year? $300,000? If a man can't live on 300,000 tax-free dollars a year, he can't live on anything."

"How long do you have on earth? You can kid and enjoy yourself up to about 65, and how old am I? Thirty-five. I don't have but thirty years. Out of those thirty years, I've got about nine years of sleeping. I've got two years of traveling. Watch television, watch movies — I've got a year of entertainment. That's twelve years out of my life. What's that leave? Eighteen? So I've eighteen years to live. In eighteen years, I won't have time to work on no more businesses, or watch no businesses. I'm going to go fishing. I'm going to take my little children out to the carnival. I want to take a trip to Hawaii and just lay in the pool and holler room service and sign checks. I don't want no headaches, no phone calls. So what I'm saying is, I don't want nothing to do with no businesses, don't want no investment, don't need no lawyers to watch nothing."

"I'll tell you something. Who had more money than Howard Hughes?"

Me, happy he asked the question: Not many people.

"All right! Did it help him when his heart stopped?"

Me: It didn't.

"You see, we're all going to die soon. You will die. Everybody on your staff will die. Everybody reading this article will die. I don't care if you're black, white. Joe Louis is going to see God quicker than all the people that's written about him. Joe Louis, you feel sorry for him, but he's going to feel sorry for you when your ass burns to eternity for ever and ever and ever. Why are you so worried about money, about how much money you got? I'm with Allah! It scares me to think that he's watching me. And blessing me, a little nigger from Louisville, Kentucky, who can boast of making $40 million, who can keep it all and not give it away. He blessed me to be healthy, to be world famous, to have pretty children — and to hear that my brothers are hungry, my brothers are hungry."

Me: If you gave it all away, people would still be hungry.

"Hold it there, hold it! You talk like some atheist. I know there's four billion people. Why did God let them be here? He's testing us to see what we're going to do about them. If I can help but one a week, I'm going to bed happy. I'm going to get myself straight. You see, there's no God in this country. Money is God. With the white man, mainly, and many blacks who have followed. God is money! Money! Money! Money! You even named your magazine *Money*!"

Me: Even you are going to need money later on. What have you done about that?

"I'm not saying which bank it's in, because we could go to court, you see, and then it would be in your book. But I have the money in different countries, in different banks. I'm not crazy. I have countries where I have loaned money to banks — Muslim banks in oil countries. They can say I've gone bananas, they can take me to court, but give me a plane ticket and I've got countries I can go to where I already have palaces. *Given* to me. One in Riyadh, Saudi Arabia, one in Tripoli, Libya, and one in Istanbul, Turkey. They remodeled a castle in Turkey, on the ocean, plus 400 acres. I can live in the Muslim world. They're everywhere. If I'm in trouble, you won't see me. If I get in such shape that I'm so embarrassed, I'll get on an airplane. And I'll hit one of my Muslim countries."

"So I'm not going to be a Joe Louis. *No Joe Louis*!"

Chapter 32

Newsletters

32.1   1953 Newsletters

1953

PBM-1	07-03	Servant Advice
PBM-2	07-10	Art in Southern Rhodesia
PBM-3	07-29	Easy Living
PBM-4	08-17	Preparation for Federation
PBM-5	08-27	Meet the Cunninghams
PBM-6	09-07	Confederate Party
PBM-7	09-17	Federal Party
PBM-8	10-05	Native Hospital
PBM-9	10-14	New Native Hospital
PBM-10	11-04	Nyasaland Native Riots
PBM-11	11-18	Federal Election Preview
PBM-12	11-29	Constitutional Crisis
PBM-13	12-05	Rhodesian Election Fracas
PBM-14	12-10	Election Predictions
PBM-15	12-17	Election Results

32.2   1954 Newsletters

1954

PBM-16	01-16	Apartheid in Higher Education
PBM-17	02-22	Apartheid in Native Housing
PBM-18	02-22	Native Opposition
PBM-19	03-15	Economic Integration
PBM-20	04-05	An Example of Economic Integration
PBM-21	04-25	Frozen Labor
PBM-22	05-17	A Quick Look at The Federation
PBM-23	05-31	Rhodesian University
PBM-24	06-30	Nationalists vs. The Trade Union
PBM-25	07-27	Meet Otto Schwellnus
PBM-26	08-19	Economic Integration in Primary Industry
PBM-27	08-29	Racial Peace in Swaziland
PBM-28	09-23	Zululand Troubles
PBM-29	09-27	African National Congress President
PBM-30	10-15	Malan's Retirement
PBM-31	11-24	The Cape Coloreds, Part I: Development
PBM-32	11-24	The Cape Coloreds, Part II: Beginnings of Reaction
PBM-33	11-24	The Cape Coloreds, Part III: Anti-European Organization
PBM-34	12-02	Nationalists Choose a Prime Minister
PBM-35	12-29	The United Party's "New" Native Policy

32.3   1955 Newsletters

1955

PBM-36	01-17	Concrete Steps Toward Territorial Apartheid
PBM-37	02-11	African Trade Union
PBM-38	03-02	Pygmies of the Ituri Forest
PBM-39	03-12	Settler
PBM-40	04-04	The Captain of the Reine Astrid
PBM-41	04-30	Native Labor in the Belgian Congo
PBM-42	05-23	The National Liberation Movement vs. Nkrumah
PBM-43	08-28	Wrap Up

Chapter 33

Bridge Chapter

I started this memoir with a promise to myself – and, by reference, to you, the putative reader. This was not to be a tedious, step-by-step recounting of my life (I was born, went to such and such schools, majored in such and such subjects in college, held whatever jobs with whatever companies, and so on and on). I was just going to touch the high points, provide a few telling details, and move on.

The surprise of winning a darkest-Africa journalism fellowship, the shock of getting there, the coping with the impossibility of repairing a British sports car in a remote Belgian colony, the game-ness of a wellborn St. Louis spouse in dealing with a mechanical/geographical emergency — these were a few of the high points of my Africa Fellowship. Except for the inescapable fact that the life of my son, Bill, had begun (I think) in Ndola, Northern Rhodesia, I had learned only a tiny bit about myself, and a passing moment in world history.

The Ford Foundation-funded Kampala conference about black African higher education produced a lot of laughs and some impossible suggestions. Ned Munger's second wife Betty ("Elizabeth the Second" was the cocktail-time term when Ned wasn't there), was a superior sort of South African who felt that black African men should be taught masonry and become better bricklayers. I ventured a neophytic observation that French colonials seemed to want Africans to end up at the Sorbonne, and Brits seemed convinced that African education should be aimed at eventual admission to Oxford or Cambridge. Portuguese settlers loved colonial Africa so much they wanted to marry it, not educate it. I hadn't spent much time with Belgians, who seemed tough and remote.

I had begun thinking about the end of my fellowship, and thinking about *not* wanting it to end. I wrote to Mr. Rogers about the "shallowness" of my Africa experience, saying that I had been looking at colonialism from the wrong end of a geopolitical telescope. Looking back at European policy-makers through this lens, I said, I could make out only vague figures who shaped "ideal" African societies that didn't fit African realities. Instead of flying straight back to New York from Africa, I proposed visiting Lisbon, Paris, Brussels and London to meet Africa-policy makers at their various foreign offices.

From Kampala, Uganda, Julie and I drove through the Ituri Forest in the Belgian Congo (where a tribe of waist-high pygmies re-trapped a tiny bushbuck we'd ordered them to set free) and then boarded a trans-shipped and rebuilt wood-burning Mississippi steamboat for a dreamlike ride down the Congo River from Stanleyville to the capital, Leopoldville. The MG followed, by barge.

The Captain of the Reine Astrid

[Newsletter PBM-40 was submitted 04/04/1955 from the Belgian Congo]

The long, slow voyage down the Congo River from Stanleyville to Leopoldville on the stemwheeler Reine Astrid is one that appeals to most of the senses and satisfies many of the appetites. I am almost ready to include it in my personal list of favorite trips—the plodding of a loaded oil tanker across the summer Caribbean from Venezuela to the United States, the rush of the air-conditioned train that runs the 90 miles from New York to Philadelphia in 90 minutes through some of the most pleasantly uninteresting scenery in the world and a day's drive almost anywhere in New Hampshire or Vermont in October.

The Congo trip has most of the requirements. The boat itself

The *Reine Astrid*, Congo River steamboat, in 1948.

is perfect, a high, square, white-painted "building" which was originally intended for use on the Mississippi when it was built in 1928. It has scrubbed wooden decks and varnished mahogany stateroom doors, twin stern wheels and stubby twin smoke stacks, an open lounge that runs from one side of the boat to the other on the top deck and a bottom deck filled with tubes, boilers, noise and heat. On each side are hung useless steel "lifeboats," always half-filled with rain water and impossible to lower because of the cordwood piled on the bottom deck beneath them. Steam hisses from one pipe or another from the time the fire is built in Stanleyville until it goes out at Leopoldville.

You float down the river, staying close to one bank or the other. The forest is thick and rich green; there are villages of huts, dugout canoes and swimming children. There's the bustle of the dally stop for wood, the quiet of the few hours after lunch when the sun beats down and people are taking siestas in the stuffy cabins, leaving you to enjoy the coolness of the lounge made to seem even cooler by the glaring sunlight on the River. An efficient refrigerator keeps the beer and the Coca-Colas icy, an efficient cook serves the steaks rare and the mayonnaise unrancid. In the evenings there is talk and the shower of bits of red-glowing wood from the smoke stacks. The trip lasts for seven days, the river widening and narrowing, passing islands and piling floating clumps of green plants against the wharves of sluggish river towns.

But the comfort and the relaxation lose some of their savor when you get to know the captain of the Reine Astrid. The captain looks like Lord Byron in shorts, with dark untrimmed curls, dark eyes and an olive skin turned a golden brown by the sun reflected from the River. He isn't unusually tall or short and wears no badges of rank—just unvarying white shorts and white shirts, with white socks rolled down over his low-cut street shoes. The first time I saw him was in Stanleyville, the afternoon we went aboard the Reine Astrid. There was no way of knowing he was the captain. He was sitting at a table in the lounge, leaning forward in one of the wicker armchairs talking loudly to three other men. They were drinking cold beer in frosted green bottles and laughing and I took them for port officials or veteran Congo travellers. It was plain they were not new passengers like myself; they took no notice of the last minute bustle of loading and seemed perfectly at home.

The next time I saw him stands out more vividly in my mind. It was the same day, in the afternoon as I was going ashore to give the keys of the car to the man in charge of loading it on the boat. I walked down the deck a few feet behind the captain, went through the door to the lounge and headed for the top of the companionway stairs. At the top of the steps stood an African, dressed in tattered khaki and barefoot. In his hand he was holding a dog-eared brown folder, apparently some kind of identity card or permit to seek work. As the captain approached, the African held out the card to him and began to say something in French. The captain didn't even break his stride. With a quick motion he twisted the African's arm, forcing him to face back down the stairs. Then he kicked him, hard, and the African stumbled and half-fell down the flight of steps to the second deck. The captain moved on to the bar and I followed the African down the stairs. He was standing at the bottom, looking up at the captain's white-shirted back.

The look on his face was frightening. Europeans who subscribe to the Natives-are-just-like-children theory would say he looked like a child who had been beaten, perhaps unjustly. They would add that, like children, Africans do not bear grudges or carry feelings of hostility over from one time to the next.

I saw the look of a man who had been taught that the way to find work was to speak the white man's language, fill out the white man's registration card, and go to the white man without pride, holding the card in his hand and speaking politely. And when he had done all that, he found that complying with the white man's rules meant getting kicked. He did not look like the kind of man who was taking his tumble down the stairs as part of the normal white-black relationship. He looked at the captain with stark hatred; and when I passed he looked at me the same way.

When a river boat is under way you see very little of the captain. He spends all his time on the bridge, following the channel of the river with the precision of something out of Mark Twain. There are always two Africans with long graduated poles standing on the bows feeling for the bottom and every 10 or 20 minutes the channel switches from one side of the river to the other or from the east bank of an island to the west bank of the next. The captain eats, sleeps, washes and drinks on the bridge, only coming down to run along the deck shouting orders during a landing and to drink beer with his friends from ashore when the boat is tied up. This is especially true in the narrow section of the river from Stanleyville to beyond Coquilhatville, about five days' steaming.

One evening, as we were nearing Coquilhatville, we were sitting in the lounge sipping *Grand Marnier*. It was after dinner and a waning full moon showed the dark wall of the forest slipping by. We were debating whether to play a second game of Scrabble when behind us, along the deck towards the bridge, we heard loud shouts and a collection of expressive French curses. Turning, we saw the captain with two of the African members of the crew. As we watched he hit one of them in the face—then turned to the other and told him to stay where he was standing. The captain chased the first African down the deck—he came running into the lounge and scurried down the companionway to the lower deck.

Then the captain walked slowly back to the other African who was standing with his back to the rail. He shouted something to the African, hit him in the face and told him to get out. The second African didn't run. He stared at the captain for a moment, then turned on his heel and walked away with a certain amount of dignity with the captain screaming insults at his receding back.

I had a long talk with the captain the night before we reached Leopoldville. True to passenger-ship tradition, the last night was meant to be a time of great festivity with a specially elegant menu and dancing after dinner. The menu was elegant indeed —- chicken cooked in a piquant sauce and a flaming pancake for dessert – but the dancing proved something of a flop. There weren't enough women to go around and what women there were had long since passed the time of life when dancing on a Congo River boat would seem like fun. It was like any other night except for the men's neckties and the appearance of the captain after dinner dressed in long white trousers.

After a few abortive attempts at dancing, I joined the group sitting at the captain's table. There were four of us; a bearded Belgian touring the Congo in search of investment possibilities, an official of an insecticide-fertilizer company returning from a field trip, the captain and myself. The Belgian was chaffing the captain when I sat down. During the day's steaming the boat had hit a sandbar, with enough speed to pass over it, but also with enough force to make the collision apparent to everyone aboard. A few minutes later the boat had struck another.

"What a captain," the Belgian was saying. "Here we find ourselves in the widest part of the River and you cannot find a channel." He smiled broadly to prove he was speaking in fun, but the captain was not in a cheerful mood.

"Ah, passengers," he sighed. "I wish I were back on the open sea on a cargo ship instead of on this packing box. You do not understand that I took the shallow channel to save us eight hours going the long way. I knew the sand was there; I also knew that I could pass over it. If you want a different life, change places with me. I would like to see you direct this boat all by yourself, with no other European aboard. Except, of course," he said with a casual sweep of his hand, "the passengers."

The Belgian seemed hurt. He sank back in his chair and pulled deeply on his grenadine soda. There was a painful pause in the conversation. The company official sat silently, observing us all with a smug detachment and the captain ordered another whiskey.

To end the silence I mentioned to the captain that I, also, had been to sea. At this he brightened and began the first of what turned out to be 45 minutes of sea stories, most of them dealing with personal violence. He began with the days during the war when he first went to sea and ended with a tale of two years ago when, as chief mate of a cargo vessel he was threatened by a drunken boatswain with a six-inch knife in a rum-soaked port in South America. "Then, like a fool, I left the sea and came here," he said, despondently pointing towards the bridge.

"Is it so bad then?" I said.

"It is terrible. Do you know that I left Leopoldville on this trip with a crew of 16? And that there are now only seven left to run the boat? The captains of the cargo boats do not have to keep to a strict schedule. But I, who must direct the boat which breaks down most often and which needs to stop for wood once, sometimes twice a day, must keep a very precise schedule. Who gets the devil if we are late? Me, And the passengers" – he seemed to be talking as one sea-faring man to another – "are brave enough to tell me that I should not touch the sand when it means saving many hours."

This was too much for the Belgian. He rose heavily from his chair, scowled at, the captain and went off to revive the dancing. The company official seemed interested. He called the waiter and ordered whiskeys all around. Then he asked the captain, "Why do the Natives leave the ship?"

The captain said, Oh, they say that the work is too hard. Tonight, when you were eating your dinner, I saw that the steam pressure was going down. So I went down to the engines to see the trouble. All the Natives were sitting about, the fire was dying and no one was putting wood into the furnace, I said "What is this?" The Natives said that they did not have enough to eat and they were tired. It was too much work, they said, for only seven men. So I was forced to beat them with a stick of wood until they went back to work."

"It is like this during all the voyages. It happens that a Native says he will not work. So I say, "*Eh bien*, come to my bathroom." They know what it means to come to my bathroom. I take them there and I lock the door behind us. Then I tell them to take down their trousers." He glanced about to see if any tender-minded women were within hearing distance.

"Then I beat them with a good stick until they say they will go back to work. Many times they refuse to take down their trousers. So I say very well and I take my handcuffs —- very heavy steel. I take the two circles together like this and put them on my hand." He went through the motions of putting on a set of brass knuckles. "Then I hit them, hard, in the mouth. I do not have to do it twice —- they say they will go back to work. You have seen the one with the mouth like this?" He puffed out his lips and assumed a mournful expression. It was the handcuffs that did it, two days ago. "

"But those Natives, they are worse than children —- they are savages. They say that they will go back to work and then, *pouf!* The next time we stop for wood they are gone and I must continue with a smaller crew. Every time I return to Leo with more than half the crew vanished." He shook his head, then swallowed the rest of his drink.

"What does Otraco[1] say to you when you return with less than half the crew? I asked."

"Oh, they complain all the time. Tonight after dinner you wrote your complaints on the paper, *hein*? They go to the company, you see, and if there are bad complaints they call for me. "What is this?" they cry. "A passenger says his cabin was not properly cleaned." And then they give me a very bad time. But the steward knows that if this happens *I* will give *him* a very bad time when I return to the ship." He made a fist and shook it threateningly, We do not have many complaints. "

"And if they talk of the disappearance of the crew I say, "if you are dissatisfied, discharge me." They never do it for they know they will never find another captain for this old box. All the other captains are afraid of the Reine Astrid. She is too old and it is too much trouble to stop for wood all the time. And, when there is a strong wind, she is very hard to manage, I am the only captain who does not lose time with her by sticking in the sand. The company knows that if they have published a schedule they must keep it even if it means replacing half the crew each voyage."

The captain got up. "You must excuse me," he said. "We must stop several hours tonight before we go into the basin at Leo. I am afraid we cannot meet again. Tomorrow I am too busy." He shook hands very formally all around, then went off down the deck towards the bridge.

---

[1] The shipping company which runs the river boats.

Chapter 34

Gold Coast Gold

I saw the captain once more before I left the boat. The day we arrived in Leo, in the middle of getting the baggage ashore, I saw him rush across, the gangplank and run up a long ramp to the pier. He threw his arms around a pretty young woman, then kissed the small child with her. He picked up the child and walked back towards the boat with the woman, talking happily. The sun was bright and sharp and his white shorts and his shirt gleamed dazzlingly in the sun.

Men of physical violence like the captain are rare in the Belgian Congo – the government sees to that. It is fairly certain that the government knows of the captain's brand of discipline and will do away with him when someone is found to replace him or when the *Reine Astrid* is scrapped. But in the meantime he is there, carrying on the good work of the South African *herrenvolk*, the old Rhodesians, the Kenya settlers, the palm-oil ruffians and the Arab, European and American slavers.

The Congo Government is proud of the job it is doing to eliminate the color bar in practice as well as theory. It points to its *immatriculés* and its African railway engine drivers as symbols of the bright, new Congo. It is odd that the Africans you talk to seem to accept immatriculation. An *immatriculé* is an African who has proved to the satisfaction of a review court that he has accepted and adopted European civilization. He is given a card which is of great assistance in gaining good employment, moving about freely and eating in good restaurants. The system has only recently been introduced, and there are now somewhere between 60 and 150 Immatriculants in the Belgian Congo. What they object to is the attitude of white men towards them. They point out that it is not necessary to act like the captain to think like him.

Julie and I checked out Léopoldville (and French-colonial Brazzaville, across the river), then drove along the north Congo Riverbank in French West Africa. A lot of mahogany trees were being harvested by German-speaking crews along the way, and their trailer weight made the mud ruts so deep that when we slipped off the road our MG wheels couldn't touch bottom. The MG would then sit on its chassis, tires in the air, unable to move until a timber truck had to stop ahead of (or behind) us. Cheerfully, a work gang of black Africans would lift the car (including Julie and our unborn son) to the side of the road, and when their truck passed, come back and make us mobile again with our left wheels on the center hump and our right ones on high ground off the road.

We eventually reached the Atlantic-coast port of Pointe Noir, where we boarded a French passenger ship (the *Père Foucauld*), bound for Lomé, capital of French Togoland on the Atlantic coast. From there it was but a short drive across the border to Accra, capital of Britain's Gold Coast colony.

The "gold" of the Gold Coast was never nuggets or bars of the yellow metal. It was human gold — slaves. Accra was one of the principal ports from which thousands of chained black Africans were shipped as layers of cargo, to die at sea or to plant and harvest the sugar cane of the Caribbean or the cotton crops of the American South. Even as a slang term, "Gold Coast" didn't apply in the 1950s. No resort hotels soared above the Atlantic beaches, no glittering casinos offered roulette or *chemin de fer*. The only "hotel" in Accra was a pinewood-and-tarpaper barracks at the airport, built to shelter American Air Force crews who had ferried warplanes from the U.S. to Brazil, to West Africa, and finally, to Britain. The rooms were noisy wooden boxes, the showers were down the hall and the dining room a primitive space decorated with posters and graffiti.

The motivating force behind the dining-room service was "dash," the West

African/pidgin-English term for "tips." Tips were also important aboard the *Pàre Foucauld*, and fellow ICWA Fellow Dave Reed, who'd boarded ship with us in Lomé,) had run out of cash by the time we reached Nigeria, where he was disembarking. We had to scrape the bottom of our cash reserves to lend him tip money to get him out of the clutches of the cabin stewards and deckhands that offloaded his Chevrolet Carryall from ship to dock in Lagos.

Result: We had no cash left in Accra to "improve" food service at the Airport Hotel, and a fund transfer from Guaranty Trust in New York to Barclay's Bank (D.C.O.) in Accra took FOREVER. When we complained about the non-service to a member of the wait staff he finally replied, in Pidgin, "Why you no show me your hand?" ("Why aren't you tipping me?"). I tried to explain that a money transfer from the U.S. was inexplicably delayed, but the notion of a white traveler in West Africa without cash was an obvious, downright lie. Service dried to a trickle. Finally, Colin Hatherly (a Nestle Corporation representative living at the hotel) and Stanley Simons (a buyer of winnowed Gold-Coast diamonds for his family jewelry firm on Manhattan's West 47th Street), came to our rescue with loans, and mealtime normality was restored.

Colin Hatherly's "job" for Nestle was to watch cocoa ripen. He made regular visits to Gold-Coast cocoa-growing regions, sent weekly crop reports (and, closer to harvest time) daily cables to headquarters in Switzerland. If the crop was looking good, on time, and plentiful, Nestle's "cocoa-futures" buyers could more or less relax. If the opposite was looming, "futures" contracts could be bought early and cheaply enough to be extremely profitable. I found Colin's job (and the topic of futures contracts) interesting as an ICWA newsletter topic, and when the MG's gas tank got emptier and emptier because of our fruitless, petrol-burning trips to the bank (there was no reliable phone service between the hotel and Barclay's), I asked him for an opportunity to travel with him to the cocoa plantations.

We were friends, and Julie and I had earned his trust sufficiently to make once-an-evening trips with him (and Stanley Simons) to the airport to check her pre-natal weight on the PanAm baggage scale. But, as he explained, no matter how friendly we were, there was a chance that I could be serving as a lookout for Hershey's, or Mars Candy, or Cadbury, or Suchard. Company policy was that no one could tag along.

Stanley would have been happy to have me travel with him, but he moved only from the hotel to his office in downtown Accra — which was nowhere near the bank. I did go along several times and saw West Africans come in with Coke and whiskey bottles filled with diamonds of all colors and sizes (mostly small and dark, although once in a while Stanley found a yellow or white reason to be excited, he told me). Stanley was one of four "foreign" traders (a Brit, a Netherlander, a South African, and an American) permitted to deal with West African winnowers. The business basis was not an "auction." Traders didn't seize on a winnower's lucky strike and bid against each other. Depending on past dealings and local reputations, winnowers would approach the foreigner of their choice. The buyer would spread the gems out on a white surface and sort them according to color and size. He would then settle down with a magnifier and a strong light and examine the gems more closely. Then bargaining then began and prices were set.

Stanley had a partner, "Mama Bee". She was large, good company, and fun.

The three of us had lunch in downtown Accra from time to time. Whether she was with us or not, Stanley made no bones about the fact that his partner was the most important part of his business operation. "Market women," it was said, were the best business people in Accra, and Stanley boasted that Mama Bee was one of the absolute best.

Chapter 35

The Ear of the Asantaheni

When our money transfer arrived at Barclay's bank, Julie and I were back in business. We repaid the dining-room advances from Colin and Stanley, "dashed" the waiters and room servants, filled the MG petrol tank, and settled our outstanding hotel charges. The Gold Coast was scheduled to become independent Ghana in a few months, and the election of a Ghanaian Parliament loomed. To get the lay of the political landscape, I headed the MG for the colony's second city, Kumasi, capital of the ancient, up-country, Ashanti kingdom.

No love was lost between Ashanti tribesmen and the "coast people," who were mostly supporters of the Peoples' Progressive Party ("PPP") of the favorite for Prime Minister, Kwame Nkrumah. Back in the bad old days of a thriving slave trade, predatory bands of coastal raiders would make forays north, seize groups of Ashanti, and transport them to southern ports along the Atlantic Coast for sale and export as slaves.

A resonant spokesman for the Ashanti was a black Britain-educated newspaper editor and editorialist, Joseph Apiah. When I got to Kumasi (after a memorable "palaver" with a villager along the way whose incredibly valuable goat had a fatal encounter with the front bumper of my MG) I called on Mr. Apiah for an exploratory interview. He suggested that I could gain better access to Ashanti voters if I had the imprimatur of the Ashanti King, the "*Asantaheni.*" Mr. Apiah agreed to arrange an introduction, and go with me to

311

the Asantaheni's throne room.

It was more "audience" than interview. The Asantaheni, being no ordinary mortal, did not speak with visitors directly. He had two assistants on such occasions, one being the "ear" of the Asantaheni, seated to his right, and the other the "voice" of the Asantaheni, on a chair to his left. If a visitor had a question, he spoke it to the Asantaheni's "ear." The "ear" then translated the question into an African language and passed it on to the Asantaheni. The Asantaheni considered the question, then turned to his "voice" and delivered his response, The "voice" then gave the answer to the visitor. This was a time-consuming process, but quite convenient for the Asantaheni, who had plenty of time to ponder the question — and his answer (or non-answer, or re-question:"What was that again?") — before delivery. My queries, mainly about Ashanti political attitudes toward coast people, produced more re-questions than answers, so I learned just about nothing, which is what I suspect the Asantaheni had in mind.

Being new in town, I became something of a celebrity among friends of Colin Hatherly and Joe Apiah and the local representative of the oil company, Texaco, whose name now escapes me. They introduced me around, and also introduced me to a favorite Kumasi evening pastime, a local version of "Capture the Flag." A grassy traffic circle lay at the southern entry to the town. On the shady edge of the circle, away from the setting sun, stood three or four stores, one of them well-stocked with one-litre bottles of chilled Beck's beer. On the store's flat roof, overlooking the circle, folding canvas chairs stood lined in staggered semi-circles. Below, set in the circle, were five flag poles. The flags hoisted on them were either the Ashanti flag or the banner of the PPP.

As the sun set and work tapered off, crowds of men (black and white) migrated toward the traffic circle. On the circle itself, PPP and Ashanti activists flexed their muscles, determined to tear down rival flags and replace them with their own. Fistfights and mass wrestling matches broke out between individuals and clumps of individuals. Above, bottles of Becks were wagered on the outcomes. Cars and ambulances carried way the injured and the fallen. Wins and losses were measured by the number of Ashanti and PPP flags hauled down, re-hung, and hauled down again. There was no final score announced, but some general good or bad feeling determined the overall result of the day's skirmishes. And, of course, the final total of flags on poles was considered by some — but not all — of the spectators — who trickled off to pre-prandial pink gins or gin-and-tonics and then to supper itself.

Life was interesting in the Gold Coast, but Kwame Nkrumah's victory in Ghana's first parliamentary election became so sure a thing that back in Accra, Julie and I found planning our departure more interesting than the endless beach parties organized by local Lebanese businessmen to entertain PanAm stewardesses during their layovers.

The idea of leaving became even more interesting when a letter from Mr. Rogers used the word "splendid" to describe his reaction to my idea of returning home by way of Portugal, France, England and the Netherlands. "While you're in England," he said, "be sure to stop in at New College at Oxford. It's an important center of Africa studies, not only at Oxford, but for all of Great Britain." He'd written to a friend of his there, he said, and knew that all of his colleagues would greatly appreciate my news and views of current developments in British Africa.

Rather than rely on trains, rental cars, taxis and buses in Europe, we decided to ship the MG to Bordeaux, pick it up after our PanAm DC-7 dropped us off in Lisbon, and drive the car around the continent as I carried out my foreign-office interviews. To do this we would have to leave the car at the Gold Coast deep-water port at Takoradi, pay for its shipment in advance, fill out the *carnet de passage* as proof that the car had never legally left Southern Rhodesia (and therefore had never had to pay import or export duties in any African territory as it entered or left). Trouble was, we were scheduled to fly away before the car could be shipped, so we got Stanley Simons to agree to drive the car to Takoradi and take care of the formalities. His driver would follow him and bring him back.

Off we took. Lisbon was lovely and comfortable, and the fluent French Jim Billington and I had learned from Miss Baker (Merci, Mademoiselle Boulanger!)

at Lower Merion High School helped me struggle through the Foreign-Office interviews. Africa seemed to be far from the forefront of the minds of the policy people I met. Comfortable smiles of agreement were the principal response when I told them that many of the Africans I'd met in Angola and Mozambique seemed to yearn for a return of the reliability of colonialism.

I was even more grateful to Miss Baker when the train from Lisbon deposited Julie and me in Bordeaux. I'd buy a diamond with complete confidence from Stanley Simons on 47th Street in New York, but he'd forgotten to fill out the MG's carnet when he dropped the car off at Takoradi in the Gold Coast. Physically, its gas tank safely empty, the car sat in a Bordeaux warehouse. Legally it was still somewhere in Southern Rhodesia, or Nyasaland, or the Belgian Congo, or wherever, liable for all sorts of customs fees or potential seizure as contraband in France.

What a test of my mastery of the subjunctive, the conditional, the bureaucratic, pluperfect verberie of France! It took two and a half hours and a visit to at least two superior customs officers with my much-stamped passports before I could successfully plead my case and convert a *cheque de voyage* into francs enough to fill the tank with *essence* and drive the MG off the dock and onto *les rues de France! Le jour de gloire était arrivée!*

Chapter 36

Oxford in July

In summertime, your first Oxford walkabout fulfills your dreams. Slumbering spires and low, windowed, brown stone walls surround courtyards of lush-green lawn beyond porters' lodges. At any moment you expect to find Lord Peter Wimsey or one of the Waugh boys ambling toward you in a blazer and significant necktie.

This is how it seemed in July 1955, when Julie and I took a black, high-ceilinged Austin cab from the Oxford train station to New College to meet Britain's once-and-future Africa policy-makers. I'm writing this more than six decades later, and I wasn't making diary notes at the time, so the expanse of my recollections is broad, and probably faulty.

My Executive Director, Walter Rogers, had written to the rector of the College before I arrived, and he (or his assistant) was surely waiting. A room had been booked at a nearby "B and B" and our New College greeter probably had the driver take Julie there to deposit our bags after welcoming us at the porter's lodge. Both terms — "B&B" and "porter's lodge" — were new to us (there were no "Bed-and-Breakfasts" in Africa and certainly no university porters' lodges; we'd spent our two-year fellowship in rented houses, hotels and "guest houses.")

We learned that if we wanted crisp B-and-B bacon, we had to order it "burned." If we wanted the room warmed (and Julie, being pregnant, often did, even in summer) we had to insert shillings into the gas-burning fireplaces.

There was no air-conditioning and (we could tell by the absence of radiators and air ducts) no equivalent central heating in winter.

I ate lunch with faculty and graduate students. I gave two or three talks about current trends in European colonial policy south of the Sahara. I had private talks with university friends of Rhodesia's Godfrey Huggins and Nestle's Colin Hatherly and was increasingly and endlessly surprised at the impression the academic Brits gave of expecting the policies and political geography of British Africa to continue more-or-less as "normal" in the aftermath of World War II. Julie and I drank sherry and a bit of white wine with faculty and graduate students in the afternoons. Leaving Julie behind, I ate lunches and dinners at New College's "high table" and washed them (the dinners, anyway) down with vintage claret. Heady stuff!

After a pleasant (for me) but rather distant (for Julie) early-summer week or ten days at Oxford, she and I set off for London, and home.

Home! Our first "home" visit was to my parents in Philadelphia, since it was near our New York landing spot at Idlewild. To the naked eye (and our eyes felt quite "naked") changes were highly visible from the window of the trains from New York, to Philadelphia, to Wynnewood (PA). Our memories were that when we'd left for Africa in 1953, passenger cars were all one color — black, mostly, with an occasional dark maroon or Navy blue. Now, in 1955, the cars in the parking lots along the way seemed to be multicolored — two-toned, particularly the Oldsmobiles and Fords — and decked out with a lot of additional chrome around the wheels and radiator grilles.

With motherhood approaching, Julie "showed" her pregnancy, but because of our travels and ever-changing diet, she had not gained a lot of weight. We both looked and felt "normal" and were eager for whatever lives awaited us. Settled in with my parents, I called Walter Rogers at the ICWA office in New York to arrange a thank-you visit.

As far as I could tell, WSR (in letters from Peru, my fellow Fellow Bill MacLeish called him "Whizzer" and I'd begun doing the same) had not changed a bit. Nor had Miss Pluntze. We chatted, hit the high points of the years I had been away, went down the street for lunch, chatted some more. He asked me about post-fellowship plans, and I talked about getting back into journalism. I thanked him some more, and he said that I probably should thank Cleon Swayzee at the Ford Foundation. Mr. Swayzee handled Africa projects there, he said, and much of my fellowship had been funded by him. He asked Miss Pluntze to call Mr. Swayzee and set up a lunch when it was convenient.

It was convenient the next day, and we met in a restaurant — which one, I don't remember. Mr. Swayzee asked what I foresaw for the subcontinent as colonialism faded and nationhood loomed, and I repeated what I'd been saying at Oxford. "You haven't talked much about that trip," Mr. Swayzee said. "What did you think of it?"

I told him I was surprised at the Oxonians' expectation that colonial African life would go on — changed somewhat, of course, but altered only slightly from the white-dominated agricultural past.

"Interesting," he said. "This seems to be the Churchillian line these days, but things don't seem to be going his way."

The conversation moved easily on in a friendly vein, but along around 4 in the afternoon I felt it was time to start saying goodbye. I began to talk in that direction.

"Hold on," said Mr. Swayzee. "What about the Oxford idea?"

"What Oxford idea?" I said.

"You mean Walter hasn't told you? That trip to Oxford. They were looking you over as a D. Phil. candidate. ("D.Phil" is OxfordSpeak for "Ph.D.") They've agreed to accept you, and Walter's arranged for us to pay for it. He never mentioned this to you?"

"Not a word."

"Oh, that Walter! Now that you do know, what do you think of the idea?"

"It's a surprise to me, and I'm honored. But I don't know the details," I said.

"Well, write to the people at New College, and let us know," he said. "And, Congratulations! You've obviously had a splendid fellowship!"

Chapter 37

Two Roads Diverge

An Oxford Ph.D.! I didn't know it at the time, but this was Mr. Rogers' way of launching the next stage of a continuing relationship between himself, promising ICWA Fellows, and established international scholars. He would position a new recruit at major colleges and universities to produce a coordinated flow of serious writing and education about World Affairs and international policy.

Journalism was a fine way for a bright young man to start, but newspaper and magazine articles were ephemeral and fleeting. Informative and entertaining, perhaps, but no way to have a significant, lasting effect on the way important men made policy, took action, and changed the way the world behaved and thought. With funding pledged by the Ford and Rockefeller Foundations and concept support from more than a dozen major college presidents visited personally by him and former ICWA Fellows Phillips Talbot and Edwin Munger, he had launched an international-policy organization at a higher level of influence — at universities, major four-year colleges, and graduate schools.

He called it the American Universities Field Staff, or AUFS. "Staff" members — he called them "Associates" (as in "Associate Professors") — would be men deeply interested and involved in international understanding and studies. They would carry out serious research and make it accessible through their writing. For three or four continuous years, they would be based in their particular countries or regions of the world. They would teach as adjunct or traveling faculty at "member universities" where they would focus on major international issues, write in depth about them, teach courses that would go above and beyond conventional knowledge and understanding, and share their findings with fellow faculty. Their writings would become textbooks or academic papers. In effect, they would be advanced and exploratory adjunct faculty at many colleges and universities.

Mr. Rogers didn't ask me directly to become an Associate of the Field Staff. I think he saw promise in me, and thought it would be a good idea to develop it and "see how things turned out." He had done the same with Ned Munger, sending him to the University of Chicago for a Ph.D. in Geography when he finished his Africa fellowship. He did the same with Dennison ("Denny") Rusinow (a D. Phil. at Oxford after Denny had finished a 1940s ICWA fellowship on the growth of Communism in Yugoslavia and eastern Europe), and Granville ("Red") Austin after a multi-year India fellowship. And (as I look back) Albert Ravenholt (China), Roger Reynolds (Japan), Doak Barmett (China), David Binder (Communism in the Balkans), Dick Nolte (the Middle East), Walter Young (Manchuria), Geoff Oldham (China), and on, and on, and on.

I wrote to the New College people about Oxford advanced degrees in sub-Saharan Africa and found out (more or less — mostly more) what was involved in a D.Phil. I would have to choose a topic of study — traditional tribal politics, for example, or the role of paramount chiefs in transitional societies. I would have to consult with faculty and researchers inside and outside of Oxford to find out who had the greatest expertise in providing the lectures and reading for my chosen topic. Since I had no previous Oxford degree, I would have to spend three years (three years) in residence in Oxford "reading" and discussing material both ancient and modern about my topic or topics close to its fringes. I could travel in and out of Africa for a summer or two interviewing sources old, new, orthodox, revolutionary, literary, contemporary, black, white, brown or sepia.

Where would Julie and (as it turned out) baby William Thornton Martin III (named for his grandfather and great-grandfather) live? And his baby brother(s) or sister(s)? How would they grow? What would they learn? What would they and their mother do while their D.Phil.Candidate father read, and studied, and traveled, and wrote, and grew into understanding of the inevitable Dissertation? And assembled an advisory committee, and prepared to defend his Dissertation thesis? (Or theses? Or revised thesis?)

Julie and I traveled to her family and friends and relatives in St. Louis and southern Illinois and pondered these questions. I eased "expense money" of $600 from ICWA for presumed "furniture storage" while we were out of the country and with the money bought Julie's father's low-mileage, four-door Ford sedan (black) and traveled back and forth between Philadelphia, New York and St. Louis until William Thornton Martin III ("Bill") was born on October 29, 1955.

And, on one of those trips, I responded to the invitation I'd received in the Gold Coast in April to stop in at the Time-Life Building in New York and talk with Jay Gold, the Articles Editor of LIFE magazine. I'd sent him copies of two or three of the monthly newsletters I'd written for ICWA.

"These were pretty good," said Mr. Gold (Need I say he said, "Call me Jay?"). "Particularly the one on the steamboat ride on the Congo River. We could use it now, if you'd like, and we'd like you to try a few more."

"What would I get paid?" I asked. "Would I go on salary?"

"No, you'd be a free-lancer. We'd pay the going rate," he said. "Fifteen hundred dollars, plus an extra five hundred apiece for any of your photos we could use. Do you have photos of the trip?"

"No. I wasn't thinking about photos at the time. There may be a couple still in the camera. I'd have to check."

"Go ahead and check," he said, "but I doubt whether we could use them anyway. I'd have to get an okay from higher-up to send a photographer to shoot the story, and that would take a while. But the story will keep."

"Free-lancing won't do for me," I said. "I've got a pregnant wife, and I need a salary."

"You're talking like a TIME writer," Jay said. "I'll give them a call." He opened an in-office phone book and dialed the phone on his desk.

"Ed," he said. "Jay Gold. I've got a TIME writer here in my office you ought to talk to. When can you see him?" He made a note. "Tomorrow at ten-thirty? Twenty-fifth floor?" He arched his eyebrows quizzically in my direction. I nodded. "Done," he said. "He'll be there. I'll send down a couple of his writing samples."

"Ed Cerf," he said to me. "Assistant Managing Editor. Good guy."

Unaccustomed to Time-Life working hours, I walked into the building lobby at nine a.m. the next day and rode the elevator up to 25. When the doors opened there was no living person in sight. And, as I found, not in the offices that opened off the corridors. There was no reception area. No receptionist. No one. I walked around the corridors, and finally found what seemed to be an office boy, pushing a wheeled cart loaded with newspapers.

I asked for Ed Cerf. "They don't come in 'til after ten," he said. "I'll show you his office. You can read his papers." He led me to an anteroom, pointed to a chair, and put copies of the New York Times, the New York Herald Tribune, the Daily News, the Daily Mirror, and the Wall Street Journal on a table. All dailies! All different!

"Does he get these every day?" I said.

The delivery guy looked at me blankly. "Every day," he said, and left me to my reading.

New York was a newspaper town! I'd already seem the Times that morning, but the Herald Tribune was more reader-friendly. Even more-so were the Mirror and the Daily News tabloids. How anyone could get through them in a single morning was a mystery. I was still buried in them when a trim fellow in a cord suit and bow tie walked in.

He smiled in my direction, "Peter Martin?" he said. I said yes. "Give me a minute. I'll be with you." He opened his office door and went in, stripping off his suit jacket. The door closed, and about five minutes later he came out. His bow tie was undone, the ends hanging down from the points of his button-down shirt.

"Come on in," he said. "Have a seat."

His desk was more table than desk. He sat down in a swivel chair, and pointed at a couple of sheafs of stapled paper in front of him.

"Nice pieces," he said. "I've been steamboating with you and the captain of the Queen Astrid," he said. "Is he typical? Do Belgians in Africa tend to be racist?"

"No," I said. "Far from typical. Most men in his position never lifted a hand against a black man. They said that the blacks were like children, and they treated them that way."

He leaned back, put his hands behind his head, and we began to talk about white-black and black-white relations in British and Belgian Africa. We talked about Indians and "coloreds" (mixed-race non-whites) as well, and at last he said, "Well, I think you'll do. When can you start?"

"I just got back from Africa, and I need a vacation. Also, my wife andI have a baby coming. How about October?"

"A vacation?" he said. "What was that Africa jaunt?"

"That was work," I said.

"Oh," he said. "October it is." He looked through a desk calendar. "Let's say October ninth That's a Monday. How much salary do you want?"

"My foundation was providing five thousand dollars a year, plus expenses. That was tax-free."

"Let's say eight thousand a year. By the time you realize that's not nearly enough, you'll either have had a raise or be out of here."

I let that sink in. "It sounds okay to me," I said. We stood up and shook hands. He looked at the pile of newspapers on the edge of his desk. "Take the Herald-Trib for the trip home," he said. "It's a good read."

He was right. In the years that followed, I started off most office days by reading the Herald Tribune. No one else seemed to, and when the news of the day was discussed in story conferences I almost always came out with a Herald-Trib tidbit that put me ahead of the others in the room.

He was right about something else. Four months into my TIME life I realized that $8,000 a year was not going to be enough to cover rent, commuting, and expenses for a growing family in Westchester County. Before Christmas, I'd been raised to $18,000 a year. And roughly six months later, to $25,000.

Chapter 38

Swinging London

Talk about tempting, low-hanging fruit! Nothing seemed as lusciously luring to a new Color-Projects TIME Senior Editor as staid, grey, fog-shrouded, Burburried London, when the Beatles, and Mary Quant, and Carnaby Street, and a pleasure-seeking Princess Margaret came into their own and set the town a-swinging from the Old Vic, to Picadilly, to Harrods, and to the new late-night, West-End gambling casinos in 1950.

I read about it in the New York press, savored the music and the sense of an old town kicking off its shoes and dancing new dances in its stockinged feet and put the term "Swinging London" on my monthly planning-lunch menu with Managing Editor Otto Fuerbringer. Sometimes Otto and I met in a private dining room on a top floor of the old Time-Life Building at 50th Street and Sixth Avenue, but as he got used to me and more comfortable, we met at what he called "his club", the Knickerbocker, on Fifth Avenue at 52nd Street. It was a newish club in an oldish, white-painted brick building, but then Otto was a newish Time editor in the old-established Time-editing lineage of Henry Robinson Luce and Briton Hadden and T. S. Matthews.

"Swinging London"? Otto said dubiously, after a glance at my story list. "London? Swinging?"

I explained that cities, like human fads and epochs, had their time and then went and then came again. There was a song lyric, "London swings like a pendulum do," and London had come again, and was swinging, I said. Otto wanted eye-witness testimony, and I was ready to provide it. I called the Time travel bureau, and was quickly booked to fly business class and spend a week at the Dorchester Hotel, off Hyde Park. I'd never been there before, but I'd learned to trust the travel bureau.

I learned that "trust" and first-class treatment were built in to the status of a Time Senior Editorship. When I arrived at Heathrow Airport, a driver from the Time-Life Bureau was there to meet me in a black Austin "Princess" limousine. My bags had been pre-collected, and they and I were whisked off to the Dorchester. Kirk Douglas (yes, that Kirk Douglas) was checking in the same time I was, but I didn't have to wait. A second desk clerk, wearing a morning coat identical to the one on the first desk clerk, appeared and we each got checked in graciously.

My room was large, and smelled of Rogers et Gallet hard-milled soap. So, I presume, was the size and aroma of Kirk's billet. A message awaited me from Murray Gart, the London Bureau Chief, inviting me for drinks and dinner that evening. "Nothing fancy," the note said. "No black tie."

I'd known Murray when I was a TIME beginner writing for the magazine's Canada edition, and he was the Montreal Bureau Chief. Brilliant he wasn't, but nice-guy he was, and we got along well. Martinis were in sharp-cut Waterford crystal old-fashioned glasses that evening, and the steaks were seignant and tender. We shared a bottle of what he called "claret" (Bordeaux), then hopped into the Bureau limo for a look at the London gambling scene.

He had a favorite establishment, "A Pair of Shoes", and there we went to play blackjack. I played alongside him. He did well, I not so well, but I held my own using an approach Money magazine had suggested for players who wanted to limit their losses. After an hour or two he was ahead by about two or three hundred pounds. I was barely breaking even, but then he seemed to begin playing carelessly. Eventually he was down about 50 or 60 pounds, and he polished off his whiskey-soda.

"Well, that about does me in," he said. "Tomorrow's another day, but I'm not going to wait."

He lost another twenty-five or thirty pounds, and called for his coat. The proprietor came over to wish us a warm farewell and we went out to the waiting limo.

"I always like to lose a bit there when I've got a visiting fireman in town," Murray said. "It warms my welcome for the next visit. Don't worry, it's on the office expense account."

As we drove back to the Dorchester, Murray said, "Take taxis if you like, but this car or one of the others will be at your disposal whenever it suits. I've briefed the staff about what you're up to, and they're on the lookout for all new happenings on the London scene."

Days and nights went by in a glorious blur. A couple of mornings I got up early to watch bowler-hatted businessmen get off trains and buses in "The City" with their tightly furled umbrellas. More often, coffee (or tea) and toast would follow a gentle rap at the bedroom door a bit after 8, or 8;30. Morning showers were never a shock. The hot-water pipes ran under the bathroom floor, and once you'd set the shower-water temperature it was always the comfortable same when you stepped into the stall. Shoes outside the door were always beautifully shined (but NOT over-shined), and then down to breakfast with the Guardian and the New York Herald-Tribune. Eggs perfectly poached, lamb chops grilled but still bloody pink inside, a Cumberland sausage or two, hot toast not cooled in the inevitable silver-plated rack with slightly salt butter and chunky orange marmalade. And, finally, a new carafe of coffee.

Properly fortified, I could go out and browse Marks & Spencer or Burberry's or Madam Tussaud's or Harrod's Food Halls (Oh! That Stilton! And Oh! Those scones!). I was a member of the Cosmos Club of Washington, DC, which had eight (Count em! Eight!) reciprocal Clubs in London, and I could drop in and pick a lunch off the "trolley" or the Members' menu at any one of them.

To understand how London cab drivers could so perfectly deliver you to your exact destination, I interviewed those who supervised the training of neophyte cabbies in "the knowledge," the photographic memorization of London street maps and street numerology that all London taxi drivers were required

– required – to have.

Evenings, younger members of the Bureau staff escorted me to Isle of Dogs pubs, where Wannabee Beatles and Wannabee singles sang their hearts out to the slightly off-key Elizabethan twanging of guitars and the lively a-rhythm of imitation Ringo drummers.

At last, one morning before breakfast, my Dorchester bedside phone rang.

"Well," said an imperious voice, "Is it swinging? Do we have a story?"

It was Otto, calling from New York.

"It is," I said. "But there's more to it than just swinging, Otto. To understand it, you've got to counterbalance it, play it against the permanence and solid quality of the old, traditional London, the London of Steak-and-Kidney pie…"

Otto had heard enough. "You get your ass out of there, and get back here. We've got a story to do."

Swinging London, the cover story, went to press about three weeks later.

Chapter 39

Hazardous Work

Back in 2005 I was 76 years old, serving my 27th term as Executive Director of the Institute of Current World Affairs. *Casually,* between sessions of a Board meeting, Joe Battat, the Institute's Board Chair, *just happened* to ask me for my opinion about possible future Executive Directors. What qualities were needed? Who seemed to have some of them?

"I'll have to think about it," I said. And I did.

The most important thing an ICWA Executive Director did was choose candidates for Fellowships and see to it that there was enough funding available to support them for two years' work overseas. They had to be intelligent and promising, of course. They had to be open to friendship, because a Fellow's best friend (and friendliest critic) had to be the Executive Director. They had to be incorrigibly curious, able to spot fascinating situations and human happenings that cried out for examination, exploration and explication. They had to love to tell stories on paper in compelling language. They had to be good reporters and potentially fine writers.

I thought about the current crop of ICWA Fellows. There were seven in the field, three of them women. All were doing fine, but still had far to go.

How about recent Fellows? Some of them were already members of the Institute's Board of Trustees. Who among them had the most experience in dealing with talented young scholars and writers? Who knew how to go to bat for them if they got into trouble? Who were the best judges of their writing, their best career guides? Who had the experience needed to look after young people in foreign fields and precarious situations?

The most obvious choice was Steven Butler. In 1982 Steve had applied for a China fellowship, with good reason. He had lived in China, earned a Ph.D. from Cornell in Chinese studies, and was teaching the subject at Cornell. He spoke Mandarin and could read a few hundred Mandarin characters. He had married a smart and successful Chinese woman, Rose Lee, who had become Curator of Asian Art at the Denver Art Museum.

Aha! My sharp eye could spot a motivation when it saw one. Steve was teaching Chinese Studies in Ithaca, *New York*. The Denver Art Museum was in Denver, *Colorado*. Without the linkage of an ICWA fellowship, the separation of Steve and Rose would most likely result in hard-to-arrange connubial visits in St. Louis, Missouri or, perhaps, even Muncie, Indiana.

What did I think about his application? China was an okay Fellowship destination, but ICWA had already had a long succession of China Fellows, beginning with Doak Barnett and Albert Ravenholt back in the 1930s. If we were thinking about Asia, Japan had also been well-covered and studied by Mr. Ravenholt, *and* by Thomas Blakemore, a young American lawyer who had been sent to Japan by foresighted ICWA Executive Director Walter S. Rogers to learn Japanese and earn a Japanese law degree four years before Pearl Harbor in *1937*!

In the U.S. Air Force during World War II, Tom had flown the Hump and listened to the radio transmissions of Japanese pilots in Asia. At the end of the war he was seconded to Douglas MacArthur's Occupation group in Tokyo. There he had helped the legal staff rewrite and reorganize the Japanese Civil and Criminal Codes. As partner in a new law firm called Blakemore & Mitsuke he stayed on in Tokyo and practiced Japanese Law for 40 years!

We knew Japan.

But as Steve Butler developed his interest in Asia, another Asian nation was becoming interesting in its own right Korea! Ever since the Korean War, the southern half of the divided nation had sat in relative quiet on its peninsula below the 38th Parallel. It had prospered, proven itself industrially productive, but seemed otherwise politically uninteresting. But all of a sudden, in the 1940s and 50s, it was coming to life. Its students had burst into activity, protest and rioting. Its soldiers were being called upon, more and more, to put down riots. Its tear gas was gaining a staggering reputation for potency.

The neighboring west end of China, the end away from Europe and Beijing, the end with all the coal and hydrology and unknown resources at the Pacific terminus of the Baikal-Amur Mainline Railway (BAM!) was relatively unknown. A new world was there, with the deepest freshwater (Lake Baikal) on earth, with immense coal resources, with the capacity to export fuel to the oil-less and energy-thirsty industries of China and Japan. Instead of another *East* Asia Fellowship, how about a *Northeast Asia* Fellowship, beginning with Korea?

So instead of China, I suggested to Steve, how about Korea? He didn't much like the idea; he was a Sinologist, after all. Korean may have been an Asian language, but it was vastly different from Japanese and Chinese. And his wife Rose, with her Chinese origins and her curatorship in Asian Art, happened to feel strongly that Korea was an artistic backwater, an uninteresting Nowhere.

It took considerable persuasion from me backed up by Steve's increasing realization that the fellowship was for South Korea, and nowhere else, to get his agreement to spend two years there. Rose's heels left high ridges in the fellowship carpet. But off they went to Seoul. Determinedly, Rose held her nose and began work on a Ph.D. in Korean Art. (I think she doubted that there *was* such a thing.) And Steve began intensive study of Korean language and history, and set out on travel to all corners at least all *southern* corners of that divided, little known country.

It paid off. No one in the world particularly in the world's press was paying much attention to Korea, and Steve's monthly newsletters began to be avidly read, particularly when Korean governments and prime ministers began to topple and fall under student protests and civilian pressure. He wrote with perception and a kind of amused distance the kind of amused distance that had attracted Henry Luce's attention to the *Economist* back at that TIME

Yearling Dinner in 1957.

As Executive Director in the 1990s, I was following former Director Walter Rogers' rule that ICWA Fellows should avoid undue attention and pressure by not writing for outside publication but Britain's *Financial Times* had no one writing who knew Korea from the inside out. Steve's newsletters (today, we'd call them "long-form journalism") began appearing on that paper's distinctive, cream-colored newsprint in street-corner newsboxes the world around. When his fellowship was over, and liking what they read, the paper's managers made Steve their "Petroleum Editor" and moved him to London. Steve went but on one condition: The paper would pay for intensive Japanese-language lessons for him.

From Hanover, I couldn't follow the trajectory of his career as a Petroleum editor. But the Japanese lessons obviously worked. It couldn't have been more than a year before I got a letter from him giving me his Tokyo address and inviting me to stay with him and his family whenever my ICWA travels carried me over, or through, Asia and Japan.

They did fairly often, as I traveled on "RTW" (Round-The-World) airfares to interview Fellowship candidates or pay longer visits to Fellows in the field.

Those were wonder-filled, wonderful trips, as rising investment values kept our endowment full and growing. In those days, we had between six and eight Fellows coming on, going off, or in the field at any given moment. My policy was to visit promising Fellowship candidates for two or three-day interviews wherever they were living. We could eat together, drink together, joke together, hash over world issues together, get to *know* each other.

For Fellows already funded and in the field, I would wait until they'd been working and living overseas for the first year of their two-year fellowships, then visit them for a week or two (usually with my wonderfully wise, wonderfully comfortable wife, Lu – Full first name: Lucretia.) She was an important, human part of the fellowship experience.

The more I thought about it, the most obvious choice to replace me as Executive Director was Steve Butler. As a newspaper editor he had already managed ten Knight-Ritter American correspondents in the field. He had been responsible for their safety and well-being, and, I thought, for *editing* their writing. [I was wrong about this; their reports were actually edited by the foreign editors of each Knight-Ritter newspaper.] I passed my recommendation to Joe Battat, and eventually Steve became ICWA Executive Director.

But then, since I didn't want to retire, what was *I* to do? Despite ICWA's nearly 50 years of finding and funding promising young internationalists, the world seemed as troubled as ever as I left the Institute. America continued to need intelligent and able understanders, writers and teachers, and I was trained to find them. But where? And who? And how? As I pondered, it occurred to me that some of ICWA's most disciplined, most organized, most effective Fellows had been lawyers.

Just after Walter Rogers and Charles Crane founded ICWA in 1923, the United States recognized the revolutionary Bolshevik government of the Soviet Union. It bothered Rogers and Crane a super-wealthy former U.S. ambassador that they had no idea what the Soviet Union was all about. To find out, they decided to fund a new-minted Harvard Law School graduate to go to the Soviet Union as an ICWA Fellow and study the legal innards of the new country from the inside-out.

Rogers traveled to Cambridge, Mass., talked the idea over with Harvard Law professors and deans, and was introduced to a new graduate, John Newbold Hazard. In his lengthy memoir, *Recollections of a Pioneering Sovietologist*, John wrote (in the third person): "Hazard was well aware of the risks in going to a revolutionary country which he had seen in 1930 during the first leg of a trip around the world with three Yale classmates. At that time, he had decided Russia was a hopelessly poor, disorganized and undisciplined country. He even wrote his sister that he never wanted to see it again.

"The decision was not easy. He saw two more of his favorite Harvard professors. Both encouraged him to accept the nomination. It went through the Board of the Institute of Current World Affairs after several interviews with forbidding Board members, the most frightening of whom was Henry Allen Moe, the world-famous director of the Guggenheim Foundation. By August 1934 the young hopeful Hazard was on his way. He knew no Russian, no Russian history and no Marxist theory. He knew only that a career of uniqueness might result, and that was reason enough to risk going into a strange country."

John was right about the "career of uniqueness." By the time I met him, 30 years later in 1953, he had become the most famous, most accomplished, most beloved professor of Russian Law in the United States perhaps in the world. He and I began a friendship that lasted through my ICWA career, John's ICWA trusteeship and his own life, which ended in 1985.

I decided to call my International-Law Fellowship program the John Hazard Institute.

But if this was such a good idea, had others thought of it before me? Was there already an international fellowship program for young American lawyers? I called Michael ("Mike") Sovern, a professor at the Columbia University Law School who had served as consulting glitch-checker when I was Senior Editor of TIME magazine's Law Section. He had come to the TIME-LIFE Building every Friday after all the Law stories had been written and edited and looked them over for obvious errors in Law language and practice.

He had become Dean of Columbia Law School and President of the University in the intervening years, but when I showed up in his office we hadn't missed a beat. I told him what I had in mind and worried that I might be re-inventing some wheel. He grinned, leaned back in his executive chair with his hands behind his head, and told me that there were John Hazard Fellowships at Columbia, but there was no money in or behind them. He said I *had* to talk to Jerome ("Jerry") Cohen, the grand master of international law education (China division) at the New York University Law School.

I called Jerry, and he was gloriously welcoming. He'd co-taught a course with John Hazard at Berkeley, he said, and he would not only support the Hazard venture, but wanted anyone interested to contact him by e-mail or telephone. He gave me names that became the first links in a list of more than 50 leading practitioners, teachers and advocates of international law.

The most straightforward of the lot was Larry Kramer, Dean of Stanford Law School in California. "I wish you luck," he said, "but I'm not going to send a single one of our donors your way. We need their dollars right here."

He was speaking for Stanford, but as it turned out he was speaking for sixteen of the seventeen law schools I visited across the country. Sixteen. *Major* law schools.

The seventeenth, smaller and much less famous, was Southwestern Law School in Los Angeles. It was a newish law school, Dean Bryant Garth told me, named "Southwestern" to evoke echoes of better-known Northwestern Law School in Evanston, Illinois. Southwestern had an intriguing headquarters, an art-deco tower on Wilshire Boulevard that had been the home base of the May Department Store chain. As we chatted, he remarked that he'd been in Hanover, New Hampshire "visiting Aunt Harle."

"*Aunt* Harle? Harle Montgomery?" I said, my senses all a-tingle. Harle was the perennially beautiful widow of Kenneth Montgomery, a Dartmouth graduate (Class of 1925) with great personal, self-made wealth. He was high on the list of persons of interest to my wife when she was working with Dartmouth President John Kemeny in the 1970s as a major fund-raiser for the College. When I met Ken he was eagerly courting Harle *and* trying to live down a well-deserved reputation as a roving ladies' man with a wandering eye and immense sex appeal.

Harle needed reassurance, and as best I could I gave Ken my New York magazine editor's version of "advice." It seemed to work or, looking back, he and Harle probably *wanted* it to work. In Hanover and Chicago, where Harle lived, Ken, Harle, Lu and I were often a foursome. We had good times. I loved Lu, Lu loved me, Ken loved Harle, Harle loved Ken, and they eventually became *Mr. and Mrs.* Kenneth Montgomery.

As a philanthropist, Ken was generous to Dartmouth, and he and Harle established "Montgomery Fellowships" designed to bring creative, inspirational "outside" professionals (artists, playwrights, editors, authors, poets, journalists) to the College to live among the students, visit with them, lecture to them, party with them, and write and study in peace and quiet. They were there, in short, to serve as accessible resident role models.

To make the whole package more attractive to potential Montgomery Fellows, Ken and Harle bought, remodeled and furnished a large and lovely private home on Hanover's residential Gold Coast, the shore of Occum Pond near the Dartmouth Outing Club. The pond, an easy stroll from the Dartmouth campus, was the centerpiece of a neighborhood of expensive and comfortable lakefront homes Dartmouth alumni used for vacations at their alma mater when the seasons and the occasion matched a homecoming mood. The idea was that "Montgomery House" would serve as a short-term (or long-term) Hanover "home" for an unending succession of visiting Montgomery "Fellows."

As the well-traveled aunt of a young and ambitious Law-School dean, Harle loved the idea of John Hazard international law fellowships. After Ken died, she funded the first Hazard Law Fellow, an Iranian-American Southwestern-Law graduate who spent two years at the leading Law School in Tehran, earning a Master's degree in Iranian Law. (She had to defend her dissertation in *Persian*.) This first venture was such a success that the Hazard Institute's board, (chaired by Jerry Cohen) decided that we should fund Law Fellows only in countries with which the United States had diplomatic or other "difficulties."

Where next? And, more crucially, How? We had no further funding, and having helped Nephew (and Southwestern Law Dean) Bryant Garth, Harle was no longer a supporting source.

In the beginning, as the Hazard Institute was trying to find its footing, I had written dozens of exploratory letters to foundations and potential funders. One of these was a guy named Jerry Lenfest, suggested by Betsy Anderson, Executive Director of ASIL (the American Society of International Law) in Washington. ("I think he was one of John Hazard's students," she said.)

I'd never heard of Mr. Lenfest, and the response from "The Lenfest Group" was typical: a plain business-letter envelope in the cardboard carton I used as a mailbox on the back stairs leading up to my office. You could tell the envelope contained a ding-letter the minute you picked it up. It wasn't hefty enough to hold all the folded pages of legal stuff you had to sign and send back to acknowledge a grant. When I found it I was on my way out to pick up a lunch sandwich, and just dropped it back in the box.

On the way back I picked it up the letter and laid it and the sandwich on my desk. I did my thing with the mustard pack and the milk container, and slit open the letter.

"Dear Mr. Martin:

"Your letter of January 28 to the Lenfest Foundation has been referred to me as your request is outside the Foundation's scope.

"I congratulate you on recognizing John Hazard by forming the Institute in his name and instituting a program for which he would be proud.

"I enclose my contribution and hope you will soon multiply it greatly by gifts from others.

"Sincerely, H.F. (Gerry) Lenfest."

The handwritten signature: "Gerry" And below, the typewritten word: "Enclosure."

The Enclosure was a personal check for One Hundred Thousand and No/100 dollars, made out to the John Hazard Institute.

It made my day.

It made Lu's day, too. I tried to seal the letter back up so she could open it and get the same thrill, but the whole business was too contrived. All we could do was marvel at it over our martinis that evening.

Chapter 40

Through the Mandelbaum Gate

Water.

Without it, mankind and all living things could not exist. The planet on which we live, love, eat, drink, procreate, exploit, enjoy, and destroy would not and could not exist without it. It is, and always has been a source of conflict, of artistic beauty, commerce, sport, tragedy, death, destruction, violence, renewal, and literature.

Exploring the Cosmos, our solar system, and all the planetary universes beyond, water is what scientists search for if there ever is to be a world beyond ours, an existence beyond ours, a life beyond ours.

It is and was, to call a halt to this recitation of qualities and characteristics, an obvious TIME cover story and color-photography project. I was still one of the magazine's Senior Editors in those days, and in 19?? I suggested it to Managing Editor Otto Fuerbringer. Despite ... or *because of* ... its immensity, Otto immediately understood the topic as a "natural" major story. At one of our planning lunches, he accepted it at first mention. And I got to work.

The clipboards went up on the wall, and I began collecting every article, every book review, every photo caption, every passing reference to water or watery situations in every possible place and format. I talked water at cocktail parties, over lunches and dinners, in bed and out. I became a kind of constant drip. I read about it in encyclopedias, in science publications, in farm journals, in weather reports, in collections of seaborne and navigation adventures, in whatever format and wherever locale.

Did hurricanes threaten? I collected storm stories. Had archeologists uncovered ancient waterworks? Were buckets of ducats being recovered from long-forgotten shipwrecks? Were plans being laid to glean electric power from the rise and fall of tides, from seasonal wind patterns, or from normal wave motion? As arctic ice sheets melted, would the Northwest Passage become navigable? Would deserts bloom if irrigated by deep-drilled aquifers?

Was there water news? Under a so-called Hayes Commission Plan, Israelis and Arabs were supposed to share the *fresh water* that flowed south out of Israel's Sea of Galilee through the River Jordan, but Palestinians complained that their farms and orchards were getting precious little of the precious liquid. Armed force was threatened.

Onto the clipboards went the ideas, notions, the news, the rumors and the tall tales. Out to the overseas bureaus and stringers went the queries. Into my mind and itchy feet came the desire to travel, to see things for myself.

The Middle East was an immediately compelling destination. Just north of the Gulf of Aqaba, at the southern tip of the Sinai Peninsula, Israeli scientists were using the minutely variable salinity of samples of the Red Sea to freeze seawater into fresh-water snowballs!

Europe also beckoned. There, scientists were not only calculating ways to measure and store the potable melt of Alpine glaciers, but turning the dream of storing the immense tides of the Bay of St. Malo into a reliable, twice-daily source of hydroelectric power. Rising tides spread bay water across the causeway between the mainland and Mont St. Michel faster than a galloping horse, they said. Engineers were developing plans to channel those galloping tides through power turbines, trap the water, close lock-gates behind it, open the gates as the tide turned, and reverse the flow back through the same power turbines. Passamaquoddy revisited!

Understandably, Otto did not like my practice of reciting news I'd gleaned from "outside sources." He wanted new material, and he wanted it to be *our material.* (One splendid source of "new" material was the late, lamented *New*

York Herald-Tribune, which was delivered to every editor's desk every morning, but which no editor but me – and a few others – ever read.)

When I put all my gleanings together, fashioned a narrative, and added it to what I called the "menu" of one of my Otto lunches, he'd get excited. "Have you checked this out?" he'd say.

"Not yet," I'd say. And after lunch I would consult a world Atlas and make one of my favorite phone calls to the Time Inc. Travel Bureau. "I need to spend five days in France and a week or ten days in Israel," I'd say. I would then telex the Paris Bureau and our Israel stringer, Marlin Levin (real first name: *Moishe*; but in those troubled days a correspondent with a Jewish name on his passport could not travel easily in the Middle East, particularly to Arab countries.)

With my beloved 35-mm Pentax and a couple of packets of Ektachrome color film, I headed off to Paris and Tel Aviv. Paris was always a pleasing stop-over for me on my way to Europe and beyond; one of my closest Dartmouth College chums, Bob McCabe, had risen through the reporters' ranks to become *Newsweek's* Paris Bureau Chief. In Tel Aviv, however, I found a message waiting for me at the hotel:

"SURPRISED TO LEARN OF YOUR PRESENCE IN MIDEAST," it read. "PLEASE JOIN CLAIRE AND ME FOR DINNER AT JORDAN INTERCONTINENTAL AMMAN THURSDAY. ALLBEST, HANK."

What the hell? Hank? Claire? The Jordan Incontinental? Amman? What was this all about? Marlin Levin had no idea. I threw economy to the winds and phoned Otto in New York. Turned out that like his father Harry, "Hank" Luce (Henry Luce III) had married a woman named Claire. She had bought a major interest in an Australian sheep ranch and she and Hank were on their way home from an inspection visit by way of the Middle East. Since Hank had inherited a major chunk of his father's Time Inc. stock, his dinner invitation, said Otto, was something of a command performance.

But in Jordan? On the map, Jordan lay cheek-by-jowl next to Israel. But they were as separate as a couple of warring worlds. I asked Marlin whether he'd ever traveled to Jordan. No, he said. The only way to get there by land was through the Mandelbaum Gate. On *foot*.

Marlin explained. The only person who could cross from Jewish Israel directly into non-Jewish Jordan was a visiting, certified non-Jew on legitimate business. His or her passport could show no sign that he or she had ever been in Israel. American journalists or businessmen who regularly visited both Israel and Arab countries could be issued *two* U.S. passports, one for Israeli border crossings, the other – without Israeli rubber-stampings – for crossings in and out of "Arab" countries. At this point, I still had only one passport.

The "normal" thing was to fly from an outside country into Jordan carrying a passport bearing no signs of visits to Israel. By land, you couldn't take a bus, tram or train. Thanks to complicated negotiations conducted by consular officers from the United States and Jordan, a certified non-Jew could *walk* from Israel into Jordan through a boxed wooden tunnel called the Mandelbaum Gate. He could carry no Israeli currency or receipts from Israeli restaurants or hotels. His luggage could dangle no Israeli baggage tags. When he got to officials at the Jordan end of the tunnel and was asked where he'd come from, he'd have to say "New York" – or any place but Jerusalem or Israel. If I did everything right, Marlin said, he could arrange to have a taxi waiting at the Jordan end of the tunnel to take me to the Intercontinental Hotel.

First, though, I had to get certified as "Christian." Marlin drove me to the Jerusalem YMCA and I met the head man there in his office.

"Are you a Christian?" he asked.

"Well," I answered, "when I was a baby, my father tried to get me christened in Philadelphia during Prohibition with two of his journalistic pals as godfathers. But on the way to the christening they found a reliable bootlegger with some good Scotch on hand. I'm told they never got to the ceremony..."

"You're a Christian," the fellow said. And he handed me a certificate attesting to the fact.

Then, a Jordanian visa. A quick visit to a consular office, and all was arranged. Suitcase in hand, I walked through the Mandelbaum Gate Thursday morning. For the historical record, it seemed to be about a quarter of a mile long. It was windowless, but lighted. The taxi booked by Moishe was waiting, and so was a room at the Jordan Intercontinental, booked from New York.

I met Hank and Claire for drinks and explained what I was up to. Hank marveled.

"Water!" he said. "That's the mother of all cover stories! Who suggested it?" Modestly, I tried not to answer, but when Hank learned that it was my idea, he got excited. "TIME's stringer here is the mayor of Jordanian Jerusalem! He's invited all the local VIPs to cocktails and dinner with Claire and me tonight, and I want you to tell them all about it! There's a notion here that TIME's pro-Jewish, and I want to put an end to it!"

Dinner was at a local upscale restaurant where we all were going to mill around and sip champagne – or fizzy water – at cocktail time. When supper came, we were to sit on hassocks, the better to eat finger food with our fingers. About twenty or thirty guests were on hand, and Hank made a brief announcement of the importance of me and my "mission" in Jordan. I nodded companionably.

The woman nearest me turned out to be the wife of a member of the local branch of the "American Friends of the Middle East." She insisted I had to raise an important issue in my article. "They'll surely invite you for a float on the Dead Sea," she said. "They'll tell you that you can't sink because there's so much salt and minerals in the water. But what they won't tell you is, *Keep your mouth shut, and don't swallow any of it.* A friend of mine took her three children for a swim in that water, and one of them swallowed a mouthful. He died."

"Died?" I said. "Couldn't they save the child? Was there no cure?"

"The poisons were too powerful," she said. "You've got to keep your mouth shut."

I decided to heed her advice, at least at fizzy-water time, and turned to Claire Luce, on the hassock on my other side. "A sheep ranch?" I said. "How many sheep do you have?"

"Thousands," she said. "They're an investment, not pets. And if you're out among them when they're being herded, it's like being in a sea of heads and wool. It can be frightening." She paused and looked around her, and at me, in a conspiratorial manner.

"You have an important assignment tonight," she said. "Keep an eye on me, and if you see me wave a little wave, it's because I'm getting bored. You're to come and rescue me. Also, if you're any kind of reporter, you've got a bottle of whiskey somewhere in your kit. Bring it to our room after dinner for a real drink." She gave me a slip of paper with her room number on it.

Rumors about Claire Booth Luce I were that she called TIME writers and editors "Harry's boys", and she considered them to be her "boys" as well. Other rumors said there was a certain *droit de seigneuse* that went with the nickname, but since I had not encountered her before, I figured that the *droit* was not being exercised by Claire II. I made my way across the crowd of important Jordanians who were flocking into the room, downsizing Hank's effusive introduction of me and keeping an eye peeled for Claire's "little wave."

One came during an overlong complaint from a Jordanian scholar about TIME's placement of a Jewish archeologist, Nelson Gleuck on a TIME cover. I reassured the gent that he was not given the prominence as a result of "pressure from Jewish advertisers" – as the gent insisted. I quaffed a glass of champagne with him, and eased him across the room away from Claire. I heard various versions of the Dead Sea "death" of the five-year-old (they ran from serious poisoning to a seriously upset stomach), heard unscientific accounts of sea-water conversions, of organized Dead-Sea floats, and (during dinner) about the source – and freshness – of the grilled scallops.

As the crowd thinned out, Claire waved, and she and Hank came over to me. "I've had all the champers I can hold," Claire said. "If you're anything like a good reporter, you've got a bottle of whiskey in that kit of yours. I'm dying for a real drink. Bring the bottle and a glass to our room." I was not only one of Harry's boys. I was one of Hank's boys. And Claire's boys."

In the Luces' room after dinner, we swilled whiskey and I talked about me, my watery cover-story idea, and my background with the Institute of Current World Affairs.

"ICWA started in the Middle East," I said. "Our founder, Charles Crane, was one of the two heads of the King-Crane commission, which was sent here from the Versailles Peace Conference to explore what was to become of the remains of the Ottoman Empire. King was President of Oberlin College. Crane, a wealthy industrialist with long interest in the Middle East, was growing desert products – dates, figs and such – with artesian well-water on his California ranch. He met Ibn Saud of Arabia, and to seal their friendship, offered the king the services of one of his hydrologists, Carl Twitchell. Twitchell didn't find much irrigation water in Arabia, but he found something more interesting – underground petroleum resources.

"The King wrote to Crane about the discovery: 'Your man Twitchell says the petroleum could be developed. I am unused to the ways of western business, but if you could manage this aspect of the development, we could divide the proceeds between us.'

"Crane wrote back that he had not offered Twitchell to the king with any expectation of payback. Twitchell, however, was interested. When he heard about Ibn Saud's offer, he got in touch with Standard Oil of California. Result – in the long run – Anglo-American."

"Fascinating," said Hank. "And what does your ICWA do?"

"We seek out promising young internationalists, and fund them to spend a minimum of two years living in foreign countries the U.S. doesn't understand well enough."

"Sounds like a good idea," Hank said. "Does it work?"

"Seems to," I said. "Some of our Fellows have become ambassadors, professors, novelists, foundation directors, even Japanese music composers and TIME magazine editors. I was one of those Crane Fellows. In the 1950s I spent two years living in subSaharan Africa from Cape Town to Senegal and back."

"Fantastic," said Hank. "I'm now running the fellowship program of the Luce Foundation, and we get a lot of first-class applications I have to turn down. Give me your ICWA address, and I'll send them on to you."

The foundation talk went on as the Scotch poured ... which wasn't for too long. I'd only bought a fifth of Johnnie Walker Black to save weight and space in my carry-on bag. With three of us lapping it up, it didn't last more than a couple of drinks.

Chapter 41

Through the Israeli Water Grid

The morning after my fifth-of-Scotch Amman evening with Hank and Claire Luce, the phone rang insistently next to my bed - and next to my head - at the Jordan Intercontinental Hotel.

"Mister Martin?" It was the hotel operator. "Your guide is here."

"Guide? I didn't ask for any guide."

"Your guide from the Ministry of the Interior. He's waiting in the lobby."

"Ministry of the Interior?"

"The *Israeli* Interior Ministry. He says he's assigned to you." Things began to unscramble. The Israelis obviously had a long reach.

"Give me a few minutes. I haven't even shaved."

"He says take as long as you like. He can explain over breakfast."

I got up, shaved, showered, and threw my pajamas and toilet kit into my bag. Then down the elevator. Waiting at the bottom was a youngish, blond-haired man reading a copy of TIME. He got up, smiled, came over, held out a hand.

"Tswee Hulka," he said, or something close to that.

"Tswee?"

"Zed double-U Eye. It's Czech."

"But you're with the Israeli Interior Ministry?"

"Yes. I'm an immigrant. Actually, a hydraulic-engineer immigrant, which is why I've been assigned to show you around."

Over breakfast Zwi explained that TIME's Israel stringer, Moishe Levine, had passed on word of my plan to do a color-photo portfolio about world water resources, and that I'd said that Israel was a key starting point. For Israel, he said, water was not only an ISSUE, but a highly sensitive issue. *The* IS-SUE. "It's as though someone said he wanted to photograph our defense communications systems. Water is Israel's life-blood, and photographs of where it comes from, and where it goes, and how, and why, could give an enemy the kind of map he'd need to bomb us back into a desert. We want to show you what we've accomplished, but we don't want to give you a map of our vulnerability."

"So?"

"So, if you don't object, I'm going to be with you every mile of your water-resource exploration. I'll be warning you about what you can photograph, and what you can't. And I won't always be completely clear about why or why not. If you do object, I think your photo essay just can't happen."

"That's pretty clear. How would this work?"

"We're providing you with a car and driver. You and I will ride in the back seat, and I'll point out places and things of interest. We'll stop and eat, and spend a night here and there, if necessary. If you want to stop and make photographs, just say so. You and I will get out, and I'll tell you what it's okay to shoot. If photos are not okay, I'll say no. In your cable to Moishe, you were pretty clear about what you were interested in, and most of it presented no insurmountable problems. And I've thought of a few things that might even make your project better."

It was clear that his people had intercepted every word I'd telexed to Tel Aviv from New York and Jordan.

"When do we start?" I said.

"Now, if you're ready," he said. And that morning we were off

"First stop, the Sea of Galilee," said Zwi. "You were right in your message to Moishe," he added. "There is a Johnson Agreement, under which we and the Jordanians share fresh Galilee water fifty-fifty as it flows into the Jordan River. We've established a pumping station next to the source of the river to cope with our share. The station is at the head of a waterdistribution grid that sends the water south through the Negev Desert into Sinai. It's like an electric-power grid in Canada or the United States. It redistributes water all the way to the Gulf of Eilat on the Red Sea. So far, the Jordanians haven't done much about using their share."

"We're going back into Israel?" I said. "Do we drive through the Mandelbaum Gate?"

Zwi laughed. "No need," he said. "Diplomacy has conquered red tape."

And sure enough, after the car - an ordinary-looking black sedan with an extra-wide back seat - was loaded, we drove off. "We're going into the Galilee pumping station," Zwi said. "No pictures 'til we get inside and I say so." We parked and walked up an incline toward a grey mountainside ... part of which rolled open like a garage door as we got close. Inside, we turned left and made our way along a metal catwalk. Every so often, set into what seemed to be solid rock, there was a metal door. Wherever we walked, there was a humming sound.

"These are the entryways to the pump housings," Zwi said. "Inside are reservoirs that hold tens of thousands of cubic liters of water. On a scheduled basis, we take a certain amount from them, and feed it into the grid. The flow stays constant; the water levels don't."

"What do you water with it?" I asked.

"You'll see," said Zwi. He picked up what looked like a small phone and said something into it. The car stopped after a bit and Zwi fiddled with the door handle. He opened the door, and we were sitting in a parking lot high above fields of green growing things. "This is one of the kibbutzim that I help manage," he said, pointing down. "We grow table vegetables here - lettuce, cabbage, kale, broccoli. It feeds us, and with what we don't eat, our animals."

I looked, admired, asked quantity and price questions. Then we drove on. After another half-hour or so we stopped again. Outside this time was a field of ripening grain of some sort. "Wheat," said Zwi. "We mill as much of our own flour as we can. We also grow our own hops and barley for beer. Vodka is a bit beyond us, I'm afraid." He chuckled.

We stopped for dinner, and to check in at a hotel. The next morning, after a fine 'American' breakfast. We stopped in one of the lushest orange groves I've ever seen - thick green leaves, large fruit ripening from pale green to bright orange, the trees separated by aisles wide enough for a Jeep or tractor to get through.

"This is a special side-trip," Zwi said. "It's Sde Boker, David Ben-Gurion's kibbutz. He lived here after he retired as Prime Minister in 1963, but he managed the Suez Crisis and the Sixday War from the Knesset and froom here. To us, this is like Benjamin Franklin's home in Philadelphia and Independence Hall." I saw Ben-Gurion's simple bedroom and office, and spent a comfortable night in an inn at the kibbutz. The next day we set off for Eilat and the Red Sea.

"You were right in your telex to Moishe," Zwi said. "We are freezing sea water into fresh, but it hasn't produced the gushing fountain you might expect. Not yet, anyhow." I could see an expanse of ocean ahead on the left as we drove through the resort, and we pulled up beside a pair of immense blue-enameled tanks. Curving steps ran up the outside of the tanks, and there was a set of steps on each tank.

"You take these steps, and I'll take the ones on the other side," said Zwi. "I'll be facing you when we get to the top." He disappeared, walking around the base of the tank, and I climbed up, up, up. The tank lid was off when I got to the top, and Zwi and I were facing each other across what seemed to be a huge bed of snow. It was actually ice, finely shaved ice.

"You could make terrific martinis on-the-rocks with this stuff," I called to him.

"Scoop some up in your hands," he yelled back. "Make it into a ball. See if you can hit me!"

And we had a short snowball fight with fresh-water ice balls high above the shores of the Gulf of Eilat.

For one of the few times in the magazine's history. Otto Fuerbringer ordered up a "double-truck" cover illustration. That is, the cover art (a color photograph of water - nothing but water - as wide as two normal issues of the magazine) lay folded under on the newsstand and when it came in the mail, but unfolded dramatically in the reader's hand. No mention was made of my snowball fight on the Gulf of Eilat.

Chapter 42

The Man Who Fingered Nelson Mandela

When William Thornton Martin III arrived in our lives in 1955, my then-wife Julie and I were back from my two-year journalism fellowship in sub-Saharan Africa, and it was time for us to settle down to serious, "mature" life as parents, citizens, home-makers, and Middle-Class familyhood. "Thornton", as we then called him, was named for his grandfather and great-grandfather, William Thornton Martin and Jr. Great-Grandfather Martin had emigrated from Ireland to Charlottesville, Virginia, at the time of the great Irish Famine of 1840. He worked in a hardware store, which eventually became W.T. Martin Hardware. The name still hangs over Charlottesville's main pedestrian mall.

I got a job as a "Contributing Editor" (writer) at *TIME,* and the setting for our domesticity was a small-but-comfortable, barn-red, two-story, restored, wood-frame house (with separate two-car garage) on half of a two-acre lot rising above Croton Lake reservoir on Crow Hill Road in the town of Mt. Kisco in Westchester County, New York.

Milk was delivered by truck, and so were clean diapers in a "Dy-Dee Wash" delivery van with a musical horn that played the tune to "Rock-a-bye Baby". (When it played, you were supposed to think the company's slogan, "Rock-a-Dry Baby", painted on the side of the truck, and get ready to turn over the previous days' soilage to the driver.)

Below us, from the living-room window, you could see Pines Bridge, an old-fashioned steel span built at the turn of the century, and a fine country restaurant, the Pines Bridge Lodge. The bridge connected our chunk of Westchester County to the next-north chunk containing rural Somers, Yorktown Heights and Katonah.

The hour-and-a-half commute from Manhattan to Mt. Kisco was by an antique, creaky collection of too-hot and too-cold passenger cars pulled first by an equally creaky electric switch engine on the New York Central's commuter line from Grand Central to the Bronx, and then by an ancient diesel locomotive to White Plains and northern Westchester County.

That ride took forever, so the wiser choice was to drive fifteen minutes west from Mt. Kisco to the Croton-Harmon station on the Central's Hudson Division. There you could park, buy a morning *New York Times,* and ride for 50 minutes in electrified speed and comfort to New York City along the River, with riverboats (and, sometimes in winter, ice-breakers and wind-powered *ice boats*) churning and skimming beneath the Palisades on the New Jersey side.

It was far from Africa, and so were we, until one day I got a phone call from Millard Shirley, a professional photographer we'd come to know in Johannesburg. Millard had retired from the U.S. Navy after World War II, and had moved, with a lovely array of cameras and dark-room equipment, to the comfortable northern suburbs of the golden city. He had a wide circle of friends from the worlds of business and politics, twin tennis courts, and a full household of Zulu and Xhosa servants. Weekends, he and his wife presided over a nonstop pleasurefest of tennis matches, meals, sandwiches, gin-and-tonics and cold bottles of Lion and Castle lager beer. We happily fell into line and the fun as, from time to time, he hosted celebrations of the publication of a photo in *Paris-Match* or *Look* magazines.

Eager to establish a reputation as a publishable free-lance writer even during my fellowship, I'd submitted some article suggestions to Marty Sommers, Foreign Editor of my father's *Saturday Evening Post.* One of them was to fill a gap in a series they'd run on "Cities of the World." They'd done one or two on North African cities (Cairo, I recall, and – I think – Marrakesh or Casablanca) but nothing from sub-Saharan Africa. I suggested Johannesburg, and also a story about life and work 8,500 feet underground in a South African gold mine in the Orange Free State. I got positive responses ... and the editors needed photographs. I assigned Millard to take them, and traveled with him around Jo'burg, and to the President Steyn Mine in the Free State town of Welkom.

We had fun, became friends as well as professional traveling companions, and stayed in touch even when Julie and I went home to the States.

Julie and Thornton were not in Mt. Kisco when Millard called from New York - she may not even have arrived from St. Louis, where Thornton was born. I was alone, and rather than have *me* make an extra trip into the city, I suggested that *he* take the train up to Mt. Kisco. We could visit, go out to dinner, he could spend the night and ride the train back to Manhattan the next morning.

Up he came. I met him at the station. Old times got talked, martinis got poured, remembrance flowed. Millard marveled at my "suburbaness." I asked him about life in South Africa after *apartheid* "soft-liner" Prime Minister Daniel Malan left and was succeeded by "hard-liner" Hendryk Verwoerd. I told him that after my Johannesburg article appeared in the *Post*, the city council issued a warrant for my arrest - not because of any specific thing I said, but because one of the photos that appeared with it, showing the contents of a "typical" housewife's handbag that included a pistol. The picture "denigrated" South Africa, they said.[1]

"I may have taken that photo," Millard said.

"Did anything happen to you?" I said.

"No. Luckily, I don't think I even got a photo credit in the magazine."

"I *did* get a copy of the picture you got of me with the black gold miners in the President Steyn mine," I said. "It's hanging on my office wall at TIME, and I'm grateful for it. It's just about the only visible evidence I've got to

[1] *Cities of the World: (No. 14) Johannesburg* by Peter Bird Martin. The Saturday Evening Post, November 26, 1955, pp. 40-41

Peter Martin (right) investigating the life and work of native workers in southern Africa's primary industry in 1954. He is pictured here 8,500 feet underground at the President Steyn gold mine near the town of Welkom in the Orange Free State. The "gold" appears as a thin layer of black dust in the wall of the mine. Miners drill blast holes in the wall above and below the layer of gold ore. The motivation is to take as small amount of waste rock out as possible as workers drill in narrow spaces.

prove I ever was *in* South Africa."

"God, do you remember how hot it was down there?"

"I remember how you had to struggle to get that giant Speed Graphic camera onto the mine-elevator cage, and into those fiendishly low working spaces. It was amazing you got any photos at all."

"These days, I've gone modern. I've got a thirty-five millimeter single-lens reflex. Have fast film, I can tell photo editors. Will travel."

"That's what Bob Hope told my father he said to Vaudeville booking agents: *'Have tux, Will travel'*"

"Nowadays, I even have a tuxedo!"

We poured ourselves in to the family Ford and drove next door to the Pines Bridge Inn. The first couple of glasses of a bottle of *Châteauneuf du Pape* were poured, toasts were raised to absent wives, and steak slices were examined for rareness.

After a pleasant dinner, as the cheddar cheese and apple pie got washed down with coffee, a question popped into my head that had been nagging at me ever since Millard phoned. I blurted it out.

"Millard, are you CIA?"

The coffee cup, which had been hoisted toward his lips, stopped suddenly in mid-air. He looked behind and around him a couple of times, and lowered his voice to an anxious whisper.

"Peter, *please* don't ever say that where anyone could *hear* you! It could be the death of me! What gave you the idea?"

"The word in South Africa was that you worked for LIFE and *Paris-Match,* and I saw the issues you showed me. But I've been watching both magazines, and I've never seen any Millard Shirley photos since then. It got me to wondering."

He looked around and behind again.

"It seemed a good cover," he said, his voice low. "I was trained as a photographer and how to work a darkroom in the Navy. And when I got out, I had no job, no - quote - 'profession'. And the Agency had nobody at the professional level they could trust in South Africa. I was asked if I'd be willing to keep my eyes and ears open as a press photographer. There'd be no cloak-and-dagger danger, no stuff like that, so I said yes. I married the girl I'd left behind me, went out to Johannesburg, set up a basement dark room, and became Millard Shirley, professional photographer.

"They wanted me to get to know middle and upper-middle people, so they funded the house with the tennis courts and paid me an expense account big enough to have servants and give parties. They even paid for golf lessons and a membership in the Wanderers' Club. Not bad!

"I took some pictures, and they somehow appeared in *Paris-Match.* By luck, a photo I shot of a lion-kill on a game-park safari was published in *LIFE,* and there was my background. It wasn't 'til you came along and needed a photographer that the profession actually worked."

I picked up where he paused. "And you worked your ass off, a mile and a half under all that rock under the Orange Free State," I said. "And got some damned good pictures."

He went on: "And now my cover's working, and I can provide good authentic looks at what's happening down there. I'm good at my job. I'm not hurting anyone, I'm making good contacts, and I'm useful. I'm doing what you did on your fellowship, Peter, learning what's going on inside a society and reporting to people who need to know. For God's sake, don't blow my cover!"

"I need to think about this, Millard," I said. "Let's sleep on it, and talk about it tomorrow morning."

We did. Over breakfast, he told me of some of the reporting he'd done. He'd used some of my newsletters from South Africa and the Belgian Congo, which somebody at the Agency got hold of, to flesh out some of his reports. This was not good news. The rule of the Institute of Current World Affairs in those pre-electronic days was that the monthly 'newsletters' we were required to write for the Trustees were not supposed to get circulated in the countries or colonies we lived in.

Millard's points were cogent and well made. He wasn't doing anything underhanded or evil, as far as I could tell. On the way to the station I promised to keep quiet about his work. He went back to New York and South Africa. 1 went back to work at *TIME*. And that was that.

Or was it? The Johannesburg *Sunday Times* reported in 1990 that Mandela had been riding in a private car to a secret rendezvous in South Africa in 1962 when he was stopped at a roadblock and arrested. Who fingered him? None other, said the *Sunday Times*, than "Millard Shirley, a CIA agent who had close relations with a member of the South African Communist Party."

Mandela was convicted of "sabotage," sentenced to 27 years in prison, and sent to Robben Island in the Atlantic Ocean off the coast of Cape Province. Ever since, I've wondered what might have happened if I'd blown the whistle on Millard. As it turned out, on Robben Island Mandela became the soul and ideal spirit of peaceful resistance. He read Shakespeare to other inmates, encouraged them in nonviolent opposition to *apartheid,* and was a teacher rather than a rabid revolutionary. He *became,* I tell myself in moments of self-questioning, Nelson Mandela, the inspirational first elected President of a free South Africa. And then I wonder, did he *have* to go to prison for 27 years to accomplish this?

Surely, no. Or, maybe yes.

Elzbieta Czyzewska, Polish Actress Unwelcome in Her Own Country, Dies at 72

ARTS

By BRUCE WEBER

JUNE 17, 2010

Elzbieta Czyzewska, a star of Polish movies and television in the 1960s whose marriage to the American journalist David Halberstam made her an outcast in her home country, and whose career frustrations in the United States became a cautionary tale for immigrant artists, died on Thursday in Manhattan. She was 72.

Her death, at New York Presbyterian Hospital, was caused by esophageal cancer, said Nancy Weber, a friend.

In the 1960s Ms. Czyzewska (her name is pronounced elzh-BYET-uh Chuh-ZHEF-skuh) was, quite simply, the most popular actress in Poland, creating, in comic and dramatic roles, a consistent persona that was both fiercely feminine and fiercely independent. "Pride of Her Generation" was the caption with her photograph, in 1965, on the cover of a Polish national news magazine.

But her life took a turn the same year, when she starred in a production of "After the Fall," Arthur Miller's dramatized account of a marriage, seemingly drawn from his to Marilyn Monroe. It was a significant cultural event in Warsaw, and Mr. Halberstam, a correspondent there for The New York Times, interviewed her, attended the opening and danced with her at the cast party.

Elzbieta Czyzewska in the 1961 film "Erotica," directed by Jerzy Skolimowski. The film made her a national sex symbol in Poland. Credit: The Museum of Modern Art

They married a few months later.

It was later that year, after Mr. Halberstam wrote an article about anti-Semitism in Poland, that he was accused of slander against the government and subsequently expelled from the country. Ms. Czyzewska eventually joined him in New York, but in 1968 she returned to Warsaw to make a film with the celebrated director Andrzej Wajda, "Everything for Sale." Mr. Wajda was denounced for hiring her, and in a letter published on the front page of a state-run daily newspaper, she was denounced as well. After the film was completed, she did not return to Poland until the 1980s, long after her marriage to Mr. Halberstam — who went on to become a best-selling author — had dissolved. He was killed in a car accident in 2007.

Ms. Czyzewska had early stage successes in the United States, most notably in a 1974 production of "The Possessed," Albert Camus's adaptation of the Dostoyevsky novel about violent nihilists in 19th-century Russia. Directed by Mr. Wajda at the Yale Repertory Theater, it featured a cast of then unknowns — Meryl Streep and Christopher Durang among them — and Ms. Czyzewska, who played a crippled woman, seemingly mad, in a performance that was singled out by critics and is still remembered by theater scholars.

"I can still see her hands, her fluttering hands, and those staring eyes," Robert Brustein, then head of the Yale Rep, said about Ms. Czyzewska's performance, 14 years later, in New York magazine. In a telephone interview Thursday, Annette Insdorf, a film professor at Columbia, recalled the same performance. "I was haunted by it," she said.

But Ms. Czyzewska was hampered by her accent and her Eastern European speech patterns — which one biographer of William Styron, who knew her, said Styron had appropriated for the title character of "Sophie's Choice" — and never had the opportunities to achieve stardom in America.

Her luck, in fact, was legendarily bad. In the mid-1980s, she was cast in the original production, in Woodstock, N.Y., of "Hunting Cockroaches," Janusz Glowacki's dark comedy about a Polish émigré couple — a writer and an actress — who are being stifled in New York City. She was Mr. Glowacki's adviser on the project, and the role was at least in part derived from her circumstances. But when the show opened in Manhattan, the director, Arthur Penn, cast Dianne Wiest.

Ms Czyzewska was said to be the model for the title character in the 1987 film "Anna," an "All About Eve"-ish tale about an actress, once famous in Eastern Europe, whose life has become a struggle in New York and who opens her home to a younger émigré actress, a version of herself, who succeeds suddenly and spectacularly.

David Halberstam, 73, Reporter and Author, Dies

ARTS

By CLYDE HABERMAN

APRIL 24, 2007

David Halberstam, a Pulitzer Prize-winning journalist and tireless author of books on topics as varied as America's military failings in Vietnam, the deaths of firefighters at the World Trade Center and the high-pressure world of professional basketball, was killed yesterday in a car crash south of San Francisco. He was 73, and lived in Manhattan.

Mr. Halberstam was a passenger in a car making a turn in Menlo Park, Calif., when it was hit broadside by another car and knocked into a third vehicle, said the San Mateo County coroner. He was pronounced dead at the scene.

The man who was driving Mr. Halberstam, a journalism student at the University of California at Berkeley, was injured, as were the drivers of the other two vehicles. None of those injuries were called serious.

Mr. Halberstam was killed doing what he had done his entire adult life: reporting. He was on his way to interview Y. A. Tittle, the former New York Giants quarterback, for a book about the 1958 championship game between the Giants and the Baltimore Colts, considered by many to be the greatest football game ever played.

Tall, square-jawed and graced with an imposing voice so deep that it seemed to begin at his ankles, Mr. Halberstam came into his own as a journalist in

David Halberstam in Vietnam.

the early 1960s covering the nascent American war in South Vietnam for The New York Times.

His reporting, along with that of several colleagues, left little doubt that a corrupt South Vietnamese government supported by the United States was no match for Communist guerrillas and their North Vietnamese allies. His dispatches infuriated American military commanders and policy makers in Washington, but they accurately reflected the realities on the ground.

For that work, Mr. Halberstam shared a Pulitzer Prize in 1964. Eight years later, after leaving The Times, he chronicled what went wrong in Vietnam — how able and dedicated men propelled the United States into a war later deemed unwinnable — in a book whose title entered the language: "The Best and the Brightest."

Mr. Halberstam went on to write more than 20 books, including one on the Korean War scheduled to be published in the fall.

"I think the work he was proudest of was his trilogy on war," his wife, Jean Halberstam, said last night. Besides "The Best and the Brightest," she was referring to a study of United States policies in the 1990s called "War in a Time of Peace: Bush, Clinton and the Generals," and the Korean War book, "The Coldest Winter."

Mr. Halberstam's range, however, extended well beyond war. His interests roamed from basketball to the auto industry, from the 1949 American League pennant race to the rise of modern media conglomerates in the 20th century.

"A writer should be like a playwright — putting people on stage, putting ideas on stage, making the reader become the audience," he recently told an interviewer for NY1 News.

Over the years, he developed a pattern of alternating a book with a weighty theme with one that might seem of slighter import but to which he nonetheless applied his considerable reportorial muscles. "He was a man who didn't have a lazy bone in his body," said the writer Gay Talese, a close family friend.

Almost invariably, Mr. Halberstam wrote about sports in those alternate books. "They were his entertainments," his wife said. "They were his way to take a break."

As a result, his book on the media, "The Powers That Be," was followed by a basketball book, "The Breaks of the Game." A study of the decline of the American automobile industry and the Japanese ascension, "The Reckoning," was followed before long by "The Summer of '49," on an epic pennant battle between the New York Yankees and Boston Red Sox.

Other works included "The Fifties," a look at a decade that he argued was more monumental than many believed; "The Children," about the civil-rights movement of the 1960s; and "Firehouse," a study of the tight-knit world of New York firefighters, focused on 13 men from a firehouse near his Upper West Side home who went to the World Trade Center on 9/11. Only one survived.

David Halberstam was born on April 10, 1934, in New York City, to an Army surgeon, Dr. Charles A. Halberstam, and a schoolteacher, Blanche Levy Halberstam. His older brother, Michael, became a well-known cardiologist in Washington. In 1980, Michael Halberstam was shot in his home and killed by an intruder.

David Halberstam in 1993

After World War II, the Halberstam family moved to Westchester County. David attended school in Yonkers, and then went to Harvard, where he graduated in 1955. By then, his commitment to journalism had been sealed. He was managing editor of the student newspaper, The Crimson.

After graduation, he went south and wrote about the nascent civil-rights movement, first for The West Point Daily Times Leader in Mississippi, then for The Nashville Tennessean. In 1960 he joined The New York Times, first in the Washington bureau, then as a foreign correspondent based in Congo.

It was when he went to South Vietnam in 1962 that he began to leave an indelible journalistic mark.

He soon saw that the American-backed government in Saigon was corrupt and failing — and he said so. William Prochnau, who wrote a book on the reporting of that period, "Once Upon a Distant War," said last night that Mr. Halberstam and other American journalists then in Vietnam were incorrectly regarded by many as antiwar.

"He was not antiwar," Mr. Prochnau said. "They were cold war children, just like me, brought up on hiding under the desk." It was simply a case, he said, of American commanders lying to the press about what was happening in Vietnam. "They were shut out and they were lied to," Mr. Prochnau said. And Mr. Halberstam "didn't say, 'You're not telling me the truth.' He said, 'You're lying.' He didn't mince words."

President John F. Kennedy was so incensed by Mr. Halberstam's war coverage that he strongly suggested to The Times's publisher, Arthur Ochs Sulzberger, that the reporter be replaced. Mr. Sulzberger replied that Mr. Halberstam would stay where he was. He even had the reporter cancel a scheduled vacation so that no one would get the wrong idea.

After Vietnam and after winning his Pulitzer Prize, Mr. Halberstam was assigned to the Times bureau in Warsaw. There, he met an actress, Elzbieta Czyzewska, whom he married in 1965. That marriage was short-lived. In 1979, he married Jean Sandness, then a writer.

In addition to his wife, he is survived by their daughter, Julia, also of Manhattan.

By the late 1960s, Mr. Halberstam tired of daily journalism and he left The Times, not exactly on mutually amicable terms. After that, he devoted himself to books, magazine articles and even a Vietnam-based novel, "One Very Hot Day."

In the recent NY1 interview, Mr. Halberstam summed up his approach to work by quoting a basketball player. "There's a great quote by Julius Erving," he said, "that went, 'Being a professional is doing the things you love to do, on the days you don't feel like doing them.' "

Reporting was contributed by Sewell Chan, Jennifer 8. Lee, Jesse McKinley and Sam Roberts.

A version of this article appears in print on Page C13 of the New York edition with the headline: David Halberstam, 73, War Reporter and Author, Is Killed in a Car Crash.

Meet the Cunninghams

[This is my Institute of Current World Affairs newsletter written August 27, 1953 from Rhodesia during my fellowship]

May I introduce our friends, Ken and Irene Cunningham. Ken is the popular sales manager of Puzey & Diss Motor Co. — he sees that the trickle of Morris Cars (Oxfords, Minors, MG's, and Morris Sixes) that come to Salisbury move smoothly through his company's showrooms onto Salisbury's streets and onto the strip roads that bump and hump their way overland through the bush and granite boulders to Umvuma, Umtali, and Que Que. He would be the first to tell you that he is just an ordinary fellow, no different from people like him in Gatooma and Gwelo.

If he knew that I was writing a letter for the Institute of Current World Affairs about him and his family he would first laugh, as though I were kidding. Then he would josh me a bit about being crazy. And then he would forget about it and go on with his life in the usual manner—boiled eggs for breakfast, inventories at the office in the morning, meeting Irene for lunch, sales at the office in the afternoon, and then home for dinner, cooked to perfection ("The new houseboy is a wonder—only hope he stays"). In the evening he would relax as usual in his lounge (living room) with his feet up and try to coax a few American radio programs from his ornate radiogram—while "Renee" (rhymes with beanie) sits across the room tapping the tip of her pen against her teeth, writing a letter to their daughter, Anne, at school in the Union of South Africa.

They *are* very usual people. They are pleasant, generous, and genuinely glad to see us. Ken wears brown or grey business suits with a sweater under

371

his coat and a silk necktie patterned with tiny "MG's" or the Morris coat of arms. He likes his white shirts well starched and in between houseboys complains that hie collars never look right. He is about 5 feet 10 inches tall and is picking up a slight bulge under the sweater. He wears rimless glasses and a well-trimmed, sandy moustache and carries himself very straight. He probably votes for the conservative United Party.

Renee says he looked "beautiful in his uniform." Now he is well into middle-age. From the distance his face looks ruddy* Eut when you come close to him you see that the red color in his face comes from tiny red lines and blotches that a physician could diagnose in a minute. I can only guess they come from living a day-to-day, tiring life for a long time, with only a prospect of more of the same in the future.

We first met him in Bulawayo. When our Comet landed at Livingstone it was several hours late, and we were whisked abruptly into a two-motored, Central African Airways transport, bound for Bulawayo« When we had found a safe spot for Julie's bottle bag and had fastened ourselves into our seats, we found we were facing an attractive, dark-haired woman and an effervescent young girl who was obviously the woman's daughter. They laughed when Julie tried to order Bourbon from the stewardess and had to settle for Scotch.

In a short time we had struck up a shouted conversation over the roar of the engines. They lived in Salisbury, it seemed, and wouldn't we come to visit them when we got settled? Mrs. Cunningham and Julie swapped addresses and small talk about flying and the Comet (Mrs. C. had never been on the Comet, although she new all about it from the accounts of the Queen Mother's arrival at Salisbury in the newspaper). In no time at all we saw the lights of Bulawayo's city of prefabricated houses thrown up to accommodate crowds at the Rhodes Centenary Exhibition and we were landing on a grass airport and jouncing up to the low line of airport buildings.

We lost sight of the Cunninghams until we were standing at the airlines desk arranging for our continuing flight to Salisbury and trying to explain about our overweight luggage. It was paid for as far as Livingstone, it seemed, but we would have to pay 12 shillings more to take it on to Salisbury. I reached in my pocket, but the cupboard was bare—all I had was 14 American dollars—and dollars were no good, I explained that we had had no time to change the dollars to pounds and shillings, but it was no good. We needed shillings.

Then Ken Cunningham came to our rescue. He offered us 12 shillings. We said no, he said yes, we said no, he said yes, and finally we had to say yes or spend the night in overcrowded Bulawayo.

They stood and talked with us while our transportational difficulties were being ironed out. Ken muttered something about "fighting the battle of Detroit during the war" and "just paying you back for some of the hospitality I enjoyed in the States." He had driven the 280 miles from Salisbury to Bulawayo to meet Renee and Anne who had flown from Salisbury to Livingstone to visit Victoria Falls. They were going to spend the next few days at the exhibition, where Ken was in charge of the Morris exhibit, and then drive home. We would see them then, they promised.

And then they said good-bye, bustling out of the lighted (and unusually gay) airport waiting room into the darkness and their Morris Minor, chattering in a family way. Suddenly we felt very lonely.

We saw them again a week later. We found that we needed a car desperately — and since we had to see Ken to thank him and return his 12 shillings, we decided to kill two birds with one stone. We walked the four blocks to Puzey & Dies, picked our way through a glittering array of Morris cars and into Ken's office. Over the door was a sign, "K. Cunningham," but there was nothing more to indicate he was an executive. No receptionist, no secretary—not even a closed door. From his cubby hole of an office you look out over the tops of fifteen or twenty automobiles. We returned the money, then told him we wanted to buy a car and described our wants.

"Well," he said, "what you want is a Morris Oxford. But I don't want you to just take my word for it. Let's go and see what the other places have to offer." For the next two hours we traveled from one show room to another—Ken standing to one side talking to a fellow sales manager while we talked to a salesman. In the end we bought a Morris Oxford—and began to see more of Ken and Renee Cunningham.

They came to our house one evening for "sundowners" — cocktails to us — and Ken told us of his visit to America during the war. He had been sent to Detroit to learn about engines as part of lend-lease. "I learned more there and enjoyed myself more than I had in ten years in England," he said. "I told myself that when the war was all over I would go back to England, begin manufacturing, and use all these techniques I had learned."

All the while he was talking he was fighting a silent battle with Cleopatra, the cat we inherited with the house. Ken doesn't like cats, and he was unknowingly sitting in Cleo's chair. When people sit there Cleo takes it for granted that the only reason they are making a lap is for her to sleep in it. You must imagine this conversation punctuated by Ken's useless efforts to keep the cat on the floor without making us think he disliked her.

"I was in the desert when Rommel was making such a fuss," he said, "Of course I was behind the lines in a motor repair depot, but there were always jerry planes to make things hot for us. Then I went to the States, and how I loved it. Ask Renee if I didn't. I used to write her letters about how things were and what I was going to bring her when I came home." And when Ken did come home he brought things that symbolized America to him. He brought a set of Community silverplate because of the advertisements featuring the beautiful young girl with stars in her eyes greeting the handsome young man home from the wars. He brought a complete outfit of clothing for Renee and some suits for himself. And he brought Nylon stockings.

American know-how impressed Ken tremendously. When he returned to England he tried to introduce American methods in the small machine shop he helped to manage. But he could not get the necessary machines and the forms and questionnaires he had to fill out to change his manufacturing processes depressed him to such an extent that he soon gave up the idea. "There we were, back in the same old rut," he said. "Finally I couldn't stand it any more so I sold out and came here."

With Anne and Renee he went to the Union and went to work for the Morris agency in Durban. After a few years he was transferred to Southern Rhodesia and Salisbury's Puzey & Diss as assistant sales manager. Now he is sales manager and has his sights set on becoming factory representative in Canada. He has not lost that attitude of "one eye to present business and the other eye to making things better" he says he acquired in the United States. On the way back from Bulawayo and the Exhibition an auto passing in the other direction on one of the strip roads threw up a atone which smashed Ken's windshield. Windshield glass here is made so that it does not shatter, but merely bends, sending a thousand cracks through the glass which "frosts" it and makes it opaque. Ken had to stop, break a hole in the glass to see through, and continue with the cold night air whistling into his face. The next day Renee came down with a cold.

After checking at other auto agencies to see how many windshields are replaced each week because of flying stones, he went to work and invented a plastic windshield screen which is shatter- and crack-proof, perfectly transparent, and is tinted to filter the sun's glare. When he had finished his design he applied for a patent, visited a machinist he knew, and is now in the windshield screen business. In a few weeks his first screens should be on the market.

We used the American silverware to eat a Sunday dinner with the Cunninghams not so long ago. They live in an average apartment building called Avon Park on the north side of Salisbury. Anne was on vacation from school and we were going out to watch polo that afternoon. Before lunch we sat in the lounge in overstuffed chairs and watched Ken's collection of tropical fish glint and glimmer back and forth in a large tank set on the window sill. The room seemed bare to us. There were no pictures on the wall and the only furniture was the sofa, two overstuffed chairs, and the dining room table. Along one wall of the room was a very elaborate piece of furniture which, I learned later, was the radiogram (or radio-phonograph). It was as long as the couch, about waist high, and very heavily carved. It had separate compartments for the radio, the phonograph turntable, and record storage.

After Ken had poured us each a dollop of sweet sherry we sat and talked. It was one of those times that the Cunninghams were between houseboys so Renee flitted in and out setting the table and Ken talked about the sorry condition of his shirt collars. After a few minutes Anne came in and put some records on the machine. Vic Damone sang a few bars of "I'm Walking Behind You" and then Ken made her turn it off.

Anne and Julie began comparing schools and Ken and I talked about America. "There's one thing I want to do more than anything else," he said. "I want to take Renee to America and show her around. I want to buy a caravan (trailer) and drive across the country and let her see it—the whole thing." Ken figures the best way to get to the United States is to get to Canada first and then move south. British subjects are strictly limited as to the amount of pounds they can take from the sterling area. But if Ken could get sent to Canada by the Nuffield Co., makers of Morris Cars, he would have solved the whole problem. "I've dropped a word or two here and there about being sent over," he confided, "but nothing's happened so far."

He has an expansive admiration for things American. American cars are the only ones that can stand up to punishment, American cigarettes are the only kind to smoke and still expect to use your throat for breathing, American food is the only food for a civilized man to eat.

"How are you at chocolate chiffon pie?" he asked Julie. "Oh, if I could only get back to the States and find myself a piece of chocolate chiffon pie."

He is not wealthy. With his salary and the small amount Renee earns as a clerk at a local real estate agency they can just afford to live in their small apartment and send Anne to a good girls' boarding school in the Union. Anne wants to go to a University next year when she graduates, but Ken can only say "We'll see."

He drives a small car—which doesn't belong to him but is a Puzey & Diss demonstrator. He is proud of its color—maroon—because it is the only maroon Morris Minor in all of Southern Rhodesia. He is proud of their newly-acquired dachshund because it is one of the few dachshunds in Southern Rhodesia.

He has not had a new dinner coat since 1938. I found this out when I had to borrow it to attend a government house reception. He is toying with the idea of buying a movie camera like our Kodak Brownie ($39.75), but he can't

Cleopatra, nobody's slave

right now. "We just can't afford it."

He has what I call a keen sense of his position in life. When we invited him and his wife to our house for canasta the other evening he accepted readily. Then, very cautiously, he asked whether we also had invited the Soames's. Bob Soames is one of the Puzey & Dias salesmen, subordinate to Ken. When we said we hadn't, his face broke into a relieved smile, "Oh, good," he said. "It's not that I don't like Bob, it's just that business and pleasure don't mix and it's not good that we get too chummy outside of office hours" He would have felt just as uncomfortable, I feel, had we invited Mr. Diss or Mr. Puzey.

Ken may never get to America, He may never taste another piece of chocolate chiffon pie. His windshield screen may be a flop. His next-door neighbor may buy another maroon Morris Minor. Anne may not be able to go to the University next year. But Ken and Renee are optimistic. And, basically, they are realistic. I think it is this feeling of optimistic realism that has brought federation into being—that brought Rhodes and the pioneers here to this "God-forsaken spot" in the first place.

As I have said, there are dozens of Ken Cunninghams in Salisbury, and more throughout the federation. I will not call him typical; yet there is something so real about him that I say to myself "This is Southern Rhodesia. In spite of the native leaders and the politicians, Ken Cunningham and his like is what makes the whole thing tick."

Perhaps what I've tried to put into this letter is not what I have been sent here for, I am fascinated by the politics and the native problem and will write about them soon. But, perhaps by way of relaxation, I decided to take time out and introduce you to Ken Cunningham and his family. I will introduce you to more people as time goes on.

Sincerely,

Peter Bird Martin

Johanesburg

Cities of the World: (No. 14) Johannesburg[2]

By Peter Bird Martin

There's an intensity in the air of Johannesburg that affects men like cheap brandy. Perhaps it's the altitude — Johannesburg sprawls across ninety-five square miles of veld more than a mile above sea level — or it may be the mining-camp tradition. Whatever it is, the city has been embroiled in a series of disturbances grown into riots, celebrations become pandemonium and brawls ending in murder since the first gold mine was dug sixty-nine years ago.

A case in point is the recent arrival of one Danny Kaye, a comedian from the United States. At first the city seemed to be taking the event in its stride, as though it were only natural for one of the world's great comics to include Johannesburg, largest city in sub-Saharan Africa, in his itinerary. Advance ticket selling dragged along and a "greet Danny Kaye" campaign died on the vine as Johannesburg set out to prove that it was just as sophisticated as London or New York—it would take a lot more than Danny Kaye to stir up any real excitement.

Even the day of Kaye's arrival was quiet under an early-winter sun blazing down from a dead blue sky. It was one of those days when the post office, a blunt square pile of brownish rock, stood out starkly and you got the feeling you could reach out and touch the yellow mountains of waste from

---

[2]I wrote this article for the Saturday Evening Post. It appeared November 26, 1955, shortly after my Africa fellowship ended. The subtitle was "Built on the richest gold mine in the world, Jo'burg is a puritanical boom town of fabulous wealth and incredible squalor, where black men and white coexist in a fearful truce."

the gold mines that run along the southern edge of the downtown district. By afternoon, however, the city was on edge, itching for excitement, experienced special-duty policemen watched with growing uneasiness as silent crowds gathered at the gleaming new Jan Smuts Airport and the Carlton Hotel, Johannesburg's answer to the Waldorf.

At the airport all went quietly as the plane set down and Kaye stepped out. He shook hands with a few dignitaries and kidded Mayor Patmore about his chain of office before climbing into an open convertible for the long ride downtown. The crowd at the Carlton greeted the news that Kaye was on the way with a shifting of feet and a slow surge toward the street. It wasn't a conscious move; it was the result of the kind of nervousness a bundle of dynamite must feel when someone lights its fuse.

After sweeping through the jammed middle-class suburbia of eastern Johannesburg, the caravan swung into the heart of the city, growing in size as homeward-bound motorists all along the route obeyed the impulse to swing around and follow. By the time the string of cars reached the towering theaters and office buildings of Commissioner Street, it had slowed in a crawl. People ran along the sidewalks toward the Carlton, darting out into the street leaping in from of the motorcycle escort and knocking one another down in their scramble to get near Danny Kaye.

Screaming and howling, they packed Commissioner Street from wall to wall. Negotiating the corner of Commissioner and Eloff Streets, the driver pressed the crowd out of the way with his fenders and front bumper. The boyish look on Kaye's face gave w ay to a mechanical smile. Sitting on the folded top of the convertible with his feet on the back seat, he looked as though he had been squeezed into the air by the sheer weight of people pressing toward him.

As men and women snatched at his trench coat, leaning farther and farther over the car doors in their attempts to touch him, Kaye vanished through the hotel's front door. A shout of outrage greeted his escape up a flight of stairs inside, but there were cheers again when he appeared on a balcony, obviously shaken and staring in disbelief at the wild crowd below.

Within a few days, however, it was clear that Johannesburg regretted its unsophisticated enthusiasm over a mere American performer. Typically, the city went to the other extreme; audience after audience assumed an attitude of intense boredom, tittering politely when Kaye laid something particularly amusing, and yawning during the songs. Audience-participation gimmicks sagged. It became terribly fashionable not to have liked Danny Kaye, especially after word got around that his material was much the same as that which had thrilled theatergoers in London.

Johannesburgers have always been ready to go to extremes, as the city itself shows. Two extremes are obvious from the start: abject poverty and the kind of wealth people are usually described as rolling in. To find the former, you thread your car through the harrowing traffic of downtown Johannesburg, cross one of the viaducts over the railway yards and then turn west on a wide, curving drive lined with flowers, pleasant old houses and school playing fields. High on the left you can see the University of the Witwatersrand; later you pass the lush fairways of the Johannesburg Country Club.

Then, almost without warning, you're in Sophiatown, with its lines of decaying houses along tattered paved streets. It doesn't look so bad—until you learn that eight or nine people live in a single room and that the houses hide back yards full of stinking, head-high shanties built of cardboard and flattened kerosene cans. Sophiatown is being razed now, strip by strip, legislated out of existence by a South African Government anxious to do away with slums and eager to fulfill a political obligation to clear black men out of "white" areas.

But farther west you find Moroka and the Orlando breeze-block shelters, miserable places that make Sophiatown look like Nob Hill. Moroka was never meant to be a town — the city administration, faced seven years ago with the problem of what to do with tens of thousands of unhoused natives, took the easy way out. After marking off plots, the City Council spread the news that squatting was allowed. Shanties sprang up, built of mud bricks, bits of planking, wads of rags and sheets of rusted corrugated iron, pushed together to gain support from the shark next door. A "temporary measure," promised the council. "By 1953 there will be plenty of houses for everyone; then we'll tear down these eyesores."

The shacks are still there, with more people than ever packed into them. You can get out of your car and watch police moving through the alleys, probing with long steel rods for buried caches of skokiaan, a poisonous, home-fermented liquor laced with methyl alcohol. But you won't stay long unless the wind is at your back. Naked children with distended bellies play on the edges of streams trickling from overflowing buckets in the communal privies, and it's easy to believe the reports of casual Sunday list fights that develop into tribal battles. The Monday-morning paper doesn't even bother to give the names of the dead.

Sensible white men stay out of these shanty towns at night when inky darkness hides the *shebeens*, illicit drinking places presided over "skokiaan queens" seizing the brew the police didn't find. Witch doctors still weave black magic, smelling out evildoers and brewing potions to cure everything from sterility to athlete's foot. It's a rare white Johannesburger who has ever even seen the squatters' towns. Everyone knows they're there, of course, but they are strategically placed well off the main roads from Jo'burg to neighboring towns in the Transvaal.

Oddly enough, you don't have to go very far to find the city's luxury. You drive back to the university, then turn north out Oxford Road, a comfortable dual carriageway lined with palm trees and paved to suit its burden of fat American cars. Houses get bigger as you drive north, and the sprinkling of tennis courts and swimming pools becomes a rash. By the time you reach the suburbs of Houghton, Dunkeld and Illovo, the rash is epidemic. And the tennis courts are not mere trappings—the Jo'burg sun shines an average of more than eight and a half hours a day throughout the year. Even in winter, from June to October, there is rarely a cloud in the sky, although the temperature sometimes drops to freezing and a few flakes of snow fall two or three times in a lifetime.

Sprawling over several acres, the houses range in style from Tudor to service-station modern and in size from baronial to princely. All are amply staffed. In every kitchen a native "cook boy" operates a battery of American appliances.

Native "garden boys" tend the flowers. Native "nannies" take care of the children. Native drivers keep the can washed and get the *baas* safely to and from the office every day. And there's always a native "house boy" handy to make beds and the like. Luxury comes cheap in Johannesburg — servants get from fourteen to thirty dollars a month, and the best cuts of beef go for forty cents a pound.

From the luxury of the north you can swing east, then circle south through the monotonous stucco and corrugated-iron roofing of the older suburbs. Then you're back in the city itself, where brownstone landmarks studded with Victorian turrets are being ripped down at a great rate to make way for modern office buildings with expressionless marble faces. Downtown Johannesburg is getting newer every day.

A few blocks south or the Carlton Hotel the city come to a sudden hall and goldmine dumps begin. Some are old and hidden under mantles of brush, but most are still growing, reminders that the only for the city's existence is the fact that a hobo stubbed his toe on a rock here sixty-nine years ago.

Johannesburg began just that casually. It was a bright Sunday morning in 1886 when a hobo named George Walker tripped over the fateful stone while walking through the rolling veld 900 miles northeast of Africa's southern tip, in the old Boer Transvaal Republic. Or perhaps it was another hobo, George Harrison. It may even have been a third hobo named Honeyball. No one is quite sure.

The gold in that stone began a rush that hasn't stopped vet. People poured into the Transvaal afoot and on horseback, by stagecoach and wagon. One affluent prospector drove up in a hansom cab. Within a few months the president of the republic, Stephanus Johannes Paulus Kruger, was forced to send two men to the new mining camp to lay out a proper village. These were Johannes Rissik and C. Johannes Joubert, and they did the job under instructions from the goldfields' first mining commissioner, Johannes Meyer. Appropriately enough, the resulting checkerboard of surveyors' pegs, mud huts and wagons was named Johannesburg.

To this day no one remembers for certain just which Johannes the city was named for. The trouble is that Jo'burg moved too fast for anyone to stop and write a history. Keeping a diary in your tent was a good way to miss a gold strike or an available woman. You had to keep on the go, digging your claim, investigating reports of fabulous wealth on a nearby farm, finding water to drink—doing all the crazy things that made up life in a boom town built on the richest gold mine m the world.

To be sure, the glitter of gold had attracted attention to the Witwatersrand, the low "Ridge of the White Waters" that runs east and west through the city, as far back as 1853. In that year a Boer prospector had burst excitedly into the *Volksraad*, the legislative assembly of the old republic, to announce the discovery of gold. To his surprise, however, the good burghers had promptly invoked a law forbidding prospecting and sworn him to secrecy on pain of death. Gold might bring wealth to the echoing coffers of the Transvaal treasury, but it would also bring a flood of the hated British with their liberal ideas and sinful ways.

Staunchest in his opposition to anything that might bring the British to the Transvaal was the republic's third and last president, "Oom Paul" Kruger. As a boy of ten he had ridden a creaking ox wagon into the Transvaal with the *Voortrekkers*, the band of 7000 fanatically religious Dutch farmers who fled the liberalism which the British had brought to the Cape Province and Natal. He grew into a square, hulking man who read nothing but the Bible and believed with all his rock-bound soul that he had been divinely chosen to lead his people, that the Almighty had reserved a special section of Paradise for the Boers and that the African natives were descended from Ham, the disrespectful son of Noah, and were therefore destined to serve as hewers of wood and drawers of water for all time. He also believed, and with equal fervor, that the world was flat.

Under his disapproving eye the gold camps grew — Ferreira's Camp, the first and most important; then Bantje's Camp, Paarl Camp and all the others. The first arrivals roughed it in tents and wagons, but presently shacks appeared, built of mud and grass or imported iron and brick. During the rainy summer, from November to May, the mud huts naturally melted like ice-cream castles in a steam bath, but when they collapsed the occupants simply crawled out, rescued the roof and molded another home.

Water sold for $2.50 a gallon, baths were unheard of and rats and snakes were everywhere. To make things completely miserable, the only bar in town was so small that it accommodated but one customer at a time. Women were in demand, to say the least. One legend tells of a bonny young servant girl, traveling through Ferreira's Camp by stagecoach, who alighted in order to avoid the foul attentions of a male fellow passenger. One month later she was sole owner of a hotel and a gold mine, with no questions asked.

The camps grew so fast that government surveyors were forced to consolidate towns that no one had dreamed would ever meet. As a result, there are unexpected jogs and right-angle turns in the city's streets today, marking the collision of one mining camp with another.

As the camps grew, so did the numbers of fools and confidence men. Mine salting was an everyday occurrence, and one prospector, watching the initial panning of a reputedly rich mine, was outraged to see two gold teeth turn up in the suspiciously heavy yield. As it turned out, the ethics of the situation had nothing to do with his anger — what made him see red was the fact that they were his teeth, strayed or stolen a few days earlier.

Stagecoach-stopping was a popular outdoor sport among the horsy set, and most crimes which would rate front-page space in today's big Rand Daily Mail or Star were either ignored or forgotten. Gold chasing kept the people of Johannesburg much too busy to pay any attention to the holdups and worse that took place nightly in the unlighted streets.

Looking at the city today, it's a bit difficult to imagine the lurid happenings of the turn of the century. But in her attempts to achieve respectability, Jo'burg seems rather like a burlesque queen married to a purebred Bostonian; she is finding it easy to keep her bustle, but hard to forget the bumps and grinds.

For example, the city fathers have curbed night life so effectively that a wild evening means a trip to one of the ultramodern movie theaters or dinner dancing at a floor-showless supper club. Drinking in bars and cocktail lounges stops promptly at midnight and a small-town silence settles when the last streetcar has headed for the barns. But iron bars on bedroom windows and the flickering fires of "watch boys" on duty outside private homes show that danger still roams the streets at night. White women rarely go out alone after sundown, and burglars have found that a long pole tipped with a hook can slip past window bars. It's common for a white man to wake up to see his trousers floating across the room toward the window. It would seem a simple matter to grab the pole, thereby saving trousers, honor and cash, but the poles are often studded with razor blades set on edge. A quick jerk on the pole by the thief, and the grabber's hands are slashed to ribbons.

Daylight brings the less dangerous thrill of mingling with the racial kaleidoscope that pushes along Jo'burg's crowded streets. There are Zulu ricksha boys in swinging skirts made of colored strips of felt, Chinese – left over from the days when great numbers of coolies were imported to work the mines, and Basuto tribesmen wrapped in their traditional red blankets, hurrying toward the railway station and the mines farther out on the Witwatersrand. There are swarthy descendants of the Malayan slaves brought to Cape Town in the early days to work on Dutch farms, strapping blond policemen with names like du Plessis and van der Merwe, whose great-grandfathers trekked across the veld with Kruger, and well-groomed men with proper British accents who have never been outside South Africa. There are Indians and Jews, Xosa and Swazi African natives, even a few hundred Americans, all racing to make a fortune or catch an electric bus in the "City of Gold."

All told, 850,000 people—including all races, Chinese, Indian and those of mixed blood—live in Jo'burg, and everyone seems to be in a tearing hurry — except, of course, on Sunday, when the Strictly Calvinist Dutch Reformed Church does its bit to bring the rush to a grinding halt. Yet Sunday morning brings one of the most thrilling spectacles the city has to offer. To find it you must go south from the center of town into the grimy world of garages, railway lines and mine dumps. Dull yellow in the sun, the dumps tower 80 or 100 feet above the road and their sides are wrinkled with the erosion of rainy seasons, year after year. You're driving over the reef—more than a mile beneath you lies the narrow layer of gold-bearing earth that started it all.

Even the mines obey the Sunday blue laws. The wheels atop the tall steel headgears over the shafts stop spinning, the mills slow and the compounds fill with excitement. The compounds are long brick or concrete dormitories where African laborers live a bachelor life during their average stay of about a year at the mines. On Sundays they put away the head lamps, helmets, battery packs and heavy boots they wear underground eight hours a day during the week and bring out their furs and feathers.

To the accompaniment of xylophone-like "Machopi Pianos," drums, chants and hand clapping, they lash through the brilliant sunlight of a wide arena, stamping their feet in perfect unison. Waving spears and shields over their heads, they do the dances of Zululand, Mozambique, Rhodesia and Tanganyika. For a few hours they forget that they are many days from their *kraals* in the green lushness along the Indian Ocean coastline or the flat bushland of the Rhodesias to the north. In a hard, pounding rhythm that shakes the packed earth, they go through the traditional motions that have been used for centuries to celebrate marriages, successful hunts or battles.

Back in their own lands the dances might last for days if the beer held out. The Xosas, who make their own music by strapping bells around their rippling chest muscles, could keep up their jangling far into the night, but here time is limited. There are other dancers from other tribes with different costumes and songs. Somehow, however, no matter what the tribe, the rhythm stays the same. Men who come from territories thousands of miles apart, who speak different languages and pay different prices for their brides, could do their dances to each other's music. It seems to be the rhythm of all Africa.

There are sudden silences when the music fades and the dancers fall to the ground, lying motionless in the settling dust. Then, slowly, as if growing from the earth itself they rise and the rhythm begins again, first murmuring, then quickening, finally throbbing as dark feet flash high in the air, pause, then come pounding down to make ankle rattles chatter and head plumes shake.

Dancers forget that from Monday through Saturday they are sweating laborers — lashing boys, loader operators, drill boys and loco drivers. On

Sunday they are men again, warriors of the old Africa, with spears, shields and the skins of animals wrapped about them. You notice the Zulus particularly, dancing with some fierce memory of the days when their regiments were feared throughout Southern Africa and their warlike chief, Tshaka, practiced the bloody rites of human sacrifice.

Most visitors leave at noon, but the dances often go on through the hot sun of afternoon. This is the real Johannesburg, you feel, more in keeping with the past than the American-style bowling alley, the zoo or the twenty golf clubs. The Zulus were dancing like this when Paul Kruger killed his first lion and blew off his thumb with a four-pounder gun; they'll probably be dancing the same way when the last ounce of gold or uranium comes up the shaft of the last mine.

When you see the fierceness of the dancing against the harsh background of the mine dumps and the modern sky line of the city, you can begin to understand why there is such a gulf between black and white and why tensions, racial and otherwise, flourish in Johannesburg.

Discrimination against "black savages, just down out of the trees," is everywhere. Separate post offices serve "Europeans" (whites) and Africans. There are separate entrances to the railway stations, separate railway cars, separate taxis, separate buses. Even the bus stops are marked Bus Stop and Second Class Bus Stop, and the pretty red benches under the rain shelters are invariably stenciled For Europeans Only. Africans are not allowed in the restaurants, hotels and bars of the city, although they can do some of their shopping in the bazaars — overgrown five-and-ten-cent stores — along Eloff Street. "European" liquor — beer, whisky, wine and gin — is forbidden them and, in addition to the identification books which they are obliged to carry. Africans must have special permission from their employers to be on the streets in "European" Johannesburg after nine o'clock at night.

Yet even this is only the discrimination which appears on the surface. Hidden, but no less strict, are the color bars which prevent Africans from rising in industry, the armed forces and the civil service. Political rights — voting and running for office — are denied to all Africans, regardless of education, except on an unbelievably limited basis in the native "reserves." It is small wonder that Jo'burg, with its 400,500 Africans, is a natural breeding ground for racial warfare.

The city has seen two bloodier-than-usual riots caused by European fears that some of their jobs might be taken over by African Bantu. In 1913, twenty-one people were killed and forty-seven wounded by troops sent to control rioting, burning and looting by outraged mobs of striking white mine workers. And, in 1922, a strike which began in the South African coal fields spread to Jo'burg, where communist leaders built it into thirteen days of all-out guerrilla warfare. Planes bombed Fordsburg, a suburb just west of the downtown district, and South African troops opened fire on the strike leaders holed up in a house there. Casualties totaled 687 killed and wounded.

In 50,000 striking African miners marched on the city, but were met by police and put to rout after a "show of force." Force, indeed, has been used many times to keep the blacks from rioting against Jo'burg's 350,500 whites. Fear of such an uprising is one of the few things on which practically all whites see eye to eye. In other respects they are divided into two camps, those descended from the Boers and those whose British forebears came to Johannesburg to grub for gold and to open businesses.

The city's signs and traffic signals, written both in Afrikaans, the Dutch dialect evolved by the *Voortrekkers*, and in English, are visible evidence of the rift between these groups. Sweet young things with American accents have been known to get away with explaining to Afrikaans-speaking policemen that they didn't know that "*Geen Parkering*" meant "No Parking" or that a "*Laaisone*" was a loading zone. A young thing, however sweet, who tried the same explanation in a British accent would not get off so easily.

The friction between English-speaking and Afrikaans-speaking Johannesburgers goes back to the days when the British moved Into Cape Town, freeing the Boers' slaves and interfering generally with their traditional way of life. Kruger vented this hostility by imposing heavy taxes on the British in Jo'burg and denying them political rights, even though they made up more than half the population of his Transvaal Republic and produced three fourths of its wealth. His continued antagonism was the direct cause of Johannesburg's most comic-opera revolution, the Jameson Raid of 1895.

The raid followed close upon Kruger's rejection of a 92,000-signature petition for arbitration of Johannesburg's grievances. Oom Paul didn't mince words. "Go back to your people," he thundered at the British delegation, "and tell them that I shall never give them anything! ... And now — let the storm burst!"

Storm-maker No.1 was Cecil Rhodes, then prime minister of the Cape Colony. Dedicated to two things—making a fortune in gold and diamonds and extending British power along the line of a British railway from Cape Town to Cairo — he drew up a simple plan. A revolution would flare up in the city on December 28, 1895. An old friend, Dr. Starr Jameson, would just happen to be on the border between Rhodesia and the Transvaal with 1,500 men; to save British lives he would march south, enter the city and thereby put an end to the Boer republic. It was a simple, straightforward plan, but it didn't work.

One reason for its failure was the attitude of the British in Johannesburg. Many of them were interested only in making money, and revolutions left them cold; those who did favor a revolution couldn't make up their minds what to do if they won. Some wanted to force concessions from Kruger, others to eliminate him completely. Finally, a member of the revolution committee gave the entire show away in an overenthusiastic public speech, and Rhodes decided to call the whole thing off. He sent Jameson three telegrams to that effect; Jameson ignored them all. On December twenty-ninth, only a day late, he blithely cabled Johannesburg that he was on his way. Unfortunately, all the members of the revolution committee were at the races, so there was no one in the office to take the message.

Also unfortunately, the man whom Jameson had assigned to cut the telegraph line to Pretoria went about his work in a thick fog of champagne. With great care he snipped several lengths of wire from a farmer's fence and buried them deep in the ground. Jameson set out with a force of about 700 men — all he had managed to collect for his gallant mission — and with a Boer telegrapher reporting his every move to Kruger in Pretoria. Two thousand Boers under General Cronje were sent out to head him off, and a "peace committee" took over Johannesburg. Jameson marched all night, and by the following afternoon he was within twenty miles of the city. There the revolution ended. Cronje closed the trap, and that evening Jameson was paraded through the streets or Krugersdorp, Oom Paul's home town, looking rather sheepish.

The main effect of the raid was to hasten the coming of the Boer War, an extraordinarily bitter conflict which settled absolutely nothing. The British won the battles, but lost the country: descendants of the Boers control South Africa today through the Nationalist Party; they are even talking of establishing a republic outside the British Commonwealth. Johannesburg is just about back where it started—bigger, of course, and more cosmopolitan, but still divided into airtight compartments. An Afrikaner at an English-speaking party is as rare a sight in Jo'burg as snow.

Separation into communities seems to come naturally here. Even Americans, famous elsewhere for ignoring social and language barriers, have hived off by themselves to form American social clubs, bowling clubs, luncheon groups and sewing circles.

But then, Johannesburg doesn't make much fuss over Americans, either — not below the rank of Danny Kaye. They are handy people to have around when a new machine has to be ordered or a question of uranium production comes up. Otherwise they are nothing special, and the city, pointedly, doesn't bother about making itself attractive to tourists, whether they are loaded with dollars or not.

There are no clip joints, no girlie shows, no sidewalk sellers of phony fountain pens and native handicrafts. Restaurants are for eating, bars are for drinking, and Americans are ordinary mortals. These are plain definitions, and many Americans, tired of being taken for walking fountains of currency, like it that way.

The future of Johannesburg is open to speculation. One pertinent question is: "What happens to a gold-mining town when there's no more gold to mine?" American experts, finding rich deposits of uranium in ore blasted loose with the gold, may have answered that one.

An even worse problem that must soon be faced by the city—and by South Africa as a whole—is what to do about the mounting tension between black and while. As the Africans become more and more conscious of the disadvantages under which they labor, they also become more dangerous to the future of Jo'burg, both as discontented laborers and as potential communists. South African laws forbid Africans to form trade-unions or to strike — but Johannesburgers have a long record of ignoring inconvenient laws when the lime comes to take power into their own hands. Things seem peaceful enough now, but Jo'burg's excitement isn't finished, not by a long shot.

About the Author

Peter Bird Martin was funded by the Ford Foundation for a two-year journalism fellowship in colonial subSaharan Africa from 1953 to 1955 before returning to New York as a magazine writer. He wrote about Latin America at Time for eight years, then served as Senior Editor of the magazine's Medicine, Press, Law, Science and performing-arts sections from 1964 to 1970.

Peter was assigned to invent new, smaller magazines for TIME to take the place of LIFE. These eventually became Money, People, Well and Entertainment magazines. Money and People are still published, and Well has been incorporated into the New York Times.

In 1978, Peter was elected Executive Director of the Institute of Current World Affairs (ICWA), the Hanover-based foundation that had sponsored his Africa journalism fellowship. He then retired from Time Inc. and managed ICWA's international fellowship program from Hanover. He found and funded 75 promising young internationalists for two-year fellowships in every continent.

Credits

- Page 1: The Time of My Life Copyright © Peter Bird Martin 2020 - All rights reserved.

- Page 1: Photo by Jon Gilbert Fox of Peter Martin (with globes) perched on Jon's ladder in Peter's office at Wheelock House in Hanover, New Hampshire. Jon Gilbert Fox © Used by permission.

- Page 5: Beffa Brothers Buffet, St. Louis, circa 1952. Rights status not evaluated.

- Page 11: Harry Lundeberg, president of the International Seamen's Union (1938-1957) and Secretary/Treasurer of the Sailors' Union of the Pacific, wearing his "Stetson". Rights status not evaluated.

- Page 26: Publicity photo for Lilly Christine, New Orleans Burlesque Dancer. Copyright unknown.

- Page 75: 1954 MG TF Roadster (Peter's Folly), in Darmstadt, Germany. Copyright © Peter Bird Martin - All rights reserved.

- Page 86: Henry R. Luce, on the March 10, 1967 cover of Time, shortly after his death. Time Incorporated © All Rights Reserved.

- Page 100: Copyright © Wall Street Journal. All rights reserved.

- Page 140: William Buckley/Conservatism Can Be Fun. Time Incorporated © All Rights Reserved.

- Page 146: Apollo 9 liftoff on March 3, 1969. Copyright © Smithsonian Institution.

- Page 153: Topography of Sri Lanka, obtained from the Shuttle Radar Topography Mission of STS-99, aboard the Space Shuttle Endeavour. Public Domain.

- Page 155: Raquel Welch. "One Million Years B. C." [1966], Directed by Don Chaffey. The photo copyright is believed to belong to the distributor of the film, the publisher of the film or the graphic artist.

- Page 171: Raquel Welch - Time Cover - November 28, 1969. Epoxy resin sculpture by Frank Gallo. Copyright © Time Incorporated.

- Page 273: Jackie Kennedy weds Aristotle Onassis in 1968. Jim Pringle/Associated Press

- Page 356: Peter Martin (right) investigating the life and work of native workers in southern Africa's primary industry in 1954. He is pictured here 8,500 feet underground at the President Steyn gold mine near the town of Welkom in the Orange Free State. The "gold" appears as a thin layer of black dust in the wall of the mine. Miners drill blast holes in the wall above and below the layer of gold ore. The motivation is to take as small amount of waste rock out as possible as workers drill in narrow spaces. Rights status not evaluated.

- Page 361: Elzbieta Czyzewska, Polish Actress Unwelcome in Her Own Country, Dies at 72. Copyright © New York Times

- Page 362: Elzbieta Czyzewska in the 1961 film "Erotica," directed by Jerzy Skolimowski. The film made her a national sex symbol in Poland. The Museum of Modern Art.

- Page 365: David Halberstam, 73, Reporter and Author, Dies. Copyright © New York Times

- Page 366: David Halberstam in Vietnam. Horst Faas/Associated Press.

- Page 368: David Halberstam in 1993. Mark Lennihan/Associated Press.

- Page 379: Cities of the World: (No. 14) Johannesburg. Copyright © Saturday Evening Post.

Index

Printed in Great Britain
by Amazon